THE SIMMERING POT COOKBOOK

THE SIMMERING POT COOKBOOK

Alice Devine Loebel

Photographs by HERBERT LOEBEL

Illustrations by VLADIMIR F. HERVERT

Macmillan Publishing Co., Inc.
NEW YORK
Collier Macmillan Publishers
LONDON

Macmillan Publishing Co., Inc.,
866 Third Avenue, New York, N.Y. 10022
Collier-Macmillan Canada Ltd., Toronto, Ontario

First Printing 1974

The Simmering Pot Cookbook is a revised and
enlarged edition of *The Stockpot and Steamer
Cookbook*, published by Macmillan Publishing
Co., Inc., in 1969.

Printed in the United States of America

Library of Congress Cataloging in Publication Data

Loebel, Alice Devine.
  The simmering pot cookbook.

  Published in 1969 under title: The stockpot and
  steamer cookbook.
  1. Stocks (Cookery) 2. Steaming (Cookery)
I. Title.
TX819.S8L6   1974   641.7'3   73-10567
ISBN 0-02-574030-X

Contents

ACKNOWLEDGMENTS

My thanks to all my friends who so generously gave me family recipes, and tasted, praised and criticized my recipes.

My thanks to my editor, Mrs. Eleanor Freide, for her encouragement and for making the expansion and revision of this book possible.

My thanks to Mr. Nicholas Wedge for his invaluable help with the manuscript, and my thanks to my husband for his patience and lovely photographs.

THE SIMMERING POT COOKBOOK

(1) KITCHEN ECOLOGY

The children's rhyme "Little drops of water,/ little grains of sand,/ make the mighty ocean/ and the pleasant land" can be paraphrased today to read: "Little drops of phosphates,/ little plastic cans,/ make a lifeless ocean/ and an ugly land."

In the security of our homes in the cities or suburbs, we tend to live in comfortable isolation from the most terrifying reality man has ever faced. Quite simply, the past few decades have produced greater destruction of our planet's ecological system than have all the previous centuries of recorded history. Nature's life-sustaining rhythms have been broken or altered to such an extent that many experts wonder if we haven't passed "the point of no return."

In our role as homemakers, it is often difficult to see that individual actions do have an effect—either in contributing to further destruction or to the survival of our planet. You may think that your little bit of trash or waste does not count. But, indeed, it counts a thousandfold!

For survival's sake, we must get back in tune with the cycles of nature, with the total environment. This does not mean that we have to forgo all manufactured comforts and conveniences. But it does mean that we have to use our raw and manufactured materials with respect and, most important, make the effort to recycle or dispose of them wisely. In brief, we must reawaken our inner sense of awareness to our surroundings.

To determine if you are working within nature's system, halt a moment to take an objective look at how you accomplish your multitude of kitchen chores. Observe all the kitchen materials you use. If the residue, including the wrappings and empty containers, do not go to a recycling plant, are they constructed so that they will disintegrate into the earth, water or air to become sustenance for life-giving micro-organisms? If not, they do not biodegrade. (This important new word, coined within the last couple of years by the conservationists, is derived from the Greek *bios*, meaning "life" or "living organisms"; and from "degrade," meaning "to break down." In short, anything that is biodegradable can be broken down by nature into a harmless substance by the action of such living beings as micro-organisms in the soil, etc.)

Further, count how many of the materials you use every day, without a second thought, that are made from limited natural resources . . . and how recklessly you may consume our diminishing fossil fuels. (Fossil fuels, derived from coal, petroleum and natural gas, are the remnants of leaves, skeletons, and other organisms of a geological age long, long past. Society's need for these fuels, coupled with the exploding population, is literally depleting them at a breakneck speed.)

The kitchen is a powerful corner in which to begin your work to improve the environment. Here more fuel is consumed, and more nonbiodegradable materials are used, than in any other area of the home. This room alone contributes more to pollution than all other rooms in the house.

There is much to be done. Let's get on with the work and not bemoan the mess we have inherited or thoughtlessly created. The thought of taking on additional work to clean up the earth may seem insurmountable; but, I assure you, the physical work will not be as strenuous as it was for our forebears, who had to clear the land, build the villages, harvest the crops and accomplish their multitude of chores in order to survive.

Check the following points to see how you can incorporate

them into your day-to-day living. Make the effort; put your energies into *sustaining* the system that sustains you.

FOOD

• The stockpot is one of the best ways to recycle food. Save all savory scraps, vegetable peels and vegetable waters; all the steak and roast drippings, chicken carcasses, roast bones and steak bones for your stockpot. They are filled with nutrients which find their way into the stock through long simmering (see recipes).

• Freeze or refrigerate any leftovers, and plan your menus so that they are tastefully and attractively used. A friend of mine, whose father was a banker, told me that he spoke of leftovers as "a balance carried forward"—such a nice thought.

• Refrigerate any leftover green salad; put it in a blender, add tomato juice and an ice cube, and you have a "family" gazpacho.

• After squeezing the juice from an orange or lemon, grate or finely slice the rinds and freeze for future use as a sprinkling over a fruit salad or a dessert. Grated orange rind is also delicious with buttered beets (see recipes).

• Put lettuce into a brown paper bag and put it into the crisper of your refrigerator. It stays crunchy and crisp for three to four days, and you have avoided using and disposing of another plastic bag.

• Pour any leftover wine into a jar, cap and save for the stockpot.

• Ardent coffee lovers tell me that unused coffee can be bottled, capped and refrigerated for two days. For a quick cup of coffee, just heat and serve. Or the coffee can be poured into an ice-cube tray and frozen. For a refreshing glass of iced coffee, put three or four cubes into a tall glass, add cream and sugar, and stir.

• Place any unused fresh onion into a jar, close tightly and refrigerate; it will stay fresh for weeks.

• When cooking with a double boiler, make it do double duty. I do not find that the lower portion is large enough to cook the vegetables for a whole meal, but I do put in a potato, a carrot, a beet or some other vegetable I might want for a salad, hash, or to add to a soup. Also, it is an easy way to hardboil a few eggs.

• To drain bacon or any fried foods, use a flattened brown paper bag instead of paper towels. You will be recycling your oversupply of bags (unless you carry your own string or cloth bag for shopping—which, by the way, is a good habit to cultivate). And you will be avoiding the needless use and disposal of paper towels.

• Cook by steaming. This method uses less water, so vegetables retain much more of their flavor. Stock may be used instead of water (see recipes). To relish the sublime taste of your own garden vegetables, do steam them until they are just bite-tender. They are so good!

• Mix appropriate table and cooking scraps with canned cat or dog food. Your pets will appreciate this.

• Do not put hot foods into the refrigerator or freezer. It takes a lot of extra fuel for the machine to cool them, whereas the normal kitchen temperature does it without wasting precious energy.

• Peel vegetables directly into a container if the peels are to to be frozen for the stockpot. It not, peel them onto a paper bag or an old newspaper to make the clean-up easier. Do not waste fresh paper towels or wax paper.

• Store cereals, beans, pastas, sugar, flour and any dried foods in empty glass jars instead of in plastic containers.

• If you live in the city and have a weekend country place, you can put your city garbage into a covered metal container and take it with you to the country for the compost heap (see *Composting*, p. 22). If there are field animals nearby, put it out for them. (I suggest this only if you commute by car; otherwise, unless the container is tightly sealed, it might be a bit unpleasant for your train companions!)

• Give any leftover soda or tonic water which has lost its fizz to house plants.

• Sprinkle used coffee grounds around your geraniums.

• Used tea leaves are a good fertilizer for rosebushes, plants and shrubs. If you use a tea bag, open it up and sprinkle the leaves around the plants.

WATER

I was raised on a vast cattle ranch in southern Arizona. On this burning, arid desert, water was more precious than gold. Open warfare, as well as legal trickery, was employed by the early settlers to gain water rights.

Pioneer parents taught their children how to survive in this seemingly hostile environment. The subject of our first lesson was always water. "Never, never go into the desert without water. If you go by foot, take a small canteen over your shoulder; if by horseback, tie a canteen or waterbag securely to your saddle; and if by wagon, carry a large drum of water for yourself and the horses." The lesson was a long one: "If you're thrown from your horse when riding alone on the desert and commit the unpardonable sin of not holding on to the reins, your horse will gallop back to the ranch, leaving you stranded without transportation or water. The hike back to the ranch can be long and hazardous. So after picking the jumping cactus from your pants and bewailing your stupidity, you limp off to the nearest mesquite tree for shade. Then, before anything else, you find a small, smooth pebble and place it under your tongue to slake your thirst. If this accident occurs in the middle of the day, stay under that mesquite tree until later in the day. Then you start walking, hoping to reach the ranch before dark. The pebble keeps your mouth and throat from becoming parched."

If a stream trickled through several ranches the land titles gave each rancher the use of this water. But the upper ranchers had the obligation to treat this stream as sacred. No contaminating wastes which would affect the lower ranches were ever dumped into it. If the rancher did not heed this survival law, the full fury of his neighbor, as well as the full power of the local court, would descend upon him.

Perhaps I place too much importance on water because of my childhood. However, the appalling fact is that today's average family of four uses five hundred gallons of water per day. Five hundred gallons! A great portion of this exorbitant amount is wasted in our kitchens, and as the water table of the nation drops alarmingly, it behooves us all to treat this precious element judiciously.

I speak of water as an "element," as it was considered in biblical times. There can be no life as we know it without water, so for me it remains an element. Rejoice in it, give thanks for it, but use it with care.

Anticipating society's ever-increasing need for water, there are studies in progress to prove the feasibility of purifying all household liquid wastes (effluents) and recycling them for everyday water needs in the large housing complexes. If water is not conserved, the system may have to be realized.

Check the following list to save your water and to help keep it clean:

• Keep all faucets closed; repair a dripping or leaking faucet immediately.

• When you turn on a faucet, remember to run the water on something or into something; do not let it run for naught . . . down the drain.

• Do not wash or rinse dishes under a running faucet. This lazy and not-too-hygienic method of turning on the hot-water faucet and washing and rinsing each dish is extremely wasteful of both water and power (see *Dishwashing*, below).

• Keep a bottle of water in the refrigerator for drinking so that you won't have to run quarts of water for one cool glass of water.

• If you have a pilot light, keep a kettle of water over it. This gives you warm water without having to run the hot faucet needlessly; and you are making use of heat you are paying for. Further, if you want boiling water for a cup of tea, it takes but a moment to bring this warm kettle to a boil.

• The disastrous effect of detergents on our underground and surface waters is well documented; instead of using detergents to wash your dishes, use a cake of plain soap, soap flakes, or a powdered soap (see *Dishwashing*, below).

• When you defrost your freezer, the melted frost is distilled water. It can be used in your steam iron or car battery—the ultimate in water recycling!

• I debated whether to place the electric disposal under the subject of "Water" or "Power." I decided on "Water" because home disposals use so much water that they are not permitted in many large cities. The basic reason—and thank heavens for it— is that sewers are not able to handle the additional water the thousands of disposals would dump into the system. In the country your food scraps should go into the compost heap or to the animals, not via the disposal into your septic tank.

• An aside: If you live in the country, why not put a rain barrel under the water spout of the roof? Rainwater is wonderful for washing hair, and it can be used to water the garden or shrubs.

DISHWASHING

When you begin the preparation of a meal, fill a dishpan or the sink half full of warm soapy water. As dishes are used, put them into the soapy water. When your cooking is finished and all the pots and pans are collected, wash them in these suds, rinse them quickly, and let them drain dry (or wipe with a clean cloth). Use the soapy water to wipe up the stove and counters. Your kitchen is now in tiptop shape for the final preparations of the meal, and you will have plenty of space for the after-dinner clutter.

Automatic Dishwashing: My gloomy forecast is that if water becomes more scarce, particularly in the arid zones, there is the possibility that the dishwasher will be banned, as it uses from fifteen to eighteen gallons of water per load. However, today it is the detergent which is upsetting the environment. At this writing there are seventy communities in eleven states where detergents are banned.

Why wait for detergents to be banned in your community? I wash our dishes in the dishwasher with the following mixture: 1 cup powdered soap, I cup washing soda, and 1 tablespoon Borax. Put into a glass jar, cover, and shake until thoroughly mixed. I use 1½ tablespoons of this mixture per load of dishes. (For our hard-water area this amount is correct; I have no over-flow of suds from the machine, and the dishes are clean. The amount of formula used would have to be adjusted in a soft-water area or in a home with a water-softening system.) I find this formula works satisfactorily, except that it occasionally leaves a slight film on *some* of the glasses and silverware. If this occurs, the film is easily removed by a quick wipe with a clean cloth. An alternative, if you like using this formula, is to wash the glasses and silverware by hand, and put only the dishware into the dishwasher. Either method requires just a speck more work, but isn't it better than having to abandon the use of the dish-washer? Or better than continuing to pour detergents into our waterways?

In addition to the foregoing suggestion, in order to keep our automatic dishwashers—and what a blessing they are—humming, I recommend the following procedure:

• Rinse the dishes in a pan of water before putting them into the machine; a dirty cooking pot works fine, because while the dishes are getting rinsed, the pot is being soaked with the same water. Think a moment: Is it common sense to rinse a dish, which is yet to be washed, in clean running water? Do not rinse dishes under a running faucet. This increases the water used for each load of dishes up to twenty or more gallons—a shocking waste.

• Wash only a full load of dishes. If you wash half or a partial load, you waste water and power.

• To save power, turn the dry cycle off at half or three-quarters of its regulated time. The drying time depends upon your machine, but I find a load of dishes does not need the full drying cycle.

Hand Dishwashing: Dishes are cleaned, and bacteria removed, by being washed in hot, soapy water and rinsed with hot water. (If there is sickness in your home the dishes should be scalded with boiling water.) Dishes can be washed, rinsed, and dried by hand; or washed, rinsed, and left to drain dry. If you have had to give up your dishwasher, or if you're just not too familiar with that "old-fashioned" hand method, here are step-by-step instructions:

1. Put a kettle of water on to heat, unless you have a really hot hot-water system.

2. Scrape all scraps from the plates and empty any liquids from the glasses and cups.

3. Empty any food left in the cooking or serving dishes into containers and store in the refrigerator or in the freezer, depending upon how you plan to use these leftovers.

4. Next to the sink, stack the glasses, then the silverware, then the china, and lastly, the pots and pans.

5. Half fill the sink or a dishpan (I prefer an enamel dishpan to a plastic dishpan because the enamel pan is more secure if

you need to move the pan when it is filled with water) with hot water, add a cake of plain soap, soap flakes or powdered soap, and stir up a good suds. (My grandmother always added a teaspoon of vinegar; she said it made the glasses sparkle.)

6. If your sink is large enough, and you do not have a double sink, place another pan in it for rinsing the dishes; otherwise, place the rinse pan on the sink. If you prefer, you can eliminate the rinse pan by placing a dish drainer on the sink with a drainer tray underneath it, so that the rinse water drains into the sink.

7. Begin by washing the glasses with a dishmop, a brush or, if you are wearing rubber gloves, wash them directly. Place them in the rinse pan right side up, or in the dish drainer. Wash and place the silverware around them.

8. Pour hot water or the now-boiling water from the kettle over the glasses and silverware. Refill the kettle and return it to the stove.

9. With tongs or rubber gloves, turn the glasses upside down and wipe them and the silverware with a clean linen cloth. Or leave them to drain dry in the dish drainer. Few dish drainers are large enough for all your dishes. The glasses dry rapidly and can be removed to make room for the chinaware. The silverware can be drained dry too, but it might be spotty unless the rinse water is really boiling hot. Hand-wiped silverware keeps its polish much longer than silver left to drain dry.

10. Continue with the washing and rinsing of the chinaware, and wipe dry or leave to drain dry.

11. Lastly, the pots and pans are scrubbed, rinsed and wiped.

POWER

Today we must face the fact that more than fifty percent of the power we consume requires the burning of fossil fuels which pollute the air and diminish a natural resource. Therefore, for the conservation of our resources and for cleaner air, we should not be capricious in pressing that ON button. The following is a list of suggestions which can save energy and lessen your fuel bill.

• Keep all your electrical equipment clean; it will run more efficiently and need less repair. Clean filters, defrost the refrigerator and freezer regularly, and don't forget to vacuum the lint from underneath all standing appliances.

• Buy the simplest type machine. The extras, such as an ice maker, an automatic defroster, or a soaking and sanitation cycle in the dishwasher all use extra power—and are they really necessary?

• Make a survey of the electrical equipment you have in your kitchen and discard (at a recycling center) whatever is excessive. Do you really need a bun warmer? Plate warmer? Toaster oven? Electrical wrap dispenser? Electric broiler? Egg cooker, coffeemaker or electric can opener? There are many efficient wall, as well as hand, can openers available, and I assure you, if you use one it will help firm up those arm muscles!

• When you go away on weekends or for a vacation, don't forget to turn the refrigerator to its lowest point.

• If there is a pilot light on your stove, see that it is properly regulated.

• Get all the light you pay for! Dusty light bulbs and bulb enclosures can reduce your room light by fifty percent. Therefore, remember to clean them with a damp cloth wrung out in warm soapy water with a splash of ammonia added to it, and wipe dry with a soft cloth.

• Plan to bake two or three dishes when you use the oven. Make it a complete oven meal or bake some extra dishes to freeze for future use. If you do this you are using all the heat and receiving full value for the cost of the fuel.

• Thoroughly wet and wring out a chamois cloth to remove cat or dog hairs from upholstered furniture. To vacuum them off is tedious and energy-consuming. Of course, the simplest method is not to allow your pets on the furniture!

KITCHEN MATERIALS

Our kitchens are overflowing, and will continue to overflow, with plastic, metal, glass and paper products. I strongly believe that we should curb the quantity of these products we buy, reuse those we do buy as long as possible, and finally, recycle all those that can be recycled.

To systematically recycle kitchen materials requires organization and effort. For me, recycling is an act of thanks for the use of a natural resource. Recycling should be a community affair; neighbors should take turns in hauling the material to the recycling center. Meanwhile, to collect the items to be recycled, you will have to find space in your home or garage for three large containers: two for the glass (clear glass is put into one container and colored glass into the other), and one for metals.

I hope the following list of substitutes for modern kitchen equipment, and suggestions for its care, will be helpful to you.

Plastics: Almost all plastics are made from petroleum products, another ebbing natural resource. They do not biodegrade nor can they be recycled. Burning is the only way to dispose of them. As our market is swamped with thousands of plastic products, it is easy and frightening to envision the piles and piles which are burned daily, discharging more ugly black smoke into our atmosphere. Those not burned will be floating in our waters or littering our land forever. It seems mandatory to me that we make a real effort to cut down on our wasteful consumption of these products.

The only exception I know of at this writing is a biodegradable plastic that is available for lids: lids to cover the paper containers for take-out orders in diners and restaurants. These plastic lids biodegrade within thirty to ninety days when exposed to sunlight. Can the answer be to our world glutted with plastics to store them in darkness? Or that each container carry a red label, warning that it will disintegrate after so many days of exposure to sunshine? The possibilities are enormous!

• Plastic Food Containers: I recommend that you buy the best quality, as they will last a lifetime. A substitute for plastic containers is glass jars.

Plastic containers are marvelous for freezing, but, even though I have read it is risky, I continuously use glass jars for freezing liquids (soups, sauces, vegetable waters, etc.) and, with care, you can too. It is important to remember to fill a glass jar only three-quarters full, this leaves room for expansion; also, the food must be cool before it is placed in the freezer, or the glass will break. To defrost, remove the jar from the freezer and thaw it at room temperature. You can speed the thawing by putting the jar in a pan of warm water, but do not put it in hot water or it will break.

• Plastic Bags: After these wonderful catchalls are used, they should be washed and reused. Do not throw them away until they are torn and unusable. To wash a plastic bag, use hot water and soap. I find that the easiest way to dry a bag is to pull it over a large bottle; the water on the inside runs out, and there is enough space between the bottle and the bag for the air to circulate and dry it out.

A substitute for plastic bags, besides glass containers, is the brown paper bag. I find it will keep salad greens crisp for days. Wash the greens, put them into a paper bag, twist the top closed, and place in the crisper drawer of the refrigerator.

Paper bags are also good for storing ice cubes in the freezer.

If you object to the appearance of brown paper bags for wastebasket liners, use white paper bags instead of plastic bags.

Insofar as you can, avoid buying vegetables or fruits in sealed plastic bags because you cannot inspect the freshness or condition of the contents. Also these bags usually have small holes in them and are, therefore, not reusable.

• Plastic Wraps: Instead of covering leftover foods with plastic wraps, put them into glass jars with secure covers.

Do not cover the salad bowl, into which you have placed your washed salad greens, with a plastic wrap. Instead, wrap the salad greens in a clean linen cloth, or put them into a paper bag and place in the refrigerator. The greens will stay crisp and cold until serving time.

Metals: Metals are a natural resource, seemingly in an unlimited supply. However, to assure a supply for future generations and to keep the earth tidy, recycle them.

• Aluminum Foil: A miracle product. What did we do without it? It is made from a plentiful natural resource, bauxite; but unfortunately, to manufacture it an enormous amount of electrical energy is needed, most of which is generated by not-too-plentiful fuels. Therefore, this wonder product should be used with cherished concern. Wash and reuse your aluminum foil until it is unusable. And remember, it can be recycled, so put all used foil in with the cans for the recycling center.

Is it such an advantage to line your broiler pan with aluminum foil? I have found that it is easily pierced by a sharp bone or too strong a jab of the fork, so the broiler has to be washed anyway. Also, it is difficult to remove from aluminum foil all those drippings and crispy bits of the steak or roast which should be saved for the stockpot. I think the use of aluminum foil in the broiler is false economy.

Instead of using aluminum foil as a liner in the bottom of the oven, put a large cookie sheet on the lower shelf. This will catch any spills and is easily and quickly washed. Further, I quote from an aluminum wrap box: "Protect oven from foods that boil over with piece of wrap a little larger than dish holding food. Place it on shelf 2-3 in. below food. Do not cover entire shelf or greater portion of it—nor line oven bottom. *Harmful heat concentration may result."* So use your cookie sheet!

Instead of wrapping your cheeses in aluminum foil, put them into a large glass jar with a small rag well moistened with vinegar; secure the cap, and the cheese stays fresh for two or three weeks.

Leftover foods keep as well in a glass container with a secure lid as they do wrapped in foil.

• Aluminum Containers: We all love these wonderful containers used for so many commercially frozen foods; use them until they fall apart, then put them in with the metal cans for recycling.

One reuse for the aluminum container is to cook a frozen vegetable in it in the oven. When you are having an oven dinner, place the frozen vegetable in the aluminum pan, add no water, just a dab of butter and seasoning.

• Tin Cans: A misnomer indeed. They are made mainly from aluminum or steel and some are washed with tin. If cans which do not contain aluminum were buried in the earth they would in time (lots of time) biodegrade. However, I think it is more efficient and helpful to our environment to recycle all cans. Your recycling box will hold many more cans if they are flattened. To do this, remove both ends of the can, put the can on the floor, and step on it.

• Aerosol Cans: The unhappy features of these cans are: (a) they may explode if stored in too warm a place, (b) they cannot be incinerated, and (c) they are expensive. Further, if certain propellants (the gas which is used to make the spray) are inhaled, they could be dangerous to your health. I do not find that these cans are needed in the kitchen because a rag and powdered cleanser are just as efficient as a spray cleanser. And, tell me true, don't you think hand-whipped or beater-whipped, cream is a lot tastier than that which squirts from the nozzle of a can?

Glass: The principal ingredient in the manufacturing of glass is sand (silica), which the earth has given us in abundance. However, glass does not biodegrade in one's lifetime. Actually, it takes many centuries for it to disintegrate, so it becomes litter unless it is put to use or recycled. When it is recycled, it is melted down to make new bottles, ground up for use in road construction, or used in other ways.

• Nonreturnable Bottles: I wish they had never been invented. They cannot be reused in the kitchen, or at least I cannot find a use for them. They should be recycled as should any unused jars or broken glass. The metal tops of the bottles should be put into the metal recycling box.

• Glass Containers: If they have a tight-fitting cover they are one of the best food containers available. Besides their obvious and numerous uses in the household and workshop, another use is found in the current hobby—and a good one it is—of making drinking glasses from old wine (or other appropriate) bottles. I have read of building walls with old bottles, and of making a surface for the patio with them. To do this the bottle is placed upside down and pushed into the earth until all the bottoms are even. They should make an attractive surface but, would be, I fear, quite slippery when wet.

• Cologne and Perfume Bottles: There are many uses for these exquisite bottles—and in the kitchen too. They can be used as carafes, oil and vinegar cruets, water bottles and vases. To remove the clinging fragrance I suggest this method: Wash the bottle and stopper in hot soapy water; fill with plain water, add one tablespoon of ammonia, replace the stopper and let stand a few hours. Empty this water and fill again with fresh water to which one teaspoon of baking soda has been added; replace the stopper and let it stand. After a few hours, rinse and smell. If the fragrance still lingers, tear a piece of old newspaper into strips, and wad it into the bottle; replace the stopper and let it stand overnight. The paper will absorb any remaining odors, and you will have gained an odorless and attractive container.

Paper Products: Paper is biodegradable, but only newspapers, magazines and cardboards can be recycled. Therefore, as the bulk of our kitchen papers cannot be dumped into the water or plowed into the earth, they are burned, thus adding more smoke to our air. Papers coated with wax or plastic are not biodegradable. They, too, must be burned, emitting a heavy, unhealthy smoke.

I often wonder if the reforestation programs of the paper companies can keep pace with our insatiable consumption of this essential material. The companies say they can, and I hope they are right. However, let's give them a hand by recycling and being economical in the use of all paper products.

• Wax Paper: Alas, in most cases I cannot find a substitute for this splendid product. However, here are two minor substitutes for its use in kitchen clean-up chores: (1) Sift and measure flour or sugar onto a plate instead of wax paper; the plate can be wiped off and put away, and (2) peel vegetables or fruits directly into a container or onto an old newspaper or paper bag, instead of onto wax paper.

• Freezing Paper: Again, what can be substituted for this needed product? Reuse it as often as you can and use it sparingly.

• Paper Towels: There is one good substitute for the paper towel, and that is rags. Good old clean rags. You may recall your grandmother's ragbag. This bag was filled with clean worn-out clothing, towels and linens. The buttons, snaps and hooks were removed from the clothing, and the rags were cut into various sizes. It supplied the household with everything from bandages to mops and dishrags. Why not start a ragbag in your home today? You will be recycling worn-out clothing and will save money otherwise spent for paper towels, mops, sponges, etc. Of course absorbent materials such as flannels and cotton make better cleaning rags than nylon or polyester materials.

In an emergency, when I do use paper towels for drying clean objects, such as salad greens or fruit, I flatten them out to dry and reuse them later for a messy cleaning chore.

• Paper Napkins: Why not use cloth napkins? A friend of mine taught me an inexpensive and easy way to make them: One yard of cotton calico print or a cotton polyester print (50% cotton, 50% polyester), makes four napkins. Tear the one yard of cloth into quarters and tear off the selvage and scissor-cut edges. Fringe the sides while watching your favorite television show. I recommend using a material with a colorful small pattern. For twelve napkins, choose three different patterns and mix the sets. The napkins are ample in size (which pleases every man) and they add great charm to your table. These napkins launder easily and no ironing is needed for the cotton polyester material; just wash, dry, and fold. Personally, I prefer the 100% cotton napkins as they are more absorbent, and the texture is softer. It takes but a minute to iron them. However, try a set of both and decide for yourself, but do eliminate those ugly wadded paper napkins from your table!

To introduce anew the use of cloth napkins, each family member should have his own napkin for the week. If you want to avoid the chore of polishing those inherited silver napkin rings, you can paint each member of the family's name on a spring wooden clothespin, and clip it to the napkin. And there are attractive and colorful inexpensive napkin rings available in wood and plastic. Each member of the family receives a fresh napkin on Sunday, and unless you serve lobster in the shell or barbecued spareribs, it should last him through the week.

• Disposable Paper Plates and Glasses, and Plastic-Coated Papers: These are a real waste in the home. If you find too many glasses are used by the family, don't give them a paper or plastic-coated glass to throw away after one use. Give each a real glass or an enamel mug, and paint his initials on it. Stand it on the sink and ask him to use it for his drinking container throughout the day.

After they have been washed out, you can reuse the plastic-coated containers, in which cottage cheese, milk and other foods are sold, for storing food in the refrigerator or for freezing.

If you have been using plastic-coated paper items for picnics, why not make the next picnic a special occasion? Put in your basket a cotton cloth, cotton napkins and real glasses, dishes, and silverware. It will make such a romantic setting, right out of a Renoir or Seurat painting.

KITCHEN CLEANSERS AND CLEANING

Sitting on your kitchen shelves are many biodegradable cleaning agents. Some of these cleansers may require a little more elbow grease, but by using home cleansers you save money and contribute to a cleaner environment. Before listing home cleansers, I want to say a word about soap.

Plain soap cleans wonderfully well, so well in fact that when a surgeon washes up before and after an operation he uses an antiseptic soap, not a detergent. If a child eats soap, he may get a stomach ache, but it will not be lethal; its fumes can be inhaled, for they are not harmful; it is the kitchen's best friend.

Following is a list of home cleansers I have used successfully. If you ask your grandmother what cleansers her mother used to keep the kitchen clean, I am sure she would be able to triple the list:

• Copper and brass can be cleaned by mixing thoroughly 1 cup flour, 1 cup salt, and 1 cup vinegar. Pour into a glass jar and cover securely. To clean a copper pot, put 1 tablespoon of this mixture on it, rub, rinse in hot water and dry. If the paste hardens, add a little water and vinegar, and stir well. To clean brass, rub on this paste, allow to dry and rub off with a dry cloth.

• A quick pick-me-up for your copper pans is to sprinkle salt on the pan, and with a leftover lemon-half, rub until the tarnish is removed. The lemon softens the hands too.

• A leftover piece of lime rubbed on a cutting board will re-move the odor of any strong foods.

• Flour is marvelous for shining stainless steel; just take a dry cloth, dip it into dry flour, and rub. The steel will gleam. Also to remove spots from stainless steel, moisten a cloth with vinegar and rub over the spots.

• Plain baking soda is excellent for cleaning the inside of the refrigerator or freezer: Mix 3 tablespoons of baking soda to a quart of warm water; it will not only clean, but deodorize as well.

• For cleaning woodwork, tiles, etc., I find that this mixture does an excellent job: 1 gallon warm water, 1 cup ammonia, ½ cup vinegar, and ¼ cup baking soda.

• For cleaning windows, use ½ cup ammonia and 1 tablespoon vinegar to 1 quart warm water. The windows really sparkle.

• Salt is a fine scouring agent for a metal or porcelain sink; it sterilizes as well as helps keep the drain pipes open.

• I have never had a clogged drain pipe, so I have not been able to try this home remedy; but since it is from a reliable source, I shall include it in case this misfortune befalls you: Pour 1 cup baking soda down the drain, add ½ cup vinegar, cover for 1 minute—and the drain should become unclogged.

KITCHEN INSECTS

Most of the common household insects can be eliminated by simple methods; it is not necessary to use a lethal insecticide:

• If you have ants in your kitchen, sprinkle the area where you find them with cayenne pepper; or take slices of lemon and place them along the path of the ants.

• A deterrent for flies is to grow pots of basil or mint and place them near the kitchen door or on the open windowsill. Besides keeping the flies at bay, you have lovely herbs for your cooking.

• If you use a poison to rid your kitchen of cockroaches, and have pets, you run the risk of killing the pets as well as the cockroaches. If you should be plagued with these tenacious insects, I suggest you try this formula: Mix lime (available at any hardware store) with salt and water and paint it around the area where the cockroaches are found. We have escaped being infested with cockroaches, so I have not had the opportunity to test this recipe; but, again, its source is dependable, so I recommend its use.

COMPOSTING

Even if you have only a small plot of land, do start a compost heap. It converts waste material into humus, which makes garden soil more porous, hold water better and provides excellent plant food.

A neighbor and friend who has great success with growing flowers and vegetables gives the following advice for keeping the composting process simple:

Take a 4-foot-wide wire mesh or piece of snow fence, and form a cylindrical container 4 to 6 feet in diameter. Chicken wire will do if it is strengthened by wiring it to four posts set in the ground. Set this up, preferably in a shady place, and dump into it leaves from the lawn and kitchen scraps (which do not go into the stockpot), such as peelings, parings, discarded lettuce leaves, and the like, but *no* meat scraps, bones, or fat, because they create an odor and attract animals. Pea, bean, and tomato vines can be used also, but don't add weeds which may have seeds that can cause future trouble. Also welcomed by the compost heap is hair. Human hair, animal hair and fur. Hair and fur are pure protein and when added to the compost heap they break down into nitrogen, an important requirement for good soil.

The heap should be kept moist to cause decomposition; so keep the heap fairly level or depressed toward the center to hold the rains and melted snow. This explains why you should put the heap in a shady spot where the sun won't dry it out. It helps, too, to sprinkle some soil through the heap to add micro-organisms that do the converting.

The waste material will settle as it rots down with moisture and as you keep adding waste. When it becomes compact and from one to two-feet deep, remove the fence and set it up in a new place to start another heap. In this way you will have one heap to use while another is being made, and one fence serves a dual purpose.

This method produces humus in about eighteen months. There are other methods for making a compost heap in a shorter time, but they are complicated and require more work.

(2) STOCKS

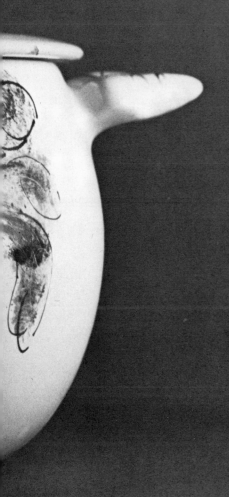

*"Stock is everything in cooking . . . Without it,
nothing can be done. If one's stock is good,
what remains of the work is easy; if, on the
other hand, it is bad or merely mediocre, it is
quite hopeless to expect anything approaching
a satisfactory result."* ESCOFFIER

THE STOCKPOT

The desire to serve forth from our modern kitchens the whole-
someness and delicious foods of our grandmother's era is a uni-
versal wish. Despite the overpackaged and refined foods in today's
markets, it can be done. You can do it if you are willing to make
the effort. The work will not be as arduous or backbreaking as
it was for Granny. We don't have to milk the cows, churn the
butter, butcher the beef, grind the meats for sausages, make the
bread, can the fruits and vegetables, and make the soap. But we
do have to give more thought to our food purchases and put more
effort into their preparation.

Convenience foods, such as TV dinners and commercial frozen
entrées are costly, low in nutrition, and their wrappings are pol-
lutants.

Granny's fare was fresh from the garden and completely recycled. Stale bread went into succulent steamed puddings; the
fats from bacon, sausages, and meats were saved for cooking or
soap-making; potato water was saved for bread or soup; soured
milk or cream was made into cheeses, and leftovers were disguised and served anew, or went into the stockpot.

During the era of large wood- and coal-burning kitchen stoves, whether in a palace or in a pioneer's shack, the stockpot stood permanently and majestically on the back of every stove. It simmered continuously, and the savory leftovers of meals and cooking scraps were always being added. (The stockpot was probably started fresh every month or two.) If, for example, a boiled chicken or a piece of meat and vegetables were to be the family's dinner, the pot was pulled forward to a higher heat area of the stove and the ingredients were put into the pot. When they were cooked and removed, the pot was returned to the back of the stove. The meal was enhanced by being cooked in stock, and the next day's soup or stew was enriched by the meat and vegetables. A continuous cycle! Or, as Alexandre Dumas called it, "the eternal kettle."

The stockpot is the oldest, most tried-and-true method of recycling food. The basic requirements to produce a rich and toothsome stock exist in every contemporary kitchen. It is my opinion that the preparation and use of homemade stocks should become as essential a part of our present-day cooking as it was for the pioneer woman or for the chef in the king's kitchen.

Stocks, like so many other foods, were brought to the peak of their refinement by the French. In French cooking each classic dish or sauce had its corresponding stock. A classic stock is made from a specific combination of ingredients.

The work to prepare all the classic stocks would be gargantuan, and freezer space to store them would be prohibitive. This book, therefore, is concerned with the making of a basic stock that is a combination of various ingredients, including meats, poultry and leftovers.

The purist may shudder, but it is my experience, from years of cooking and testing, that basic stock can be substituted for any of the classic meat stocks in practically all recipes. Fish stock, of course, has no substitute. Recipes for the classic stocks are included for your reference, and each recipe notes which classic stock may be used in place of the basic stock.

The rewards you will receive if you make the effort to use basic stock are: (1) you will cook more economically and ecologically, (2) you will cook more nutritiously, (3) you will add special flavor to your cooking, (4) you will save time, and (5) you will enjoy new recipes. Large promises indeed! But not one is an empty promise, as you will note from the following.

1. *Economy and Ecology*: The ingredients for making a stock include the less expensive cuts of meat, bones with their marrow, chicken wings and necks, vegetables a bit too old, tasty leftovers, carcasses of baked fowl, roast bones, roast and steak essences, vegetable waters and peelings. All of these at-hand foods go into the pot with water to cover, and the slow simmering extracts and blends the flavors to make a delicious stock. And by this process you are recycling your savory leftovers, not feeding them to the garbage can.

2. *Nutrition*: The long simmering of the ingredients extracts all the nutriments that otherwise would be discarded. For example, wine or lemon juice added to the pot extracts calcium from the bones. Also, and extremely important today, stock is fat-free. After the stock has cooked, been strained and chilled, the fat congeals on the surface and is quickly and easily removed—a blessing for everyone!

3. *Flavor*: The succulent juices of all the food in the pot are, by many hours of slow cooking, absorbed into the stock. The taste of soups, stews and sauces is enriched when they are prepared with this flavorful stock. If basic stock instead of water is added to frozen foods, dehydrated foods and canned foods, their flavor will be improved a hundredfold.

4. *Time Saving*: An ample quantity of basic stock in the freezer will lighten the chores of daily cooking for a month or two, and delicious soups, stews or sauces can be rapidly prepared with it. But do not be misled: There is no quick method of bypassing the work involved in the preparation and completion of basic stock.

However, this work is far less arduous than cooking one truly good soup, stew or sauce without it.

Freezers have eliminated the continuous cooking of stocks because table and cooking scraps, vegetable waters and peelings can be frozen in containers until the day you are ready to cook your supply of stock. Also, completed stock can be frozen for an indefinite period. Defrosting stock takes only a moment because it can be placed over direct heat. Perhaps we can update Dumas's phrase to "the eternal freezer."

5. *New Recipes*: It would be foolhardy to claim that the basic stock is a new recipe when, actually, it is a robust descendant of the stock cooked by the caveman with his first pot. However, I can claim that the use of basic stock in your favorite recipes will give them a new dash and taste.

Upon completion of your first pot of stock, try one or two of the soup recipes. I have purposely included more recipes for soup than anything else because they will give you and your family an immediate appreciation and enjoyment of stocks. And when you find out how good they are, your family's fare will include, I am sure, many more delectable and nutritious soups than in your prestock days.

The only equipment needed for stockpot cooking is (1) a large pot with a capacity of six to ten quarts, and (2) freezer space. It is as easy to cook six quarts of stock as two, but you must have freezer space for storage.

Today there are stockpots of copper, stainless steel, cast iron, aluminum and enamelware, ranging in capacity from one quart to many gallons. The ideal pot is heavy, and the lid should fit securely but lightly on top to permit a small amount of steam to escape. A few chefs are of the opinion that a stock made in a ceramic pot is superior to one made in a metal pot. I do not find this so, but if you are curious, make the comparison in your own kitchen. Remember, the ceramic pot must have an asbestos plate between it and the heat.

THE STEAMER

Your stockpot will be used for numerous top-of-the-stove recipes, but do not overlook another marvelous use: it can be converted into a perfect steamer by adding a rack, trivet or steam basket. The age-old culinary art of steaming is exquisitely simple, tasteful and healthful. Recipes for steaming poultry, meats, fish, vegetables and desserts are included in this book, as well as explicit steaming directions. The double boiler is not a steamer, because it does not allow the steam to flow freely around the food or a mold.

The steaming of poultry, meats and certain vegetables over stock can be compared to a friendship: it is a give and take—the subtle flavors in the steam of the stock are absorbed into the food, and the food returns the compliment by adding some of its flavor to the stock. When the cooking is finished, the stock's volume has been decreased and this, together with the added flavor, makes an especially rich and delicious basic stock.

If your stockpot is in use and you want to steam some food, an efficient steamer can be made from any large pot, even a roasting pan, if it has a secure-fitting lid. By the way, the roasting pan is excellent for steaming a whole fish.

Steaming a dessert in a decorative metal mold, or a lard or coffee can, was an everyday affair during the era when extra fuel had to be added to the fire to heat the oven. But today it has become rather uncommon. Steamed desserts should be gracing more tables because they are so simple to prepare, and I have found that if you cook to please a man, a steamed pudding brings him a contentment that all the glistening gelatins, frozen ices and oversweet cakes never do.

If you find the steamed recipes as delicious as I do, you may have the added enjoyment of searching for metal molds. Classic pudding molds of many shapes and sizes are available in various stores, and wonderful old metal pudding molds can often be discovered at thrift shops and secondhand stores. If the shape is attractive and there are no breaks in the metal, don't worry about the tarnish and dismal appearance of a mold; it is relatively inexpensive to have one retinned. After a tin bath, the mold emerges sparkling, decorative and ready for your use.

It is my hope that the use of the stockpot and steamer will become a pleasant habit and that they will add new dimensions to your cooking skills.

STOCK NOTES

Ingredients: The ingredients given for the stock recipes should be considered as guides. To each, except the fish stock, you may add a variety of vegetables in season, such as radish tops, fresh peapods, artichokes, etc. Also, as you gain confidence in stock preparation, you may wish to omit or add ingredients to your taste. I hope you will experiment.

Frozen vegetables may be added in place of fresh, but it is, of course, much more economical to use vegetables in season. The use of stocks, besides adding to the flavor of your meals, should be a saving for the family purse, not a luxury!

Because the stocks will be used to prepare many different dishes they should *not* be highly seasoned.

Preparation: Prepare to make your basic stock a week or two in advance by freezing in plastic bags or containers:

1. Bones from beef, lamb and veal roasts; steak bones and meat scraps; the carcasses of roasted chickens, turkeys, ducks, and, if you are fortunate, game birds. If you make a recipe calling for boned chicken breasts or any other boned meats (leg of lamb, etc.) be sure to ask the butcher to give you the bones. You have paid for them, and they will enrich your stock.

2. Drippings from beef, lamb and veal roasts and steaks; also drippings from roasted or broiled chicken. To obtain these drip-

pings, place the roasting pan or broiler on top of the stove, add a small quantity of water or wine and bring to a fast boil. Rapidly scrape all the crusty bits from the pan and pour into a container.

3. Vegetable peelings, except potato and beets, should be saved to add to the stockpot.

4. Leftover cooked vegetables, except those of the cabbage family or beets.

5. If freezer space is available, freeze the water in which vegetables—except beets, cauliflower, parsnips, and cabbage—have been boiled or steamed. To simplify the storing and freezing of vegetable waters, take a large glass or plastic container and pour into it the first bit of vegetable water. Place it in the freezer, and continue adding vegetable waters, and/or meat drippings to it, and returning it to the freezer. If glass is used, do not fill it more than three-quarters full. You will have what looks like a frozen zombie, but it is all pure goodness for the pot.

6. When your savory meat and bone scraps total approximately two or three pounds, you are ready to go to the butcher to buy any of the fresh meats you wish to add (see recipes) to the pot. Don't buy too much—remember the cache of health-giving goodies you have accumulated!

Dont's *for the Stockpot:*

1. Don't use the bone or meat of ham or pork. These should be saved for a classic ham stock or to use in a pea, lentil or bean soup (see recipes).

2. Don't add any creamed vegetables or sauces to the stockpot.

3. Don't add any cabbage, cauliflower, parsnips, brussel sprouts or beets.

4. Don't add any potatoes, potato water, noodles, macaroni, spaghetti or rice. Any of these will cloud the stock.

5. Don't add too much spinach or spinach water; it will make your stock green and slightly bitter.

6. Don't add any fish (see *Fish Stock*, p. 42).

Skimming: The question of whether "to skim or not to skim" a stock while it is cooking has provoked me to considerable experimenting and has led me into the study of nutrition. My conclusion is: Do not skim. If you do not skim, you will see sediment at the bottom of the container when the stock has cooled. This sediment is rich in nutriments; it is absorbed into stews, soups and sauces and, I believe, adds to the flavor. If you need a sparkling consommé, golden broth, aspic or clear stock for a delicate sauce, clarify the stock by following the directions given later in the book.

Straining: Straining a large pot of stock may pose a problem for the beginner. The following method works efficiently for me:

1. Remove any large pieces of meat with a fork or tongs.

2. Remove all large bones with tongs or a slotted spoon.

3. Remove the marrow from the marrow bones. The marrow should be served as a food or saved to be added to a soup or stew.

4. Place a large strainer over a 2-quart heatproof glass or metal mixing bowl.

5. Place a colander over a pie plate.

6. Ladle the stock into the strainer. When the bowl is full, pour the strained stock into containers and dump the pulpy ingredients into the colander.

7. Continue straining and dumping until the pot is empty.

8. Leave the pulpy mass of ingredients in the colander to drain. Press it with the back of a large spoon to squeeze out all the stock. Add this liquid to the containers and discard the pulp.

Storing: Cool the containers of stock and refrigerate overnight. Remove and discard all the fat which has congealed on the surface of the stock. The stock is now ready to be used or to be frozen for future use. In freezing stock I recommend that at least a quart of it be frozen in an ice tray. When it is frozen, put the cubes into a container and back into the freezer. When you need a small amount of the stock for braising or to add to a sauce, use 1 or 2 cubes. Each cube is approximately 2 tablespoons.

BASIC STOCK

This is the basic stock recipe, and as previously stated, I believe it is the stock to use in all recipes except, of course, the fish recipes. In each recipe where basic stock is used, I have given the individual, classic stocks used in French haute cuisine; but the basic stock may be substituted with no loss of quality in all the recipes.

BASIC STOCK

2 *to 3 lbs. various meat and bone scraps and meat leftovers*	2 *medium white turnips, washed and quartered*
2 *to 3 lbs. chicken necks and wings*	4 *cloves garlic, peeled*
4 *beef marrow bones, cut into 4-inch pieces*	2 *bay leaves*
	6 *tbs. salt*
1 *veal knuckle, cracked*	16 *peppercorns*
6 *medium carrots, washed and cut into 2-inch pieces*	6 *stalks celery, including the leaves, washed and cut into 2-inch pieces*
2 *large onions, peeled and studded with 4 cloves*	8 *sprigs parsley*
4 *medium leeks, washed and cut into 2-inch pieces, including the fresh green tops*	1 *cup of red or dry white wine*
	Vegetable waters
	Cold water

Crack any large roast bones with a cleaver.

Put all the ingredients into an 8- to 10-quart soup pot. Add cold water to cover by 2 inches. Place a loose-fitting lid on top and bring slowly to a boil. Immediately adjust the heat so that the stock simmers lazily. Stir occasionally. Simmer 4 to 5 hours. Turn off the heat and cool

When cool, strain (see *Straining*, p. 33), the stock into containers and refrigerate. When cold, remove and discard all the fat congealed on the surface. Then refrigerate the stock for immediate use, or place in the freezer for future use.

This recipe makes 5 to 6 quarts.

Variations:

a. Add one 3- to 4-lb. chicken. Remove after 1 hour of cooking, or when tender.

b. Add 3 lbs. brisket of beef. Remove after 2 hours of cooking or when tender.

c. Add 1 lb. chicken giblets.

d. Add 2 lbs. short ribs of beef.

e. Add 2 to 3 lbs. shin of beef, cut into 4- to 5-inch pieces.

f. Add 2 cups canned or fresh tomatoes, with 2 tsps. sugar.

g. Add the juice of 1 lemon instead of the wine.

h. Add 1 head of lettuce, washed and coarsely sliced.

i. Add ¼ lb. fresh or frozen mushrooms or mushroom stems.

j. For a stronger stock, remove the lid during the last hour of cooking and turn up the heat so that the pot boils gently.

CLASSIC CHICKEN STOCK

1 *4-lb chicken or a 5-lb.*
fowl
2½ *lbs. chicken necks*
and wings
1 *veal knuckle,*
cracked
1 *medium onion, stuck*
with 3 cloves
4 *medium carrots,*
washed and cut into
quarters
2 *medium leeks,*
washed and cut into
1-inch pieces, includ-
ing the fresh green
leaves

2 *stalks celery, washed,*
including leaves, cut
into 1-inch pieces
½ *tsp. dried thyme*
1 *bay leaf*
1 *garlic clove, peeled*
2 *tbs. salt*
6 *peppercorns*
3 *sprigs parsley*
1 *cup dry white wine*
Cold water

Place all the ingredients into a large 8- to 10-quart soup pot. Add cold water to cover by 2 inches. Place a loose-fitting lid on top and bring slowly to a boil. Immediately adjust heat to a simmer, and simmer for 3 to 4 hours. Turn off the heat and cool.

When cool, strain all the stock into containers and refrigerate. When cold, remove and discard all the fat congealed on the surface. Refrigerate the stock for immediate use, or freeze for future use.

This recipe makes approximately 4 quarts.

Variations:
a. Omit the veal knuckle.
b. Add 2 lbs. lean veal.
c. Add a second chicken of 2½ to 3 lbs. and remove after

1 hour of cooking, or when tender. This chicken can be served at once; or the meat can be used for a chicken salad or a chicken casserole.

d. Add 2 tbs. lemon juice instead of the wine.

e. Add 1 lb. chicken gizzards and hearts.

f. Add 1 cup canned tomatoes with 1 tsp. sugar.

g. Add 2 small white turnips, washed and halved.

h. Add ¼-lb. fresh mushrooms or mushroom stems.

i. Add 4 chicken feet. Before adding to the pot, prepare them as follows: Place in a pan, cover with cold water and bring to a boil. Remove and plunge them into cold water. Remove and discard the scaly yellow outer skin.

j. Add the carcass of a roasted chicken.

k. For a stronger stock remove the lid during the last hour of cooking and turn up the heat so that the pot boils gently.

NOTE: The meat from the large chicken or fowl may be used in making chicken croquettes.

CLASSIC BEEF STOCK

½ cup dried mushrooms
2 lbs. short ribs of beef
2 lbs. beef marrow
   bones, cut into 2- to
   4-inch pieces
1 veal knuckle, cracked
1 lb. ground beef chuck
1 large onion, peeled
   and coarsely chopped
1 clove garlic, peeled
3 medium carrots,
   washed and cut into
   quarters

2 tbs. salt
10 peppercorns
1 bay leaf
1 tsp. mace
1 tsp. dried thyme
3 sprigs parsley
3 ribs celery, including
   leaves, washed and
   quartered
1 cup dry red wine
1 tbs. soy sauce
   Cold water

Soak the dried mushrooms in 1 cup of warm water for 15 minutes.

Put all the ingredients, including the water in which the mushrooms were soaked, into a 6- to 8-quart soup pot. Cover with cold water by 2 inches. Place a loose-fitting lid on top, bring to a boil. Immediately adjust heat to a simmer, and simmer for 3 to 4 hours. Turn off the heat and cool.

When cool, strain all the stock into containers and refrigerate. When cold, remove and discard all the fat congealed on the surface. Refrigerate the stock for immediate use, or freeze for future use.

This recipe makes approximately 3½ quarts.

Variations:

a. Add 3 lbs. brisket of beef. Remove after 2 hours of cooking or when tender.

b. Add 1 cup of canned or fresh tomatoes, with 1 tsp. sugar.

c. Add 2 tbs. of lemon juice instead of the wine.

d. Add any roast beef or steak drippings.

e. Add any roast beef or steak bones.

f. For a stronger stock, remove the lid during the last hour of cooking and turn up the heat so that the pot boils gently.

CLASSIC BROWN STOCK

4½ lbs. beef bones, including at least 4 marrow bones	1 medium onion, peeled and coarsely sliced
3 lbs. veal bones, including 1 knuckle	1 medium carrot, washed and quartered
	1 cup dry red wine or water

Have your butcher crack and saw the bones into 2- to 4-inch pieces.

Put the bones, onion and carrot into a large roasting pan. Place in a 400° F. oven for 45 to 50 minutes. Occasionally turn the bones so that they brown evenly on all sides.

Remove pan from the oven and put the bones into an 8- to 10-quart soup pot. Deglaze the roasting pan with the wine or water and add to the pot. Also add:

2 medium carrots, washed and quartered	1 bay leaf
	3 tbs. salt
2 medium leeks, including the fresh green leaves, washed and cut into coarse slices	10 peppercorns
	1 cup canned tomatoes
	1 tbs. tomato paste
	1 tsp. sugar
1 large onion, peeled and quartered	1 cup dry red wine
	Cold water to cover the ingredients by 1 inch
4 stalks celery, washed and quartered	

Bring to a boil. Adjust heat to a simmer, cover with a loose-fitting lid, and simmer 4 to 5 hours. Turn off the heat and cool.

When cool, strain into containers and refrigerate. When cold, remove and discard all the fat congealed on the surface. Refrigerate the stock for immediate use, or place in the freezer for future use.

This recipe makes approximately 6 quarts.

Variations:
a. Add the carcass of a roast chicken.
b. Add 3 lbs. brisket of beef. Remove after 2 hours of cooking or when tender.
c. Add any roast beef or steak drippings.

d. Add any steak or roast beef bones.

e. Add 2 tbs. of lemon juice instead of the wine.

f. For a stronger stock, remove the lid during the last hour of cooking and turn up the heat so that the pot boils gently.

CLASSIC VEAL STOCK

3 *to 4 lbs. veal knuckles, cracked*	1 *medium onion, peeled and stuck with 2 cloves*
1 *lb. shoulder, neck or shin of veal, cubed*	1 *clove garlic, peeled*
1 *cup dry white wine*	2 *stalks celery, including leaves, washed and quartered*
1 *tbs. salt*	
8 *peppercorns*	2 *medium carrots, washed and quartered*
2 *medium leeks, including the fresh green leaves, washed and cut into 2-inch pieces*	1 *bay leaf*
	4 *sprigs parsley*
	Cold water

Put all the ingredients into a large soup pot. Add water to cover by 1 inch. Bring slowly to a boil, place a loose-fitting lid on top, and adjust the heat to a simmer. Simmer for 3 to 4 hours. Turn off the heat and cool.

When cool, strain into containers and refrigerate. When cold, remove and discard all the fat congealed on the surface. Refrigerate the stock for immediate use, or freeze for future use.

This recipe makes approximately 3 quarts.

Variations:

a. Add one 3½-lb chicken and remove after 1 hour of cooking or when tender.

b. Add the carcass of a roasted chicken.

c. Add 1 small white turnip, washed and halved.
d. Add 2 tbs. lemon juice instead of the wine.

CLASSIC HAM STOCK

No salt measurement is given, because the ham may season the stock sufficiently. If not, add salt to taste.

1 ham bone	4 stalks celery, including
4 quarts cold water	leaves, washed and
1 cup dry white wine	quartered
1 large onion, peeled and	1 clove garlic, peeled
quartered	½ tsp. dried thyme
2 medium carrots,	7 peppercorns
scrubbed and quartered	1 bay leaf
	3 sprigs parsley

If the ham bone is large, crack and break it with a cleaver.

Put all the ingredients into a large pot and bring slowly to a boil. Immediately adjust the heat to a simmer, cover with a loose-fitting lid, and simmer for 2 to 3 hours. Turn off the heat and cool.

When cool, strain the stock and pour into containers. Save the small pieces of ham to add to a soup. Refrigerate the stock. When cold, remove and discard all the fat congealed on the surface. Refrigerate the stock for immediate use, or store in the freezer for future use.

This recipe makes approximately 3 quarts.

Variations:
a. Add any pork roast bones or pork meat scraps.
b. Add any pieces of bacon rind.
c. Add 2 tbs. of lemon juice instead of the wine.

FISH STOCK

This is quick and simple to prepare. I suggest it be prepared in small quantities so that valuable freezer space can be saved for more complicated stocks. However, it is convenient to have a few cups on hand for a fish sauce or soup or for cooking rice to accompany a fish dish.

I recommend using flounder, halibut or whiting. Frozen fish can be used, but the stock will have more flavor if the head, tail and backbone of a fresh fish are added to the pot.

1½ lbs. fresh or frozen fish
1 medium onion, peeled and finely chopped
2 ribs of celery, cut into small pieces
1 medium carrot, scrubbed and finely diced

2 sprigs parsley
3 slices lemon
8 peppercorns
2 tsps. salt.
¾ cup dry white wine
3 cups cold water

Put all the ingredients into a pot and bring slowly to a boil. Cover with a loose-fitting lid. Immediately adjust the heat to a simmer, and simmer for 30 minutes. Turn off the heat and cool.

When cool, strain through a fine sieve into a container. Refrigerate the stock if it is to be used within a day or two. If not, store in the freezer for future use.

This makes approximately 3½ cups of stock.

TO CLARIFY STOCK

For a sparkling clear stock to prepare aspics and special sauces, the following method is used:

> 4 cups cold stock   1 eggshell
> 2 egg whites

Remove every particle of fat from the stock; also check to see that there is no grease in the pot. Pour the cold stock into the pot. Lightly beat the egg whites with a fork or wire whisk, and crush the eggshell.

Place the pot over medium heat, pour the egg whites into the stock, add the eggshell and beat with a whisk until the liquid begins to boil. Stop beating but watch the pot carefully. Turn heat off at once as the stock comes up to a hard boil. Remove the pot from the stove and set aside. Do not disturb for at least 15 minutes.

Pour gently into a container through a fine strainer lined with 2 layers of cheesecloth or a linen cloth wrung out in cold water. The cold cloth traps any particle of fat that might have lingered in the stock.

(3) SOUPS

SOUP NOTES

Frozen vegetables may be used instead of fresh vegetables in making soups. The cost is greater, but the time saved may make their use worth your while.

Canned broth may be used instead of your own stock, but a lot of flavor will be forfeited. Also, the can has to be recycled.

All soups, except the cold soups, should be served piping hot in heated bowls or tureens.

All pepper should be freshly ground peppercorns.

Taste before you serve. Correct the seasoning to your taste.

For additional soup recipes, see Chapter 8, "Dried Beans and Grains."

BEEF CONSOMMÉ

The difference between clarified stock and consommé is that the stock used to make the consommé is strengthened by the addition of meat and vegetables and by simmering it uncovered to reduce its volume.

Consommé may be served plain or with any of numerous

garnishes added. Consommé is the base for a few soups, but it is not used in sauces or stews.

10 cups cold basic stock,
   beef stock or brown
   stock from which all
   fat has been removed
½ lb. lean ground beef
1 medium carrot,
   scrubbed and sliced in
   thin rounds

1 leek, or 3 scallions, including the fresh green
   leaves, washed and
   thinly sliced
1 stalk celery, washed
   and finely diced
1 tsp. salt
3 peppercorns
2 egg whites

Put all the ingredients into a large pot. Slowly bring to a boil, beating continuously with a whisk or fork. When the mixture comes to a boil, immediately lower the heat to a simmer. Simmer uncovered for 1 to 1½ hours. Set aside to cool.

Line a fine strainer with 2 layers of cheesecloth or a linen cloth wrung out in cold water, and when the consommé is cool, strain it into a container.

To serve: Heat and serve in individual heated cups; or add any one of the vegetable garnishes listed or a garnish to suit your taste.

This recipe makes 7 to 8 cups.

NOTE: If all the fat has been removed from the stock, if the beef is lean and if the cheesecloth or linen cloth is wrung out in cold water, there should be no fat in the consommé. Should fat be present, chill the consommé and discard any fat congealed on the surface.

Vegetable Garnishes:

The following vegetables should be added to hot consommé, covered and simmered for 5 minutes. Allow 1 to 2 tablespoons of vegetables per serving.

Carrots: Peeled and cut into julienne strips or paper-thin rounds or finely diced.

Celery: Washed and cut into 2-inch julienne strips or diced into tiny squares.

Leeks: Washed and the white part cut into julienne strips or thin rounds.

Turnips: Peeled and cut into julienne strips or finely diced.

The following vegetables should be stirred into the boiling consommé at the last moment. Heat, but do not cook. Serve at once. Except where otherwise specified, allow 1 to 2 teaspoons per serving.

Carrots: Peeled and finely grated.

Celery: Leaves washed and finely chopped.

Scallions: Washed and cut into paper-thin round slices, including the fresh green tops, or finely chopped.

Tomatoes: Peeled, seeded and cut into julienne strips or finely diced.

Spinach: Leaves sliced into julienne strips.

Watercress: Small whole tender leaves.

Mushrooms: Cleaned and finely chopped. One small mushroom per serving.

Ginger root: Peeled and cut. One or 2 paper-thin rounds per serving.

Escarole: One or 2 leaves washed and finely shredded.

Parsley: Finely chopped.

Chives: Finely chopped.

CHICKEN CONSOMMÉ

10 cups cold chicken
stock from which all
fat has been removed
1 lb. chicken necks and
wings
1 medium carrot,
scrubbed and sliced in
thin rounds

1 leek, or 3 scallions, including the fresh green
leaves, washed and
thinly sliced
1 stalk celery, washed
and finely diced
1 tsp. salt
3 peppercorns
2 egg whites

Put all the ingredients into a large pot. Slowly bring to a boil, beating continuously with a whisk or fork. When the mixture comes to a boil, immediately lower the heat to a simmer. Simmer uncovered for 1 to 1½ hours. Set aside to cool.

Line a fine strainer with 2 layers of cheesecloth or a linen cloth wrung out in cold water, and when the consommé is cool strain it into a container.

To serve: Heat and serve in individual heated cups, or add any one of the vegetable garnishes listed for beef consommé.

This makes approximately 2 quarts.

Variations:

a. Add 1 3-lb. chicken. Remove after 1 hour of cooking or when tender.

b. Add 1 lb. chicken gizzards and hearts.

JELLIED CONSOMMÉ

If either the preceding beef or chicken consommé recipe has been followed, this consommé should be jelled when it is cold. A small amount of gelatin is added to ensure that it does not melt at the edges during serving or eating.

2 tsps. unflavored gelatin	¼ tsp. salt
4 tbs. cold beef or chicken consommé	¼ cup Madeira Lemon wedges
4 cups beef or chicken consommé	

Dissolve the gelatin in the cold consommé.

Pour the 4 cups of consommé into a pot and bring to a boil. Add the gelatin and stir until it is completely dissolved. Add the salt and Madeira. Stir and pour into a container, cover and refrigerate until set, approximately 1 to 3 hours.

To serve: Spoon into small chilled bowls and garnish with the lemon wedges.

Serves 6.

Variation:

Cut an avocado in half lengthwise, remove the seed, and slice a small wedge off the bottom so that it sits firmly on a plate. Fill the centers with the jellied consommé, add a squeeze of lemon juice and serve it as a first course. Allow half an avocado per serving.

EGG-RIBBON CONSOMMÉ

6 cups beef or chicken consommé	4 scallions, including the fresh green leaves, finely chopped
2 tsps. soy sauce	2 eggs

Put the consommé into a pot, add soy sauce and scallions. Bring to a boil.

Beat the eggs lightly. When the stock boils, stir it rapidly with a long-handled wooden spoon to make a whirlpool in the center of the pot. With the other hand hold the bowl of eggs high up and slowly pour, stirring continuously, into the consommé. The eggs, when cooked, are long, thin ribbon strips.

Serve in heated consommé bowls or cups.
Serves 6.

PANCAKE CONSOMMÉ

These thin, tender pancakes turn any consommé into an important soup which men, particularly, enjoy. Because the pancake slices can be frozen, the soup can be prepared effortlessly.

½ cup sifted flour	1 cup milk
2 eggs	Butter
2 egg yolks	2 quarts beef or chicken
½ tsp. salt	consommé
¼ cup vegetable oil	

Put the flour, eggs, egg yolks, salt and vegetable oil into a bowl and mix. Add the milk and beat until thoroughly blended. Pour into a container with a tight-fitting lid and refrigerate for 1 or 2 hours. The batter improves if it is stored in the refrigerator for 2 or 3 days.

Place a skillet, 8½ inches in diameter, over the heat. Stir or shake up the batter. Using a rolled-up stick of wax paper, pick up a small dab of softened butter and rub it around the sides and bottom of the skillet. When the skillet is piping hot, pour 3 tablespoons of the batter into it, and tilt and turn the pan so that the batter covers the full bottom of the pan. Keep the heat high. When all the pancake has a shiny, waxy surface—after about 20 or 30 seconds—turn and cook the other side. Turn the pancake out on a plate. With the wax-paper stick, pick up another piece of butter, lightly dab the skillet again and continue the process until the batter is used up.

Roll the pancakes, 2 or 3 at a time, and with a sharp knife cut into strips as thin as possible. Set aside.

Bring the consommé to a boil, taste and correct the seasoning.

Place an equal amount of pancake slices into individual heated bowls or all the slices into a heated tureen, and pour the hot consommé over them. Serve at once.

If the pancake slices are frozen, drop them into the hot consommé for barely a minute or two to thaw. Do not boil. Ladle into bowls or a tureen and serve.

From this batter you should have 12 or 14 pancakes.

Serves 6 to 8.

Variation:

Add 1 tablespoon of finely chopped parsley to the pancake batter.

ASPIC

Aspic is not a soup, but as it is made from stock, a soup base, I have included it in the soup recipes.

Aspic is beautiful. It adds sparkle and beauty to a commonplace dish. If covered, it will keep in the refrigerator for 2 to 3 weeks. It can be frozen, defrosted over a medium direct heat and put in the refrigerator to reset and use. When finely chopped,

it makes an elegant garnish for simple cold cuts and cold roasts, and deviled eggs, pâté and other canapés.

If you have aspic on hand, a cupful can be melted down, and "eggs in aspic" or a jelled vegetable salad can be quickly prepared. To seal in the moisture and preserve the freshness of cooked eggs, meats, and vegetables fresh or cooked, coat them with aspic; this method is centuries old but still a superb one.

Make some up without any specific use in mind. If you have it in the refrigerator, particularly during the summer, you will find many good ways to serve it.

5 cups basic stock or brown stock from which all fat has been removed	1 tsp. pepper
	½ tsp. lemon juice
	1 egg shell, crushed
	2 tsps. soy sauce
4 tbs. unflavored gelatin	2 egg whites, lightly
½ cup cold water	beaten
3 tsps. salt	2 tbs. brandy or Madeira

Put the stock in a metal pot. Be certain that the stock and the pot are completely free of any fat.

Put the gelatin into a small bowl and soften it with the cold water.

To the stock add the salt, pepper, lemon juice, eggshell, soy sauce and softened gelatin. Stir. Pour in the egg whites and place over a medium heat. Beat with a wire whisk until the liquid comes to a boil. Boil for 2 minutes. Remove the pot from the heat and leave undisturbed for at least 15 minutes.

Rinse out 2 thicknesses of cheesecloth in cold water; wring out thoroughly and place them in a strainer. Pour the aspic carefully into the strainer lined with the cheesecloth. Drain. Discard egg white and accumulated particles.

Add the brandy or Madeira to the aspic and pour into a

metal bread-loaf tin. Cover and place in the refrigerator to set, 2 to 4 hours.

This makes approximately 1 quart.

GROG BOUILLON

This is an elegant first course, but before giving the recipe I would like to digress briefly to speak of dinner or luncheon courses.

Every woman who enjoys cooking wants to present her accomplishments as attractively as possible. However, when help is unavailable, jumping up and down to serve many courses is nerve-racking for both hostess and guests.

I have worked out the following serving method when I have guests and no help. The first course is planned to be a bouillon. After the time allotted for cocktails has passed, I serve the grog bouillon or any other bouillon or consommé, as follows: The bouillon is ready and hot on the stove; the small attractive Chinese or Japanese bowls, in which it is to be served, are warm. I fill the bowls, place them on a tray, serve each guest in the living room, and with the same tray pick up the glasses and canapé plates. The guests drink the bouillon from the bowls; no serving plates or spoons are needed. The touch of the warm bowls, the smell and the taste of an aromatic clear bouillon gently prepares the senses for the dinner to follow.

4 cinnamon sticks	5 cups clarified basic stock, or clarified beef stock
1 tbs. sugar	
2 cups claret	6 slices lemon, cut paper thin

Four to 6 hours before serving, place the cinnamon sticks, sugar and claret in a pot. Bring to a boil and boil for 2 minutes. Place a cover on the pot and set aside to marinate. Do not put the mixture into the refrigerator.

When ready to serve, strain the claret mixture into the clarified stock and heat.

To serve: Pour into warmed bowls and float a slice of lemon on the top of each bowl.

Serves 6.

MUSHROOM BOUILLON

This is a refreshing and aromatic bouillon. You may garnish it with a thin slice of lemon in each cup, finely chopped chives or parsley. However, I prefer it plain so that the smoky flavor of the mushroom essence is not adulterated.

*1½ lbs. fresh mushrooms,
  including stems, or
  frozen mushrooms
½ tsp. lemon juice*

*4 cups clarified basic
  stock or clarified
  chicken stock
1 tsp. salt
½ tsp. pepper
2 tbs. Madeira*

Clean mushrooms and chop them coarsely. Sprinkle with the lemon juice. Put the clarified stock into a pot, add mushrooms and simmer for 30 to 40 minutes with a loose-fitting lid on top.

Remove from heat and strain through a strainer lined with 2 layers of cheesecloth. Leave the mushrooms in the cheesecloth, and with your hands twist the cheesecloth firmly so that all the juices from the mushrooms are extracted.

Pour the liquid back into the pot, add salt and pepper, place over a medium heat and bring to a boil. Add Madeira.

Serve immediately in warmed cups or small bowls.
Serves 6.

PETITE MARMITE MARIE

Petite marmite *is the name of a French glazed ceramic pot. Many French cooks believe that the pot gives a special flavor to soups. This type of pot is not commonly used in this country, but many houseware shops sell specially imported* petite marmite pots.

If you have one, do serve this elegant soup from it. The soup is simple to prepare, but the broth must be crystal clear, strong in flavor, and the few garnishes neatly diced. If possible, serve it in small white or light-colored cups or bowls so that the sparkle of the broth can be admired.

10 cups basic stock or brown stock from which all fat has been removed
1 carrot, scrubbed and quartered
2 stalks celery, washed and coarsely chopped
1 small onion, peeled and coarsely chopped
1 tsp. salt
1 lb. chopped lean beef

¼ cup carrots, peeled and finely diced
¼ cup celery stalks, finely diced
¼ cup white turnips, peeled and finely diced
¼ cup peas
¼ cup cooked chicken breast, finely diced
¼ cup cooked brisket of beef, finely diced and all fat removed

Put the stock into a large pot and add the carrot, celery, onion, salt and chopped beef. Bring to a boil, adjust heat to a simmer, place a loose-fitting lid on top and simmer for 1 hour. Strain

into a container. Refrigerate until all fat has congealed on the surface. Remove every speck of fat.

Clarify the stock according to instructions given on p. 43.

Put the clarified stock into a pot, bring to a boil and add the diced carrots, celery, turnips, peas, chicken breast and beef. Let simmer for 5 to 8 minutes.

Serve piping hot from a *petite marmite* pot or in heated individual bowls.

Serves 6.

GAZPACHO

This is a blender recipe. It is quickly prepared and can be kept in the refrigerator for at least a week. It is the perfect first course for a hot day's lunch or supper, and it is delightfully refreshing as a pickup on a midsummer's afternoon. Use fully sun-ripened tomatoes.

1½ *cups clarified basic, chicken or beef stock*	1 *medium cucumber, peeled and coarsely sliced*
1 *medium clove garlic, peeled and halved*	1 *tsp. salt*
4 *large tomatoes, peeled and quartered*	½ *tsp. pepper*
	2 *tbs. olive oil*
½ *medium green pepper, seeded and the white membranes removed, cut into thick slices*	2 *tbs. wine vinegar*
	½ *tsp. Worcestershire Sauce*
	1 *tsp. lemon juice*
½ *small onion, peeled and coarsely chopped*	½ *cup chilled basic, chicken or beef stock from which all fat has been removed*

Put the clarified stock into an ice cube tray and freeze.

Into the blender put the garlic, tomatoes, green pepper, onion, cucumber, salt, pepper, olive oil, vinegar, Worcestershire Sauce, lemon juice and unclarified stock. Cover and blend 3 to 6 seconds or until the vegetables are coarsely chopped. Pour into a jar and chill.

To serve: Pour into chilled bowls, and place 1 cube of frozen stock into each bowl. Serve at once.

Serves 4 to 6.

CUCUMBER AND YOGURT SOUP

Refreshing and delicious. If you try it on a summer's first hot day you'll become an addict like many others and continue to serve it up to and through winter's cold days.

3 cups plain yogurt

3 cups chilled basic stock
   or chicken stock from
   which all fat has been
   removed

2 tbs. olive oil

2 medium cucumbers,
   peeled and diced into
   ¼-inch cubes

3 tbs. walnuts, finely
   chopped

2 small cloves garlic,
   finely chopped

½ tsp. salt

¼ tsp. pepper

4 scallions, including
   the fresh green tops,
   washed and finely
   chopped

2 tsps. lemon juice

Put the yogurt and stock into a bowl and mix. Beating continuously, add the olive oil slowly to blend it thoroughly into the soup. Add the cucumbers, walnuts, garlic, salt, pepper, scallions and lemon juice. Mix well and chill.

Serve in chilled soup bowls or from a chilled tureen.
Serves 6.

Variation:
Omit walnuts.

COLD BEET AND CUCUMBER SOUP

If you use a strong stock in making this soup, it will be slightly jelled when chilled. It is pretty to the eye as well as delicious. Even though it is low in calories, it is filling, so don't serve it before a heavy meal. It is perfect as the first course for a summer luncheon.

6 cups basic stock, or chicken stock from which all fat has been removed	1 tbs. parsley, finely chopped
2 medium cucumbers	2 tsps. salt
2 cups beets, cooked, peeled and grated	1 tsp. pepper
2 tsps. onion, peeled and finely grated	½ cup sour cream
	1 tbs. fresh dill, finely chopped

Put the stock in a pan and bring to a boil.

Meanwhile, peel the cucumbers and cut them in half. Remove all the seeds and grate. Combine the cucumbers, beets, onion, parsley, salt and pepper in a large bowl. Add the hot stock, stir well and set aside to cool. When cool, cover and place in the refrigerator until thoroughly chilled.

To serve: Mix the sour cream with the dill. Portion out the soup into six bowls and top each with a generous teaspoon of the sour cream and dill mixture.
Serves 6.

ESCAROLE SOUP

Escarole, so good in salads, is a welcome addition to the soup pot. This is an easy, delicious and economical soup.

¾ lb. lean ground beef
¼ tsp. garlic, finely chopped
3 tbs. freshly grated Parmesan cheese
1 egg, slightly beaten
1 tsp. salt
½ tsp. pepper
2 quarts basic stock or beef stock from which all fat has been removed
2 tbs. tomato paste

½ tsp. sugar
1 lb. escarole, washed and coarsely chopped
2 large onions, peeled and finely diced
1 cup celery stalks, washed and diced
2 large potatoes, peeled and cut into small cubes
2 tbs. parsley, finely chopped

Mix the ground beef with the garlic, cheese, egg, salt and pepper. Form into balls ½ to 1 inch in diameter. Set aside.

In a large pot pour the stock. Add the tomato paste and sugar. Bring to a boil and add meatballs. Turn heat down and simmer uncovered for 10 minutes. Add the escarole, onions, celery and potatoes. Cover with a loose-fitting lid and simmer for 30 minutes.

Serve directly from the pot or from a heated soup tureen. Garnish with the parsley.

Serves 8 to 10.

VICHYSSOISE (COLD POTATO AND LEEK SOUP)

Delicious, and a must for the hot summer days.

If you are pressed for time, frozen potatoes can be substituted for fresh potatoes without any loss of flavor or texture.

I recommend adding the light cream just before serving. The potato, leek and stock base keeps well in the refrigerator up to 10 days. If it is prepared in advance, one or two cups of this refreshing soup may be made ready at once. One time I left a cup of the mixture too long, and it had started to sour. Before I was able to throw it out, a friend mixed herself a cup with the sweet light cream and swears that the touch of "sourness," or fermentation, improved the soup tremendously. I do not share her opinion, but I do have such a high regard for her taste that I pass the idea on to you.

1 tbs. butter	4 cups basic stock or
4 leeks, washed, and the white parts coarsely sliced	chicken stock from which all fat has been removed
1 medium onion, peeled and coarsely sliced	3 tsps. salt
	½ tsp. pepper
4 cups potatoes, peeled and coarsely sliced	3 cups light cream Chives or scallions, finely chopped

In a large pot melt butter, add leeks and onion. Cook over a medium heat, stirring until leeks and onion are transparent. Do not brown. Add potatoes, stock, salt and pepper. Bring to a boil, cover with a loose-fitting lid, adjust heat to a simmer and simmer for 30 to 40 minutes or until potatoes are tender.

Put the mixture through a food mill or blend in a blender until smooth. Pour into a container, cover and chill thoroughly.

To serve: Pour the mixture into a large bowl and add cold light cream. Mix thoroughly with a whisk or beater. Pour into chilled individual soup cups or small bowls. Garnish with chives or scallions.

Serves 6 to 8.

NOTE: For an individual serving, combine 1 cup of potato and leek mixture with ½ cup light cream. If you prefer a thinner soup, add more light cream.

ASPARAGUS AND POTATO SOUP

If you are a frozen-food fan, this delicious soup can be made in a couple of minutes. However, when fresh asparagus is in season, it is economically prudent to make up a generous supply and freeze it for future use.

1 bunch (approximately 2½ lbs.) fresh asparagus, or 2 packages frozen asparagus	3 medium potatoes, peeled and quartered, or an equal amount of frozen potatoes
4 cups basic stock or chicken stock from which all fat has been removed	2 tsps. salt
	½ tsp. pepper
	2 egg yolks
	½ cup heavy cream
	½ tsp. grated nutmeg

Clean the fresh asparagus, discarding the tough fiber ends, and cut into 3-inch pieces. Bring 2 cups of the stock to a boil. Add the asparagus and cook until almost tender. If frozen asparagus is used, follow the same cooking procedure. Remove the asparagus and set aside. Save a few asparagus tips for garnish.

Bring the liquid in which the asparagus was cooked back to a boil and add the potatoes. Cook until tender. When tender, put the potatoes and asparagus, together with the liquid, through a food mill or sieve, or blend in a blender until smooth.

NOTE: If the asparagus is fibrous, put the mixture through a food mill or a sieve; do not blend because the blender does not emulsify the coarse fibers.

Put the purée mixture into a pot, add the 2 remaining cups of stock, salt and pepper, and simmer 5 to 10 minutes, stirring occasionally.

Beat the egg yolks with the cream and add very slowly to the soup, stirring continuously. Add nutmeg. Heat but do not boil.

Serve in individual heated soup bowls and garnish with the asparagus tips.

Serves 6.

NOTE: If the soup is frozen, defrost and heat it in a double boiler over hot water. Give it a good beating with a wire whisk from time to time.

POTATO AND BACON SOUP

4 tbs. butter
2 tbs. vegetable oil
6 medium potatoes,
    peeled and cut in small
    cubes
4 medium onions, peeled
    and thinly sliced
6 cups basic stock or
    brown stock from
    which all fat has been
    removed

3 tsps. salt
½ tsp. pepper
½ lb. bacon, cut into 1-
    inch pieces
½ cup grated Parmesan
    cheese

Heat butter and vegetable oil in a large heavy pot. When hot, add potatoes. Cook 10 minutes over a medium heat, turning them often. Add onions and continue to fry until the potatoes and onions are golden brown. Add stock, salt and pepper. Bring to a boil. Place a loose-fitting lid on top, adjust heat to a simmer, and simmer 30 minutes or until potatoes are soft.

Meanwhile, fry the bacon pieces until crisp. Drain on a brown paper bag and crumble into fine bits.

Pour the soup into a heated tureen. Put the crumbled bacon and Parmesan cheese into two side dishes.

To serve: Ladle the soup into heated soup plates and sprinkle each with a heaping tablespoon of bacon and cheese.
Serves 6 to 8.

POTATO AND SPINACH SOUP

A soup that freezes perfectly. Watercress leaves may be substituted for the spinach. If you prepare it with watercress and want to put it through a blender, use only the leaves and the tiny leaf stems, as the fibrous stalks will not emulsify. The whole stem can be used if you put the soup through a food mill or sieve.

1 quart potatoes, peeled and diced	2 ozs. butter
	1 tsp. salt
1 large onion, peeled and coarsely sliced	½ tsp. pepper
	½ lb. spinach leaves, washed
1 quart basic stock or chicken stock from which all fat has been removed	1 cup light cream

Put the potatoes and onion in a large pot. Add stock, bring to a boil, cover with a loose-fitting lid, adjust heat to a simmer, and simmer for 30 minutes or until potatoes are tender. Add butter, salt and pepper.

Turn the heat off and add spinach. Stir until spinach is wilted. Pour the mixture through a food mill or sieve, or blend in a blender until smooth. Return the mixture to the pot, add cream and heat. Do not boil.

Serve in a heated tureen or in heated individual soup bowls.

Serves 6.

AVOCADO SOUP

This thick soup is so rich that if you serve it as a first course, keep the portions small. If it is too thick for your taste, add a bit more stock. It is easy to prepare and freezes well.

2 tbs. butter
2 medium onions, peeled and finely chopped
3 tbs. flour
1 small clove garlic, peeled and finely chopped
2 tsps. salt
⅛ tsp. cayenne pepper
¼ tsp. ground cloves

¼ tsp. nutmeg
4 cups basic stock or chicken stock from which all fat has been removed
3 medium avocados
4 tsps. lemon juice
1 cup light cream
Croutons

Melt butter in a large heavy pot; when foaming, add onions and cook them until transparent. Remove from heat and stir in flour, garlic, salt, pepper, cloves and nutmeg. Add stock, return to heat and bring to a boil, stirring constantly. Adjust heat to a simmer, and simmer for 10 minutes.

Peel the avocados and remove seeds. Dice into coarse pieces. Add to the soup, stir and cook 1 or 2 minutes. Add lemon juice.

Put the mixture through a food mill or blend in a blender until smooth. Return the mixture to the pot, add cream and reheat. Do not boil.

Serve in heated individual bowls and garnish with croutons (see p. 103).

Serves 6.

CURRIED SPINACH SOUP

Absolutely delicious. This soup can be served hot or cold, and it freezes perfectly.

6 tbs. butter
3 large onions, peeled and thinly sliced
2 large potatoes, peeled and coarsely sliced
2 cups milk
3 cups basic stock, or chicken stock from which all fat has been removed

2 tsps. salt
1 bay leaf
½ tsp. dried tarragon
1 10-oz. package frozen chopped spinach
2 tsps. soy sauce
½ tsp. curry powder
1 cup heavy cream

Put the butter into a large heavy pot, and when foaming, add the onions and cook them until transparent. Add the potatoes, milk, stock, salt, bay leaf and tarragon. Bring to a boil, adjust the heat to a simmer, and cook covered until the potatoes are tender. When the potatoes are tender, add the spinach, soy sauce and curry powder; cover, and cook until the spinach is done. Then remove the bay leaf.

Put this mixture into a blender and blend until it is mashed—about 2 or 3 seconds; do not blend it until it is a smooth homogenized mixture.

Pour the soup back into the pot and add the cream, stir and heat. Do not boil.

To serve hot: Pour into a heated tureen or individual heated soup bowls.

To serve cold: Pour into a container, cool, and refrigerate overnight. If it is too thick after it is chilled, beat in a little milk or stock. Pour into chilled individual soup cups or bowls.
Serves 6.

CAULIFLOWER SOUP

This is a delicate creamy soup. You cannot make a meal from it, but it is delicious with sandwiches for lunch or when served as a first course.

1 medium cauliflower, washed
1 stalk celery, washed and cut into 1-inch pieces
1 thick slice of lemon
2 tbs. butter
1 medium onion, peeled and diced
2 tbs. flour
1 cup of the water in which the cauliflower was cooked
3 cups of basic stock or chicken stock from which all fat has been removed
2 tsps. salt
¼ tsp. pepper
1 cup light cream

Cook the cauliflower, celery pieces and slice of lemon in boiling water. When tender, drain and reserve the celery pieces and 1 cup of the water. Discard the lemon.

Break the cauliflower into florets and reserve ½ cup of the tiniest for garnish.

Melt the butter in a large pot, and when foaming, add the onion. Stir and cook until onion is transparent. Add the flour, and cook and stir until well blended. Slowly add the cup of cauliflower water, stirring constantly until well blended. Add the stock, salt, pepper, celery pieces and cauliflower. Put this mixture through a food mill or in a blender and blend until smooth.

Return the soup to the pot and simmer for 10 to 15 minutes. Add the light cream. Stir and bring to a boil. Just before serving, add the florets.

Serve from a heated tureen or in individual heated bowls. Serves 6.

CREAM OF CARROT SOUP

This is a very thick soup; if you prefer a thinner soup, add more stock. Its flavor is subtle and its color is a soft lobster pink. I think you will enjoy serving it before a grilled fish entrée or an omelet supper.

2½	tbs. butter	1½	tsps. salt
2	cups carrots, scrubbed and diced	⅛	tsp. pepper
2	medium onions, peeled and diced	2	whole cloves
2	tbs. flour	1½	cups milk
1½	cups basic stock or beef stock from which all fat has been removed		Watercress leaves

Melt the butter in a heavy pot, and when foaming, add carrots and onions. Stir and cook until the onions are transparent. Add flour. Add stock slowly, and stir until the mixture is well blended. Add salt, pepper and cloves. Cover and simmer slowly for 30 minutes.

Remove the cloves and put the mixture through a food mill or blend in a blender until smooth. Return the soup to the pot and add the milk. Stir until it comes to a boil. Do not boil.

Serve in warmed individual soup bowls and float one or two watercress leaves on top.

Serves 4 to 6.

CREAM OF CELERY SOUP

Celery happens to be one of my favorite vegetables, so, since I cannot be objective, I restrain myself from praising this soup as much as I would like. It freezes perfectly; thaw it over a low heat or in a double boiler.

½ cup butter	1 bay leaf
1 large onion, peeled and coarsely chopped	2 tsps. salt
3 cups celery, washed and cut in 1-inch pieces	½ tsps. pepper
	2 cups milk
2 medium potatoes, peeled and cubed	2 tbs. celery leaves, finely chopped
1 cup basic stock or chicken stock from which all fat has been removed	

Melt the butter in a large heavy pot; when foaming, add onion. Stir and cook onion until golden. Add celery, potatoes, stock, bay leaf, salt and pepper. Bring to a boil. Adjust heat to a simmer, cover with a loose-fitting lid and simmer for 30 minutes or until potatoes are soft.

Remove bay leaf and put the mixture through a food mill or blend in a blender until smooth. I recommend that you use a food mill, as the tough fibers of the celery do not emulsify. Return to the pot and add the milk. Heat.

Serve in warm soup bowls and garnish with the chopped celery leaves.

Serves 6.

CELERY AND EGG SOUP

Another delicious celery soup!
During my preschool years I was raised on a remote cattle ranch in Arizona by kind, elderly grandparents from New England. From them I first heard and experienced the strict application of such adages as "Waste not, want not" and "A penny saved is a penny earned." Therefore, I cannot bring myself to discard the strained celery, carrot and onion left over from this recipe. I put them into a container, freeze them and add them to the pot when I prepare basic stock.

2 quarts basic stock or chicken stock from which all fat has been removed
1 medium onion, peeled and chopped
1 carrot, scrubbed and diced
12 stalks celery, including leaves, washed and cut into 1-inch pieces

1 tsp. salt
3 egg yolks
1 tbs. lemon juice
6 or 8 lemon slices, cut paper thin
2 tbs. celery leaves, finely chopped

Put the stock, onion, carrot, celery and salt into a large heavy pot. Bring to a boil, place a loose-fitting lid on top, adjust heat to a simmer, and simmer for 1 hour. Strain. Set this broth aside until final preparation time. In fact, it can be made a week or two in advance and frozen.

When ready to serve, bring the broth to a boil. Beat the egg yolks lightly with the lemon juice. Pour the hot broth into the egg yolks bit by bit, stirring constantly. When it is all well mixed, pour back into the pot and place over a low fire. Stirring constantly, cook for 3 or 4 minutes. Do not boil.

To serve: Pour into heated soup bowls and float a lemon slice on top and garnish with a sprinkling of the celery leaves.
Serves 6 to 8.

CREAM OF PEA AND MUSHROOM SOUP

This soup is such a vivid green that I feel it should be served by anyone of Irish ancestry on St. Patrick's Day. But don't look for an Irish ancestor or wait until St. Patrick's Day to try it. It is nourishing and delicious and can be frozen.

½ lb. mushrooms	2½ cups fresh peas, or
2 tbs. butter	frozen peas
Lemon juice	1 quart milk
2 tbs. flour	1 small onion, peeled
1½ cups basic stock or	and finely sliced
chicken stock from	2 whole cloves
which all fat has	1 small bay leaf,
been removed	crushed
½ tsp. chervil	1 clove garlic, peeled
2 tsps. salt	and finely diced
1 pinch cayenne pepper	1 tbs. parsley, finely
	chopped

Clean the mushrooms and chop them coarsely. In a heavy pot melt the butter until it is foaming, add a few drops of lemon juice and the mushrooms and cook over a high heat for 1 minute, stirring constantly. Lower heat and stir in flour; mix until smooth. Slowly add 1 cup of stock, stirring until well blended. Add chervil, salt and pepper. Bring to a boil. Adjust heat to a simmer, place a loose-fitting lid on top of pot, and simmer for 25 minutes. Give the pot an occasional stir.

Cook the peas in the remaining half cup of stock until tender. (If frozen peas are used, follow the same procedure.) Put them, together with the water in which they were cooked, through a food mill, or blend in a blender until smooth. Add the pea purée to the mushroom mixture. Set aside.

Scald the milk with the onion, cloves, bay leaf, garlic and parsley in a saucepan. Strain. Add the strained milk to the pea and mushroom mixture. Stir thoroughly and heat.

Serve from a heated tureen or in heated individual soup bowls.

Serves 6.

CREAM OF CHICKEN AND VEGETABLE SOUP

This is too filling to serve as a first course. Plan it as a main dish with fresh dark bread and a crisp green salad with cheese. It freezes perfectly.

2 quarts basic stock or chicken stock from which all fat has been removed	1 cup onions, peeled and finely diced
1 tbs. potato flour	3 to 4 cups cooked chicken meat, diced
¼ cup cold water	1 cup peas, fresh or frozen
1 tbs. butter	2 tsps. salt
1 cup carrots, peeled and finely diced	1 tsp. pepper
1 cup celery, washed and finely diced	2 egg yolks, lightly beaten
	½ cup heavy cream

Bring the stock to a boil. Mix potato flour with the water, and while stirring, slowly pour into the stock and simmer.

Melt the butter in a pan, add carrots, celery and onions. Sauté for 5 to 10 minutes or until onions are transparent, not brown. Add to stock. Add chicken meat and simmer for 15 minutes. Add peas, salt and pepper and simmer for 5 minutes.

Mix together the egg yolks and cream. Bit by bit add a small amount of the hot soup to the eggs and cream, stirring constantly. When a cup of the hot soup is blended with the egg mixture, pour it slowly into the soup, stirring continuously. Heat, but do not boil.

Serve from a heated tureen or in heated individual soup plates.

Serves 6 to 8.

CHICKEN CURRY SOUP

A country cousin of an elegant Senegalese soup, Chicken Curry Soup is similar, but quite a bit more filling, and the fried chicken pieces add a pleasant surprise. Should you want to make this a one-dish meal, put a cup of cooked rice into each soup plate and ladle the hot soup over it.

This recipe may be prepared a day or two in advance up to the point of frying the chicken pieces.

3 cups basic stock or
chicken stock from
which all fat has been
removed
3 cups cold water
2 2½-lb. chickens split in
half
1 large onion, peeled
and quartered
1 large carrot, scrubbed
and quartered

6 tbs. flour
4 tsps, curry powder
1 tsp. salt
1 pinch cayenne pepper
4 tsps. cornstarch
Seasoned flour
3 tbs. butter
¾ cup heavy cream
1 tbs. chives, finely
chopped

Put the stock and water into a large heavy pot. Add the split chickens, onion and carrot, and cover pot with a loose-fitting lid. Bring slowly to a boil. Adjust the heat to a simmer, and simmer for 25 to 30 minutes. Remove the pot from the heat, and cool the chickens in the broth.

When cool, remove the chickens and reserve the broth. Remove and discard the skin and bones of the chickens. Carve the meat into 2-inch pieces. Set aside.

Remove the fat from the broth. Strain the broth and return it to the pot.

Mix the flour, curry powder, salt, pepper and cornstarch to a smooth paste with cold water. Pour slowly into the broth, and bring the mixture to a boil, stirring continuously. When well blended, cover and simmer for 10 or 15 minutes.

When ready to serve, proceed as follows: Dredge the chicken pieces in the seasoned flour. Melt the butter in a frying pan, and when foaming, add the chicken pieces. Brown rapidly until crisp and golden. Add them to the soup, and simmer for 5 minutes. Add the cream, and heat. Do not boil.

Serve in heated deep soup plates and garnish with chives. Serves 6.

TOMATO AND DILL SOUP

An ideal soup for the summer, when you can get large, sun-ripened tomatoes. It may be served hot or chilled.

2 tbs. vegetable oil
1 medium onion, peeled and finely chopped
½ tsp. garlic, finely chopped
2 tsps. salt
½ tsp. pepper
6 large fresh tomatoes
1 tbs. tomato paste

3 tbs. flour
3 cups basic stock or chicken stock from which all fat has been removed
½ cup heavy cream
2 tbs. fresh dill, finely chopped, or 2½ tsps. dried dill

Heat the oil in a deep pot, add onion and garlic. Cook, stirring continuously, over medium heat for 2 minutes. Add salt and pepper and 2 of the tomatoes, which have been coarsely sliced, including the skin. Turn the heat up high and stir, cooking briskly for 3 minutes. Remove from the fire, stir in the tomato paste and flour. Slowly stir in the stock. Return the pot to the fire, and bring to a boil, stirring continuously. Adjust heat to a simmer, and simmer for 10 minutes.

Coarsely chop 2 more of the tomatoes, including the skin, and add to the mixture. Immediately put the soup through a fine strainer so that all seeds are removed.

Return the soup to a pot, add the cream, dill and the last 2 tomatoes, which have been peeled, seeded and cut in fine, thin shreds. Heat, but do not boil.

To serve hot: Pour at once into a large heated tureen or in heated individual bowls.

To serve cold: Chill for 4 hours or overnight in the refrigerator. Stir and pour into chilled individual bowls.
Serves 6.

SORREL AND POTATO SOUP

*A true delicacy. This is a thick soup that can be served
either hot or cold. If you prefer a thinner soup, add additional
chicken stock. It is especially good served cold in chilled bowls
on a hot summer evening. It freezes perfectly.*

*A word about sorrel. This hardy herb dates back before
3000 B.C. Today it is cultivated and marketed. The cultivated
sorrel leaves are elongated, from 5 to 8 inches in length.*

*Species of sorrel grow wild in practically everyone's gar-
den; unhappily, however, it is regarded as a weed, and frowned
upon. It is also known as sourgrass or dock, and though the leaves
are much smaller than the cultivated variety, they are every bit
as tasty. If your greengrocer does not have the cultivated sorrel,
go to your neighbor's garden and he will bless you for weeding
out this prolific plant.*

*One species of wild sorrel, found everywhere, is similar
to the clover leaf, except that it is heart-shaped. If you have any
doubt about its identity, just bite into it; if it is sour, you have the
proper herb for this delicious soup, or you might add a few of its
tender leaves to your green salad. It is interesting to note that
the shamrock is related to this herb.*

*When sorrel is cooked, its color turns beige; the small
amount of spinach added to this soup gives it color and accentu-
ates the refreshing sour taste of the soup.*

6 *cups of strong chicken stock from which all fat has been removed*

3 *large potatoes, peeled and cut into coarse slices*

4 *tbs. butter*

2 *medium onions, peeled and coarsely chopped*

4 *cups of firmly packed sorrel leaves, washed and cut into coarse shreds (approximately 1 to 1½ lbs.)*

¾ *cup fresh or frozen chopped spinach*

2½ *tsps. salt*

1 *tsp. pepper*

Sour cream

Bring the stock to a boil and add the potatoes.

Melt the butter in a small pan until it is foaming; then add the onions, stirring and cooking them until transparent. Add the onions and butter to the stock and potatoes, cover, adjust the heat to a simmer, and cook until the potatoes are tender.

When the potatoes are tender, add the sorrel and spinach, stir, cover and cook 3 to 5 minutes. Put the mixture through a blender or a food mill and return it to the pot. Add the salt and pepper; stir and cook until it comes to a boil.

NOTE: Wild sorrel (unlike cultivated sorrel), has a small, invisible fibrous stem that does not emulsify in a blender and will pass directly through the openings of a food mill. Therefore, if wild sorrel is used, it must be strained through a fine mesh sieve or through 2 pieces of cheesecloth after the soup is blended or put through a food mill.

To serve hot: Ladle the soup into individual heated soup bowls and garnish each with a tablespoon of sour cream.

To serve cold: Thoroughly chill the soup; ladle it into chilled individual soup bowls. Garnish each with a tablespoon of sour cream and place 3 or 4 thin slices of hard-boiled egg on top.

Serves 6 to 8.

MINESTRONE

A friend of mine, well known for her culinary skills, said that since minestrone is simple and delicious, she found it an ideal dish for the end of the Christmas holiday season. Serve it with a crisp green salad, French bread and a fruit compote. It freezes perfectly.

¼ cup olive oil
2 cups spinach leaves, washed and chopped
1 cup celery, washed and diced
3 cups cabbage, shredded
2 cups scrubbed carrots, diced
1 medium onion, peeled and coarsely chopped
2 tbs. parsley, finely chopped
1 clove garlic, peeled and finely chopped

2 quarts basic, brown or beef stock from which all fat has been removed
2 cups canned tomatoes
½ cup rice
½ tsp. dried thyme
¼ tsp. dried rosemary
1 pinch dried sage
2½ tsps. salt
1 tsp. pepper
½ cup elbow macaroni
1 cup cooked kidney beans*
1 cup cooked baby lima beans*

Heat the olive oil in a large pot, and add the spinach, celery, cabbage, carrots, onion, parsley and garlic. Sauté for 5 minutes over a high heat, stirring all the while. Add the stock, tomatoes, rice, thyme, rosemary, sage, salt and pepper. Stir. Bring to a boil, cover pot with a lid, and adjust the heat to a simmer. Simmer for 30 to 40 minutes, stirring occasionally. Add macaroni,

* Cooking instructions for the kidney and baby lima beans are given in Chapter 8, "Dried Beans and Grains."

kidney beans, and lima beans, and continue to cook until the macaroni are tender.

Serve in a heated tureen.
This recipe makes 3 quarts.

Variation:
Add ½ cup of any in-season vegetable, diced: string beans, wax beans, peas, turnips, etc.

OXTAIL SOUP

Oxtail has a special aromatic flavor. After a bowl of this soup one is pleasantly sated. Serve it for luncheon or supper with a green salad and hot homemade French bread.

1 oxtail cut into 1- to 2-inch pieces Flour	2 leeks, washed and cut into rounds
2 tbs. vegetable oil	1 medium onion, peeled and thinly sliced
8 cups basic stock or beef stock from which all fat has been removed	¼ tsp. Worcestershire Sauce
3 large carrots, scrubbed and cut into thin rounds	½ tsp. lemon juice Salt

Wash and dry the oxtail pieces, and roll them lightly in flour.

Heat the oil in a large heavy pot, and when it is hot, brown the oxtail pieces. Add the stock, stir and bring to a boil. Cover pot with a loose-fitting lid, adjust the heat to a simmer, and simmer for 2 hours. Add the carrots, leeks and onion, cover and simmer for 1 hour more.

Remove only the large pieces of oxtail and cut off the meat; discard the bones. Put the meat pieces back into the soup, and add the Worcestershire Sauce and lemon. Taste for seasoning and add salt to your taste.

Before serving, remove the fat. If the soup has not been cooked in advance so that the fat has congealed on the surface, tilt the pan and remove all the fat with a large spoon.

To serve: Pour into a large heated tureen or in individual heated soup bowls.

Serves 6.

BRAIN SOUP VIENNESE

The great chef Escoffier wrote that "calf's brains form the most wholesome rebuilding diet for all those who are weakened by excessive head-work. . . ." I don't think present-day nutritionists would agree with this view, but I do think they would agree that this is a good soup. It is elegant to the eye, and if your family or friends are squeamish about eating brains, don't tell them what they're eating; just serve the soup.

1 pair calf's brains, cleaned	6 tbs. parsley, finely chopped
8 tbs. butter	1 tsp. salt
2 tbs. flour	½ tsp. pepper
4 cups basic or brown stock from which all fat has been removed	

Clean the brains by covering them with cold water and soaking for 20 or 30 minutes. Remove and wash under cold running water. Cover again with cold water, to which a dash of salt or vinegar has been added, and leave for 15 minutes. Remove and wash under cold running water. Carefully remove all the membrane and veins.

In a small pot melt 4 tablespoons of the butter, and when foaming, add the brains. Sauté over a medium heat for 20 minutes. Remove the brains and set aside on paper towels or brown paper to absorb the excess butter.

In a heavy pot melt the other 4 tablespoons of butter and add flour. Cook, stirring constantly, until flour and butter are a deep, rich brown. Remove from heat and stir in 1 cup of stock. Return to heat, and stir until flour and stock are smoothly blended. Add the balance of the stock, 4 tablespoons of parsley, salt and pepper. Cover pot with a loose-fitting lid and simmer for 15 minutes.

Cut the sautéed brains into tiny pieces, about the size of a navy bean, add to the soup and simmer for 5 minutes.

Serve in heated individual soup bowls and garnish with the remainder of the chopped parsley.

Serves 4 to 6.

EGG AND MEAT SOUP

A delightful use for leftover roast, boiled beef or chicken. An excellent soup for a quick, nourishing lunch.

6 cups basic or beef stock from which all fat has been removed	2 tbs. lemon juice
	1½ cups cooked beef or chicken meat, finely diced
2 tsps. soy sauce	
1 tsp. salt	Parsley, finely chopped
¼ tsp. pepper	
2 eggs	

Bring the stock to a boil in a heavy pot, add soy sauce, salt and pepper. Beat eggs lightly. Stirring the stock rapidly, pour the eggs slowly into the pot. Add lemon juice and meat. Simmer for 2 or 3 minutes.

Serve at once in heated individual bowls and garnish with parsley.

Serves 6.

HUNGARIAN GOULASH SOUP

My sister-in-law, Edith Karel, was raised in Vienna, and this is her family's recipe. She told me that in the pre-World War II days, after the balls, and particularly during the festivities of Mardi Gras, it was customary for the revelers to stop at a restaurant for a large bowl of this soup before going home. Served scalding hot, it was supposed to overcome any ill effects resulting from drinking too much wine or champagne. I regret I cannot say whether it is effective in this regard or not, but I can say that it is an excellent soup in any season. It freezes perfectly.

1 lb. beef, shin or chuck	2 cups canned tomatoes
¼ lb. bacon, cut into 1-inch pieces	2 tsps. salt
	¼ cup red wine
4 medium onions, peeled and coarsely chopped	1 tbs. tomato paste
	½ tsp. sugar
2 tsps. paprika	¼ tsp. pepper
½ tsp. caraway seeds	3 medium potatoes, peeled and cubed into ½-inch pieces
1 pinch dried marjoram	
1 clove garlic, peeled and finely chopped	
	¼ cup flour
6 cups basic stock or beef stock from which all fat has been removed	¾ cup water
	4 beef frankfurters, cooked
	Lemon juice

Cube the beef into ½-inch pieces, discarding excess fat and tough cartilage.

Fry the bacon in a large heavy pot until it is clear. Add the onions and cook until golden, stirring constantly. Add the paprika, caraway seeds, marjoram and garlic, and stir and cook for one or two minutes.

Add the stock, tomatoes, salt, wine, tomato paste, sugar and pepper. Bring to a boil. Stir. Place a loose-fitting lid on the pot, adjust heat to a simmer, and simmer for 25 minutes.

Add the potatoes and simmer 30 minutes or until tender.

Mix the flour and water until they make a smooth paste, and pour it slowly into the soup, stirring all the while. Simmer until the soup thickens.

Slice the frankfurters into ¼-inch pieces, and add them to the soup together with a few drops of lemon juice. Stir and simmer for 5 minutes.

Serve piping hot in large heated soup plates.
Serves 6 to 8.

SMOKED BACON AND LEEK SOUP

Buy the smokiest-flavored bacon your butcher has on hand for this soup. I find that smoked slab bacon is best.

¼ lb. smoked bacon, sliced and cut into ½-inch pieces

6 cups basic stock or ham stock from which all fat has been removed

4 medium leeks, including the fresh green leaves, split in half, washed and cut in thin slices

2 medium potatoes, peeled and cubed into ¼-inch pieces

¼ lb. smoked cooked ham, cut in thin strips (the size of a kitchen match)

1½ tsps. salt

½ tsp. pepper

Fry the bacon pieces over a low fire until they are transparent, not crisp. Discard the fat and drain the pieces on a brown paper bag.

Bring the stock to a boil in a large pot, and add the leeks, potatoes and bacon. Bring the soup to a boil and place a loose-fitting lid on top. Turn the heat down to a simmer, and simmer for 30 minutes or until potatoes are tender. Add the ham strips, salt and pepper, and simmer for 10 minutes.

To serve: Pour into a heated tureen and serve at once. Serves 6.

NOTE: If ham stock is used, taste before adding salt.

GREEN BEAN AND BACON SOUP

Here is a real country soup. Serve it as the main dish with hot cornbread. It is easy to prepare and freezes excellently.

½ lb. smoked bacon
2 cups string beans, washed and cut into 1-inch pieces
1 cup onions, chopped fine
6 cups basic stock or beef stock from which all fat has been removed

2 tsps. tomato paste
2 tsps. salt
½ tsp. pepper
⅔ cup rice

Cut the bacon in ½-inch pieces, and fry over a low flame until transparent. Do not brown. Discard all the bacon fat except 2 teaspoons. Drain the bacon pieces on a brown paper bag.

Add the string beans and onions to the bacon fat, and sauté for 5 to 10 minutes or until onions are transparent, not brown.

Put the stock into a large pot, and bring to a boil; add bacon, onion, beans, tomato paste, salt, pepper and rice. Cover pot with a loose-fitting lid, adjust flame to a simmer, and simmer for 25 to 30 minutes or until rice and beans are tender.

Serve in a heated tureen or in large, heated soup plates. Serves 6.

Variation:
Ham may be substituted for the bacon; dice it into small pieces, and sauté the onions and beans in butter.

SUMMER SOUP

A hearty, nutritious soup, equally good in winter, and definitely a one-dish meal. I think it is the sweetness of the green peppers that gives it such a light, cool flavor.

2 large green peppers, washed	1 clove garlic, peeled and finely chopped
2 slices bacon, cut into ½-inch pieces	2 tsps. salt
	½ tsp. pepper
1 large onion, peeled and finely chopped	½ tsp. dried thyme
	½ tsp. sugar
1 quart basic stock or beef stock from which all fat has been removed	1 lb. lean ground chuck or bottom round of beef
	2 cups canned tomatoes
½ cup red wine	

Remove the core, seeds and white membranes from the green peppers. Dice into small pieces.

Fry the bacon pieces until most of their fat is rendered, but do not brown. Add diced peppers and onions; cook and stir until the onions are transparent. Pour this mixture into a large heavy pot. Add stock, wine, garlic, salt, pepper, thyme, sugar, beef and tomatoes. If the tomatoes are whole, dice them into small pieces.

When adding the beef, break it up so that it does not form large lumps.

Cover pot with a loose-fitting lid. Bring soup to a boil, adjust heat to a simmer, and simmer for 1 hour.

Serve in the pot, or pour into a heated tureen.
Serves 6.

WINTERBORSCHT
(BEETS AND BEEF SOUP)

Particularly good in winter, this is a warming, nourishing soup that is also pleasing to the eye.

3 cups water	1 bay leaf
3 cups basic stock or brown stock from which all fat has been removed	1 cup beets, peeled and cut into thin strips
3 lbs. short ribs of beef	1 6-oz. can tomato paste
2 medium onions, peeled and sliced thin	2 tbs. vinegar
	1 tbs. sugar
3 stalks celery, washed and cut into 2-inch pieces	1 tbs. salt
	6 Idaho baking potatoes
4 large beets, peeled and sliced	1 head cabbage, cut into 8 wedges
4 carrots, scrubbed and sliced	2 tbs. fresh dill, finely chopped
1 tbs. salt	1 cup sour cream

Put water, stock, ribs of beef, onions, celery, beets, carrots, salt and bay leaf into a large pot. Cover pot with a loose-fitting lid and simmer for 2 hours.

Add the strips of beets, tomato paste, vinegar, sugar and salt. Bring to a simmer, and simmer for 20 minutes.

Remove from fire, cool and refrigerate. When cold, discard all the fat congealed on the surface. Remove and discard the beef bones. Cut the meat into neat serving pieces. At this point, the soup can be frozen or set aside. One hour before serving, proceed as follows:

Steam or boil the potatoes in a separate pot for 40 to 50 minutes or until tender. Peel and keep warm.

While the potatoes are cooking, bring the soup to a boil. Add the cabbage wedges and cook 20 to 25 minutes.

To serve: Heat six large, deep soup plates. Into each, spoon a wedge of cabbage, a few pieces of meat and a generous ladleful of the soup. Roll the potatoes in the chopped dill, and place one into each plate. Put a heaping tablespoon of sour cream into the center of each plate. Serve immediately.

Serves 6.

MUSHROOM SOUP JOSEPHINE

This is a low-calorie soup with real flavor. It is very simple to prepare and can be frozen.

1 lb. fresh or frozen mushrooms	1 tsp. salt
4 tbs. butter	4 tsps. soy sauce
½ tsp. lemon juice	1½ tbs. potato flour
4 cups basic stock or brown stock from which all fat has been removed	3 tbs. cold water
	2 tbs. sherry

Clean the mushrooms. Set aside 4 mushroom caps. Coarsely chop the remainder of the mushrooms, including the stems.

Melt the butter in a large pot, and when foaming, add mushrooms and ¼ teaspoon of the lemon juice. Cook over a high heat for 3 or 4 minutes, stirring constantly. Add stock, salt and soy sauce. Cover pot with a loose-fitting lid, and simmer for 5 minutes.

Put the mixture into a blender and blend until smooth, or mash through a food mill. Pour it back into the pot, and bring to a simmer.

Mix the potato flour with the cold water, and stir into the soup. Stir and cook until it is thickened.

Finely dice the raw mushroom caps and add to the soup. Simmer for 5 minutes without a cover on the pot. Add the remainder of the lemon juice. Just before serving, add the sherry.

To serve: Pour into heated individual soup bowls.
Serves 4 to 6.

ONION SOUP

The excellence of this soup depends upon your basic or brown stock, which should be strong and full-bodied. Don't be in a rush to boil it up fast to tenderize the onions; rather, let it simmer slowly so that the stock and onions meld their flavors.

2 tbs. butter	8 cups hot basic stock
2 tbs. vegetable oil	or brown stock from
4 cups onions, peeled	which all fat has been
and sliced into thin	removed
rings	¼ cup brandy
½ tsp. sugar	6 or 8 thick slices French
2 tbs. flour	bread, toasted
1 tsp. salt	1 cup grated Swiss
¼ tsp. pepper	cheese

Melt the butter and oil in a large heavy pot, and add onion rings. Separate the rings as they are added. Keep the heat low, and cook slowly until the onions are transparent. Add the sugar, and cook and stir until the onions are an even golden brown. Sprinkle on the flour and mix well. Add salt and pepper.

Remove from heat and slowly add stock, stirring continuously. When well blended, return to the fire and bring to a boil. Adjust heat to a simmer, cover pot with a loose-fitting lid and simmer for 35 to 45 minutes. Add brandy.

To serve: Ladle the soup into heated individual deep soup bowls, place a piece of toasted French bread on each and heap a generous tablespoon of cheese on top of each. Place under the broiler until the cheese has melted and is lightly browned. Serve immediately.

Serves 6 to 8.

QUICK VEGETABLE SOUP

With your stock on hand, this soup is quick, easy, delicious and nutritious, and its variations are limited only by your imagination. Any fresh vegetables in season are a welcome addition.

6 cups basic stock or beef stock from which all fat has been removed	2 leeks, washed and only the white part thinly sliced
2 cups potatoes, peeled and diced	1 cup canned tomatoes
2 cups carrots, peeled and diced	1 cup noodles
1 medium onion, peeled and thinly sliced	1 cup fresh spinach, washed and chopped, or frozen chopped spinach
4 stalks celery, washed and diced	2 tsps. salt
1 small clove garlic, finely chopped	1 tsp. pepper
	3 tbs. parsley, finely chopped

Put the stock into a large pot and bring to a boil. Add all the ingredients but the parsley, and bring the pot back to a boil. Adjust heat to a simmer, cover pot with a loose-fitting lid, and simmer for 20 to 30 minutes or until vegetables are tender.

Serve in heated individual soup plates or from a heated tureen. Garnish with the parsley.

Serves 6 to 8.

Variation:
Add 2 cups of cubed cooked beef.

SOUP ALEXANDER

This recipe was given to me by a friend after whom I've named it. He brought it home from one of his visits to Greece. It demands a heady, pungent stock; any scraps and bones from a lamb roast can be added to the stock.

Lamb stock is not included in the chapter on stocks because, in my opinion, its strong and distinctive flavor limits its use. However, this soup is so delicious, it is worth making. A greater quantity of stock may be made and frozen for future use.

LAMB STOCK

2 to 3 lbs. lamb shanks	1 stalk celery, washed and coarsely sliced
1 carrot, scrubbed and quartered	1 tsp. dried thyme
1 medium onion, peeled and quartered	3 tsps. salt
1 clove garlic, peeled and halved	8 peppercorns
1 bay leaf	¼ cup dry white wine, or lemon juice
	2½ quarts cold water

Place all the ingredients in a large pot, bring to a boil, cover pot with a loose-fitting lid, adjust the heat to a simmer, and simmer 3 to 4 hours. During the last hour of cooking, remove the lid, turn the heat up high and reduce the stock to 8 cups.

Strain the stock into a bowl and cool. Remove the fat, and prepare the soup as follows:

MAKING THE SOUP

8 cups lamb stock from which all fat has been removed	1 tbs. lemon juice
	2 egg yolks
½ cup rice	Mint leaves, finely shredded

Put the stock into a large pot, and when boiling, add the rice. Cover, adjust heat to a simmer, and cook until the rice is tender. When tender, add the lemon juice and stir.

Beat the egg yolks slightly in a small bowl. Remove the soup from the heat, and with a long-handled wooden spoon or fork, stir the soup rapidly, and while stirring, slowly pour the yolks into it in a thin stream.

Serve at once in heated individual bowls and garnish with the mint.

Serves 6.

Variation:

Instead of garnishing with the mint, float a paper-thin slice of lemon in each bowl.

CHEESE SOUP

Delicious, economical and easy to prepare. Use a good strong Vermont natural cheddar, sometimes called "store cheese." For a summer luncheon, serve this soup with a fruit salad and French bread. In winter it is good anytime and perfect after a day on the ski slopes.

4 tbs. butter	3 cups milk
2 cups onions, peeled and finely chopped	3 tsps. salt
	1 tsp. pepper
4 tbs. flour	2½ cups cheddar cheese, grated and firmly packed into the measuring cups
3 cups basic stock or beef stock from which all fat has been removed	

Melt the butter in a large pot, and when foaming, add the onions. Stir and cook onions until transparent. Add flour, and stir and cook over a low heat for 5 minutes. Do not brown.

Remove the pot from the heat, and add the stock bit by bit, stirring all the while. Return to the heat and bring to a boil. Simmer for 5 to 10 minutes, giving the pot an occasional stir. Add the milk, salt and pepper. Stir and bring to a boil. Add the cheese, stir and bring to a boil.

Serve piping hot in heated mugs or bowls.

Serves 6 to 8.

CRAB CHOWDER

2 *tbs. butter*	1 *tsp. fresh dill, finely chopped*
2 *cups onions, finely chopped*	1 *tsp. salt*
½ *tsp. garlic, finely chopped*	½ *tsp. pepper*
3 *fillets of sole or haddock cut into ½-inch pieces*	½ *lb. crab flakes*
	2 *cups fish stock*
1 *cup mushrooms, finely chopped*	2 *cups heavy cream*

Melt the butter in a deep pot, add onions and garlic and cook until soft. Add fillets, mushrooms, dill, salt and pepper. Cook, stirring constantly, 3 to 4 minutes. Add crab flakes. Slowly stir in the fish stock and cream. Bring to a simmer, and simmer for 2 or 3 minutes. Serve at once.

Serve from a large heated tureen or in heated individual bowls.

Serves 6.

Variation:

Crab chunks cut into small pieces may be substituted for the crab flakes.

SCALLOP CHOWDER

2 ozs. salt pork, finely diced	2 tsps. salt
2 cups onions, chopped fine	½ tsp. pepper
3 cups potatoes, peeled and diced in ½-inch pieces	1 lb. sea or bay scallops
6 cups fish stock	4 saltine crackers, finely crumbled
2 tomatoes, peeled, seeded and finely chopped	1 cup heavy cream
	Parsley, finely chopped

Fry the salt pork pieces in a large heavy pot until golden brown. Discard all but 1 tablespoon of the fat. Add onions and cook until transparent. Add potatoes and fish stock. Cook over a medium heat, with a loose-fitting lid on top, for 20 minutes or until potatoes are tender. Add tomatoes, salt and pepper, and cook for 5 minutes. Add scallops, crackers and cream. Stir. Bring to a simmer, and simmer for 3 to 5 minutes.

Serve from a large heated tureen or in heated individual bowls. Garnish lightly with chopped parsley.

Serves 6 to 8.

NOTE: If sea scallops are used, cut them into small pieces.

HIGGINS' FISH CHOWDER

My sister has made her home on the coast of Maine for the past twenty-five years. This is the chowder served by the "downeasterners" on a Sunday night with crackers and a salad. The use of canned evaporated milk is "pure Maine," and makes a richer soup; but the soup can be made with all fresh milk.

2 cups fish stock	1⅓ cups fresh milk
2 cups water	⅔ cup canned evaporated milk
2½ to 3 lbs. fillet of haddock	
4 tbs. butter	2 tsps. salt
1 large onion, peeled and finely chopped	½ tsp. pepper
1 quart of potatoes, peeled and diced into ½- to 1-inch cubes	Paprika

Combine the fish stock and water in a pot and bring to a boil. When boiling, drop the fish into it and cover. Adjust the heat to a simmer, and simmer until the fish flakes easily when tested with a fork. With a slotted spoon, remove the fish to a dish and break it into small pieces. Set aside. Reserve the stock.

Melt the butter in a large pot, and when hot, add onion and cook until transparent. Add potatoes and the reserved stock. Cover and cook until the potatoes are tender.

Meanwhile, combine the fresh and canned milk in a pan and scald.

When the potatoes are tender, add to them the scalded milk, the fish pieces, salt and pepper. Heat, but do not boil.

To serve: Pour the chowder into a heated tureen or individual bowls, or serve it directly from the pot in which it was cooked. Garnish with a few dashes of paprika.

Serves 6.

BILLI-BI

A splendid soup.

2½ lbs. mussels	6 peppercorns
3 sprigs parsley	2 tbs. butter
1 small bay leaf	2 cups dry white wine
1 stalk celery, finely diced	1½ cups heavy cream
2 shallots, finely chopped	1 cup fish stock
1 small onion, peeled and finely sliced	1 tsp. salt
¼ tsp. dried thyme	¼ tsp. white pepper

Clean the mussels by scrubbing them with a strong brush under cold running water. Cut and scrape off the beards. Put the mussels into a large pot, cover with cold water and discard any mussels that float on the surface; also discard any mussels that are not closed. If a mussel is open or floats before it is cooked, it means that it is not fresh.

Put the parsley, bay leaf, celery, shallots, onion, thyme, peppercorns, butter and wine into a large pot. Add the cleaned mussels. Put a lid on top, bring to a boil and steam 5 to 10 minutes. All the shells should open; discard any mussel whose shell remains closed.

Remove the mussels from the pot with a slotted spoon and set aside. Line a strainer with 2 thicknesses of cheesecloth, and strain the liquid into a bowl.

Put the strained liquid into a pot, bring to a boil and add the cream, stock, salt and pepper. Stir and reheat. Do not boil.

Serve in small heated bowls. Cheese sticks are a perfect accompaniment to this soup.

Serves 4 to 6.

NOTE: The mussels should be removed from their shells, refrigerated and used to make a mussel bisque (see recipe below).

Another use for the cold mussels is to mix them with a vinaigrette (see p. 238), add 2 tablespoons of finely chopped parsley and serve them as a first course.

A few mussel shells should be saved to garnish either the bisque or salad.

MUSSEL BISQUE

3 *lbs. mussels*	1 *cup heavy cream*
1 *cup dry white wine*	½ *tsp. salt*
1½ *cups fish stock*	1 *pinch cayenne pepper*
4 *tbs. butter*	1 *pinch nutmeg*
4 *tbs. flour*	1 *tbs. brandy*
2 *cups milk*	

Thoroughly scrub the mussels and remove the beards. Discard any mussels that are open or that float.

Put the wine, fish stock and mussels into a large pot; cover with a tight-fitting lid and steam over a low heat until all the shells have opened—about 10 minutes. Remove the pot from the heat and cool.

When cool, remove the mussels from the shells and set aside. Discard any mussels that did not open.

Strain the broth into a bowl through a fine strainer lined with 2 layers of cheesecloth. Set aside.

Melt the butter in a large pot, and when foaming, add flour. Cook and stir 2 to 3 minutes. Do not brown. Remove from the heat, and slowly add 1 cup of the milk; stir and blend until smooth. Add the other cup of milk and the mussel broth, return to heat, stir and bring to a boil. Simmer and stir over a low heat or over hot water for 10 minutes.

Chop the mussels into small pieces and add to the bisque, together with the cream, salt, pepper, nutmeg and brandy. Heat, but do not boil.

To serve: Pour into heated individual bowls, or serve from a heated tureen.

Serves 6.

Variation:

If you have made the Billi-Bi Soup (see p. 98), use the mussels for this bisque. Follow the above recipe, except use only ½ cup of dry white wine and 2½ cups of fish stock. Then proceed with the recipe as given.

CREAMED SHRIMP SOUP

4 cups fish stock	4 tbs. parsley, finely
¾ lb. shrimps, fresh or	chopped
frozen	1½ tsps. salt
3 cups milk	½ tsp. pepper
1 small bay leaf	4 tbs. butter
1 cup celery, finely diced	4 tbs. flour
4 tbs. onion, peeled and	
finely chopped	

Put the stock into a pot and bring to a boil. Add the fresh or frozen shrimps, cook 5 minutes or until they have turned pink. Turn the heat off, and allow the shrimps to cool in the stock. Remove the shrimps from the stock with a slotted spoon. Strain and reserve the stock.

If fresh shrimps are used, peel and devein. Cut the shrimps into small pieces about the size of a raisin. Set aside.

Put the milk in a pan, add bay leaf, celery, onion, parsley, salt and pepper, and scald. Remove bay leaf.

Meanwhile, melt the butter in a large pot, and when foaming, add the flour, stir and cook over a low heat 3 or 4 minutes. Remove from heat. Add 3 cups of the strained fish stock in which the shrimps were cooked and the scalded milk, together with the celery, onion and parsley. Stir and blend.

Return to heat, and stirring constantly, bring to a simmer, and simmer uncovered for 10 minutes. Add the shrimp pieces. Heat.

Serve from a heated tureen or in heated individual soup bowls.

Serves 6.

TOMATO AND SHRIMP SOUP

This is a bit unusual because it combines fish stock and meat stock; but I think you will like its flavor. It is perfect as the first course for a dinner party or a special luncheon.

6 large ripe tomatoes, quartered	1 tsp. sugar
2 cups canned tomatoes	2 tsps. salt
3 large onions, peeled and coarsely sliced	¼ tsp. pepper
	5 cups fish stock
2 tbs. butter	1 lb. shrimps, fresh or frozen
1 clove garlic, peeled	
1 bay leaf	3 cups basic stock or beef stock from which all fat has been re-moved
2 medium carrots scrubbed and quartered	
2 stalks celery, washed and quartered	2 tbs. tomato paste
	Dill or parsley, finely chopped

Put the fresh tomatoes, canned tomatoes, onions, butter, garlic, bay leaf, carrots, celery, sugar, salt and pepper into a heavy pot. Bring to a boil, cover pot with a loose-fitting lid and cook over a medium heat until the ingredients are soft—25 to 35 minutes.

Meanwhile, put the fish stock into a pot, bring to a boil, add the shrimps and cook 5 minutes or until they have turned pink. Turn the heat off and allow them to cool in the stock. Remove the shrimps with a slotted spoon and reserve the stock. If fresh shrimps are used, peel and devein. Set aside.

When the tomato mixture is soft, remove the bay leaf and mash the mixture through a food mill or a strainer. Do not put it in the blender, because the seeds and skins of the tomatoes are to be discarded.

Return the mashed tomato liquid to the pot. Cook and stir over a high heat, without a lid, until the liquid is reduced to a purée. The pot must be carefully watched and stirred during this step so that the purée does not burn. When reduced, there should be 3 cups of purée.

Add the basic stock or beef stock and tomato paste to the purée. Cut the shrimps into ½-inch pieces and add to the soup. Bring to a boil and serve.

Serve from a heated tureen or in heated individual bowls. Garnish with fresh dill or parsley.

Serves 6.

CROUTONS

Croutons are such a delightful garnish that I recommend preparing a whole loaf of bread at a time. Freeze what you don't immediately use in cup-size containers. To reheat, place them in a pan in a medium oven for 10 minutes. They will be as crisp and crunchy as if freshly made.

1 loaf white bread,   ½ lb. butter, melted
   thinly sliced

Cut the crusts from the bread. With a brush, brush each side of the bread slices with butter. Stack the slices evenly and cut them into small cubes. Place on a cookie sheet in a 350° F. oven. From time to time shake and gently toss the bread cubes until they are all a deep golden brown.

Yield: 4 cups.

(4) POULTRY

POULTRY NOTES

The meat of chicken is tender and succulent, but it loses both these qualities if it is cooked too long. Besides watching the cooking time given in the recipe, from time to time test to see whether the chicken is done by using one of the following methods:

a. A whole chicken is done when the leg can be easily moved back and forth.

b. A whole chicken is done if the juices run pale pink or clear when a fork is stuck into the upper joint of the second joint.

c. Chicken pieces are done if a fork easily pierces the thickest piece.

Veal stock may be substituted for chicken stock. Also canned chicken broth may be substituted for your own chicken stock, but the dish will not be as flavorful—and you have to recycle the can.

All dishes use freshly ground pepper. It is preferable to use freshly ground white peppercorns in chicken dishes with a white sauce.

If your family does not like the skin of chicken, it is easily removed from a boiled or steamed chicken a moment before serving.

A double boiler is a marvelous utensil to use in reheating frozen chicken or chicken in a sauce. Put it over a low flame, cover and let it reheat gently, steaming in its own juices.

Taste before you serve, and correct the seasoning to your taste.

BOILED CHICKEN DINNER

Instead of using the traditional old large fowl for this recipe, I prefer to use two young chickens. They cook more rapidly, and the vegetables can go into the pot as soon as the chickens are simmering.

2 2½- to 3-lb. chickens	12 small new white potatoes, scrubbed, or 8 medium potatoes, peeled and cut in half
½ lemon	
4 cups cold basic stock or chicken stock from which all fat has been removed	
	12 medium carrots, scrubbed and cut in half
1 bay leaf	
4 sprigs parsley	6 large leeks, including the fresh green leaves, washed and cut in half
3 sprigs celery leaves	
1 large onion, peeled and quartered	
	1 lb. peas, fresh or frozen
2 tsps. salt	
½ tsp. pepper	2 tbs. parsley, finely chopped

Rub chickens inside and out with lemon, truss and place into a large pot. Add stock. Bring slowly to a boil. Adjust heat to a simmer.

Tie the bay leaf, parsley and celery leaves together, and add to the pot. Add onion, salt, pepper, potatoes and carrots. Place a loose-fitting lid on top and simmer 30 minutes.

Tie the leeks together, and add them to the pot. Add the fresh peas and simmer for 15 minutes, or until chickens and vegetables are tender. If frozen peas are used, follow the cooking-time instructions on the package.

To serve: Carve the chickens and place the pieces on a heated deep platter. Discard bay leaf, parsley, celery leaves and onion. Untie the leeks and arrange them attractively around the chicken pieces with the other vegetables. Skim the fat from the hot broth and pour 1 cup of broth over the chicken and vegetables. Garnish with parsley.

The broth may be seasoned to taste and served as a first course or refrigerated for future use.

Serves 6 to 8.

BOILED CHICKEN WITH GREEN OLIVES

Chicken, green olives and brown sugar—surely you will think it a strange marriage of flavors! However, I recommend you try it. It is delicious and can be prepared the day before it is to be served.

1 3- to 4-lb. chicken cut into serving pieces	5 cups basic stock or chicken stock from which all fat has been removed
1 medium onion, peeled	
4 cloves	
1 tsp. salt	2 tbs. butter
½ tsp. paprika	2 tbs. flour
1 tbs. brown sugar	1 2½ or 3 oz. bottle of pitted unstuffed green olives

Put the chicken pieces into a deep pot, add the onion stuck with the cloves, salt, paprika, brown sugar and stock. Bring to a boil. Place a loose-fitting lid on the pot, adjust the heat to a simmer and simmer 1 to 1½ hours or until the chicken is tender.

When tender, lift the chicken pieces from the pot with a slotted spoon. Remove and discard the skin and bones, and cut the chicken meat into large pieces. Set aside.

Strain the stock into a bowl and skim off any excess fat. Pour the stock into a pot, and over a high heat bring it to a rapid boil; continue to boil, uncovered, until it is reduced to 2 cups.

Melt the butter in a small pot, and when foaming, add the flour and cook 2 minutes over low heat, stirring continuously. Add the 2 cups of hot stock, stir and cook until the sauce thickens.

Cut the olives into thin slices and add to the sauce. Taste before adding salt; the olives add considerable tartness. Simmer gently for 5 minutes. Add chicken pieces and simmer another 5 minutes.

To serve: Serve the chicken in the pot in which it was cooked or in a heated serving dish. Serve with rice or noodles.
Serves 4 to 6.

NOTE: Green olives stuffed with pimientos may be substituted for the unstuffed green olives.

BOILED CHICKEN SALAD

A dish to be served as a salad or as a first course.

1	2½- to 3-lb. chicken	3	generous slices fresh ginger root
1½	to 2 quarts basic stock or chicken stock from which all fat has been removed	2	tbs. lemon juice
		5	to 7 tender young scallions, washed

Put the chicken into a deep pot, and add enough stock to barely cover it. Add the ginger and lemon juice. Place a lid on top and bring to a boil. Adjust the heat to a simmer, and simmer for 45 minutes or until tender.

When tender, remove the pot from the heat and allow the chicken to cool in the stock.

When cool, remove the chicken. Strain the stock into a bowl and reserve for future use.

Cut away and discard all the skin from the chicken. Carve the chicken. Remove the meat from the pieces by tearing it with your fingers into thin shreds 2 to 3 inches long. Put the shreds into an attractive glass salad bowl.

Trim off the roots of the scallions and cut the scallions lengthwise. Use only that part of the tops which is crisp, fresh and green and cut into 2-inch fine, thin slivers. Add to the shredded chicken and toss. Cover and place in the refrigerator to chill.

Make vinaigrette (see p. 238). Pour it over the chilled chicken and scallions, toss and serve.

Serves 6.

CHICKEN IN THE POT

Have you had a busy day? If you want an easy, tasty and attractive supper, serve this dish. Prepare it in your prettiest from-stove-to-table pot.

4 cups basic stock or chicken stock from which all fat has been removed	1 large onion, peeled and cut into quarters
2 2½-lbs. chicken, cut into quarters	1 bay leaf
6 medium carrots, well scrubbed or peeled	1 pinch dried thyme
6 medium potatoes, peeled	2 tsps. salt
	½ tsp. pepper
	1 cup frozen peas
	2 tbs. parsley, finely chopped

Into an attractive pot put the stock, chickens, carrots, potatoes, onion, bay leaf, thyme, salt and pepper, and bring to a boil. Cover pot with a loose-fitting lid, adjust the heat to a simmer, and simmer for 25 minutes or until the chicken pieces are tender. Remove the chicken pieces to a plate and set aside. Continue cooking until the carrots and potatoes are tender. Add the frozen peas, and return the chicken pieces to the pot, cover and cook for 5 minutes.

To serve: Sprinkle the parsley over the chicken and serve right from the pot.

Serves 6.

WHITE CHICKEN 1

This is the classic French Poulet au Blanc, and it has, I'm sure, as many variations as a hen has feathers. These two versions come from the recipe collection of an elegant French lady, the grandmother of a dear friend, who titled her hand-written book "Recettes de Cuisine du Bon Vieux Temps." The little book is a treasure, and I am pleased to include her recipes from "the good old days."

1 *4- to 4½-lb. roasting chicken*
2 *quarts basic stock or chicken stock from which all fat has been removed*

2 *cups cold water*

Truss the chicken, place it in a deep pot, and add the stock and water. Cover pot with a loose-fitting lid, and simmer over a low heat for 1½ to 2 hours or until the chicken is tender.

When tender, remove the chicken to a heated platter and keep warm.

Skim off any excess fat from the stock and prepare the following white sauce:

4 *tbs. sweet butter*
4 *tbs. flour*
2 *cups of hot stock in which the chicken was cooked*
1 *tsp. salt*
⅛ *tsp. cayenne pepper*

2 *egg yolks*
½ *cup heavy cream*
½ *lb. fresh mushroom tops, thinly sliced*
1 *tsp. lemon juice*
Parsley, finely chopped

Melt the butter in a heavy pan over a low heat. Add flour, stir and blend 3 minutes; do not brown. Remove from heat and add the hot stock, salt and pepper. Stir briskly until smooth. Return to heat and stir continuously until the sauce comes to a boil. Stir and simmer gently 3 to 5 minutes.

In a bowl, mix the egg yolks with the cream. Beat 1 cup of the hot sauce into the egg and cream mixture bit by bit. When well blended, add to the sauce, and stir and cook over a low heat until the yolks thicken it slightly.

When slightly thickened, add mushrooms and lemon juice. Cook and stir for 3 minutes. Do not boil.

To serve: Carve the chicken into serving pieces and place them over a bed of fluffy white rice or cooked noodles. Spoon the sauce carefully over the chicken pieces and garnish with parsley.

Serves 6.

WHITE CHICKEN 2

An exceptionally rich and nutritious dish, because all the chicken juices, as well as the fat, are absorbed into the vegetables. These succulent vegetables become the sauce.

1 3½- to 4-lb. chicken	1 bay leaf
Salt	2 cups celery stalks, in-
Pepper	cluding leaves, cut
Lemon wedge	into 1-inch pieces
2 medium carrots,	8 sprigs parsley
scrubbed and quartered	½ cup dry white wine
2 medium onions, peeled	½ cup basic stock or
and thickly sliced	chicken stock from
1 small white turnip,	which all fat has been
washed and thickly	removed
sliced	2 tsps. salt
1 clove garlic, peeled and	¼ tsp. pepper
cut in half	

Salt and pepper the inside of the chicken. Rub the outside with lemon. Truss.

Put all the vegetables and herbs in the bottom of a heavy pot. Add wine, stock, salt and pepper. Place chicken, breast side down, on the bed of vegetables. Place a tight lid on top and cook over a low heat 1 to 1½ hours or until chicken is tender. Remove the chicken to a hot platter, keep hot and prepare the sauce as follows:

Discard the bay leaf. Put all the vegetables, together with the liquid, through a food mill or blend in a blender until smooth. Pour into a saucepan, correct seasoning, stir and bring to a boil.

To serve: Carve the chicken into serving pieces, arrange them on a heated platter and spoon the sauce over them. Serve with noodles or rice.

Serves 6.

STUFFED CHICKEN IN THE POT

An unusual and good meal. Don't use an old fowl; be sure that your butcher gives you a fat, plump roasting hen.

1 4- to 5-lb. roasting hen	1 tbs. parsley, finely chopped
Lemon wedge	
Chicken liver	½ tsp. pepper
Chicken gizzard and heart	1 tsp. salt
	2 egg yolks
2 cups coarse bread-crumbs	2½ quarts basic stock or chicken stock from which all fat has been removed
2 small cloves garlic, peeled and finely chopped	
½ cup boiled ham, finely diced	1 cup dry white wine
	Watercress

Rub the chicken well inside and out with the lemon wedge.

Prepare the stuffing as follows: Boil the liver, gizzard and heart until tender—about 10 minutes. When tender, chop them and put them into a large bowl. Add the breadcrumbs, garlic, ham, parsley, pepper, salt and egg yolks. Mix thoroughly. Stuff the chicken. Sew up the openings of the chicken and truss.

Put the chicken into a deep pot and add the stock and

wine. Bring slowly to a boil. Place a loose-fitting lid on top, adjust the heat to a simmer, and simmer for 1½ to 2 hours or until the chicken is tender.

When tender, carefully remove the chicken to a heated platter. Remove and discard the trussing string.

To serve: Garnish with sprigs of watercress. Serve at once. Serves 6.

Variations:

a. Add additional vegetables—carrots, peas and potatoes —to the pot, and serve them on the platter with the chicken.

b. Strain the stock, remove any excess fat, taste for seasoning and serve as a first course.

CHICKEN CACCIATORE

1 3- to 4-lb. chicken, cut into serving pieces
Seasoned flour
5 tbs. olive oil
1 large onion, peeled and coarsely chopped
1 large green pepper, coarsely chopped after discarding seeds and white ribs
1 medium clove garlic, peeled and finely chopped
2 tbs. celery leaves, coarsely chopped

1 cup fresh tomatoes, peeled and diced, or canned tomatoes
1 cup basic stock or chicken stock from which all fat has been removed
2 tsps. salt
½ tsp. pepper
1 cup mushrooms, including stems, sliced
2 tsps. lemon juice
1 tbs. parsley, finely chopped

Dredge the chicken pieces lightly with the seasoned flour.

Heat the olive oil in a heavy pot. When hot, add chicken pieces and brown. Remove from the pot and set aside.

Add onion to the pot and cook until transparent. Add green pepper, garlic and celery leaves, and stir and cook 3 to 5 minutes.

Replace the chicken pieces in the pot, add tomatoes, stock, salt and pepper. Cover pot with a tight-fitting lid, and simmer 30 to 40 minutes. Stir occasionally.

Wipe the mushrooms clean, slice and sprinkle them with lemon juice. Add them to the pot 10 minutes before you are ready to serve.

To serve: Serve directly from the pot or arrange the chicken pieces on a heated platter and spoon the vegetables and sauce over them. Garnish with parsley.

Serves 6.

CHICKEN ROSEMARY

This is an uncomplicated and good recipe. Serve it for a party or for a festive family affair.

1½ tsps. dried rosemary, or 3 tsps. fresh rosemary finely chopped	¾ cup dry white wine
	1 cup basic stock or chicken stock from which all fat has been removed
2 tbs. wine vinegar	
½ cup butter	
2 2½- to 3-lb. chickens, cut into serving pieces	1 tbs. parsley, finely chopped
3 medium onions, peeled and finely chopped	2 tsps. salt
	1 tsp. pepper
	1 cup cooked ham, finely diced
2 medium cloves garlic, peeled and finely chopped	

Put the rosemary into a small dish, and pour the vinegar over it. Set aside.

Put the butter into a large pot, and when foaming, add the chicken pieces and cook until golden. As the chicken pieces brown, remove them to a plate. Don't let the butter burn. When the chicken is browned, add the onion, stir and cook until it is transparent. Return the chicken pieces to the pot, and add the garlic, wine, stock, parsley, rosemary, salt and pepper. Bring to a boil, cover, adjust the heat to a simmer, and simmer for 20 minutes or until the chicken is tender.

To serve: Arrange the chicken on a heated serving dish or platter, spoon over the sauce in which it was cooked, and sprinkle the diced ham over it.

Serves 6 to 8.

CHICKEN SAN SEBASTIAN

A truly pretty, delicious party dish. Our house is divided on the type of Italian sausages to use; I prefer the sweet; the others prefer the hot. So try both and suit your own taste.

3 tbs. butter
2 tbs. vegetable oil
2 2½- to 3-lb. chickens quartered
1 cup dry white wine
1 cup basic stock or chicken stock from which all fat has been removed
1½ tsps. salt

½ tsp. pepper
1 lb. Italian sausages, sweet or hot, cut into 1-inch slices
6 medium tomatoes, peeled, seeded and coarsely chopped
6 medium green peppers, seeded, cored and coarsely chopped
¼ lb. Westphalian ham, or any cured smoked ham, finely diced*

Put 2 tablespoons of the butter and oil into a large frying pan, and when hot, add the chicken pieces and brown them; do not let them overlap. As they are browned, place them into a large pot. Discard the fat and add the wine to the pan, stir, and bring to a boil, gathering all the crispy bits, and pour over the chicken pieces. Add ½ cup of the stock, salt and pepper. Bring to a boil, cover, adjust the heat to a simmer, and simmer for 20 minutes or until the chicken is tender. Set aside and keep warm.

Meanwhile put the remaining tablespoon of butter into the frying pan, and when hot, add the sausage slices and cook until brown and done. Remove them to a flattened brown paper

* If this ham is not available, use baked or boiled ham.

bag to drain. Discard the fat in the pan, and add the tomatoes and green peppers and the remaining half cup of stock. Cook uncovered over a low heat, stirring often, until it is a soft and thick sauce.

To serve: Place the chicken pieces on a heated serving platter, pour the tomato and pepper sauce over them, and scatter the sausages and ham over the top.

Serves 6 to 8.

CHICKEN IN WINE AND CREAM

Quite a rich dish, but it is so delicious that one should forgo counting calories.

2 tbs. butter	1 cup basic stock or
1 3½- to 4-lb. chicken,	chicken stock from
cut into serving pieces	which all fat has been
18 small white onions,	removed
peeled	3 cups dry white wine
1 tsp. salt	½ lb. small fresh or
½ tsp. pepper	frozen mushroom caps
	3 cups heavy cream

Put the butter into a large heavy pot, and when foaming, add the chicken pieces, skin side down. Turn the heat down, cover the pot and cook gently for 10 minutes.

Add the onions, salt and pepper. Cover and cook for 20 minutes.

Add the stock and wine; cover and simmer for 20 to 30 minutes or until the chicken is barely tender.

Add the mushroom caps; cover and simmer for 5 to 10 minutes.

Remove the chicken, onions and mushrooms to a heated serving dish and keep warm. Add the cream to the sauce and boil it rapidly over a high heat, uncovered, until it is reduced by one-half. At this point the sauce should be thick and smooth. Stir occasionally.

To serve: Pour the sauce over the chicken, onions and mushrooms, and serve at once.

Serves 6.

CHICKEN WITH CURRY SAUCE

A Madras curry powder is recommended for this recipe.

1 cup flour mixed with 2 tsps. salt, 1 tsp. pepper and 2 tsps. curry powder

2 2½- to 3-lb. chickens, cut into pieces

3 tbs. butter

2 tbs. oil

1 large onion, peeled and finely chopped

2 tbs. of the flour used for dusting the chicken

4 tsps. curry powder

1 tsp. tomato paste

1 tsp. sugar

1 tsp. salt

½ tsp. pepper

3 cups basic stock or chicken stock from which all fat has been removed

1 medium clove garlic, peeled and finely chopped

¾ cup heavy cream

2 tbs. parsley finely chopped

Lightly dust the chicken pieces in the mixed flour. Heat the butter and oil in a deep heavy pot until foaming, then add the chicken pieces (don't let them overlap) and brown until golden.

When the chicken pieces are brown, remove them to a plate, add the onion to the pan; stir and cook until transparent. Remove the pan from the heat and add the flour, curry powder, tomato paste, sugar, salt and pepper. Stir until blended. Add the stock slowly, stirring continuously, until the ingredients are well mixed. Add the garlic, return the pan to the heat and stir and cook the sauce until it comes to a boil. Replace the chicken pieces, cover, adjust the heat to a simmer, and simmer 30 to 35 minutes or until the chicken is tender.

When tender, remove the chicken to a heated serving platter with a slotted spoon or tongs and keep warm. Over a high heat, bring the sauce to a rapid boil, and boil, uncovered, until it is reduced to 1½ or 2 cups. Skim any excess fat off the surface of the sauce. Lower the heat and add the cream; stir until blended. Heat, but do not boil.

To serve: Spoon the sauce over the chicken pieces and garnish with the chopped parsley. Serve with noodles or rice or kasha.

Serves 6 to 8.

CHICKEN WITH BASIL

A dish that freezes so beautifully, I usually double the ingredients so that two meals are prepared with a single effort.

2 tbs. butter
1 4-lb. chicken, cut into serving pieces
¼ cup scallions, chopped
½ clove garlic, peeled and finely chopped
½ cup dry white wine
¾ cup fresh tomatoes, peeled and diced, or canned tomatoes

½ cup basic stock or chicken stock from which all fat has been removed
4 leaves fresh basil, chopped, or 1½ tsp. dried basil
1 bay leaf
2 sprigs parsley
1½ tsp. salt
¼ tsp. pepper

Melt the butter in a heavy pan, and when foaming, add chicken pieces and brown on all sides. Remove the chicken and set aside. To the pan add the scallions, and cook quickly until soft; do not brown. Add garlic and wine. Stir and boil over a high heat, uncovered, until the liquid has been reduced by one-half.

To this liquid add the tomatoes, stock, basil, bay leaf and parsley. Simmer 5 minutes.

Put the chicken pieces into the sauce, add salt and pepper and cover tightly. Cook 25 to 30 minutes over a low heat, or until the chicken is tender.

To serve: Remove the bay leaf and parsley, put the chicken pieces into a heated serving dish and pour the sauce over them.

Serves 4 to 6.

CHICKEN TARRAGON

2 2½- to 3-lb chickens
   Salt
   Pepper
4 tsps. dried tarragon
   leaves, or 8 tsps. fresh
   tarragon leaves, finely
   chopped

½ tsp. garlic, finely
   chopped
   Lemon wedge
2 tbs. butter
1 tbs. vegetable oil
4 cups basic stock or
   chicken stock from
   which all fat has been
   removed

Lightly salt and pepper the inside of the chickens. Stuff each with equal amounts of tarragon and garlic. Truss. Rub the outside of each bird with lemon.

Put the butter and oil into a heavy pot, and heat until foaming. Place the chickens, breast side down, in the hot fat, and cook and turn until they are golden brown. Carefully control the heat so that neither the fat nor the chickens burn.

In a separate pot bring the stock to a boil. When the chickens are a golden brown, pour the hot stock over them. Bring to a gentle boil. Cover the pot with a tight-fitting lid. Adjust the heat to a simmer, and simmer for 30 minutes or until tender. Remove the chickens to a heated dish and keep hot.

Prepare the following Tarragon Sauce:

4 tbs. butter
4 tbs. flour
1 tsp. salt
⅛ tsp. cayenne pepper
2 cups strained hot stock
   in which the chickens
   were cooked and from
   which any excess fat
   has been skimmed

2 tsps. dried tarragon
   leaves, or 2 tbs. fresh
   tarragon leaves, finely
   chopped
1 egg yolk
1 tbs. brandy
½ cup heavy cream
   Parsley or watercress

Melt the butter in a heavy saucepan, add flour, salt and pepper. Stir over a slow fire for 3 minutes. Do not brown. Turn off heat, and add the stock and the tarragon. Bring to a boil, and cook over a low heat 5 to 10 minutes, stirring constantly. Remove from heat.

In a small bowl mix the egg yolk with the brandy, and add 1 cup of the hot sauce bit by bit, stirring all the while. When mixed, pour into the sauce, and cook over a low heat for 3 or 4 minutes, stirring constantly. Add the heavy cream. Stir and heat. Do not boil.

To serve: Carve the chickens into quarters and place them on a heated deep platter or gratin dish. Carefully spoon all the sauce over the pieces. Garnish with small bunches of parsley or watercress at each side. A teaspoon of finely chopped fresh tarragon over the sauce is an attractive addition. Serve at once.

Serves 6 to 8.

CHICKEN AND HERBS IN RED WINE

A recipe based on a chicken-and-red-wine dish my husband and I ate in the French village of Cézanne many years ago. I don't believe this recipe is a duplication of what we enjoyed, but I do believe it is good. You may omit or add herbs to your taste. The wine should be the best your budget will permit.

When the chicken is ready for serving, the outside is a dark burgundy color, almost black, and the meat is snow white and succulent.

1 clove garlic, peeled and finely chopped

3 tbs. celery leaves, coarsely chopped

4 sprigs parsley

1 large onion, peeled and coarsely chopped

1 medium carrot, scrubbed and diced

4 cloves allspice, crushed or ½ tsp. ground allspice

2 bay leaves, crushed

2 medium slices fresh ginger root, or ½ tsp. powdered ginger

1 large pinch each of dried marjoram, oregano, rosemary, saffron, sage, tarragon, thyme and dill

1 tsp. salt

½ tsp. pepper

1 tbs. lemon juice

¾ cup hot olive oil

1 4½- to 5-lb. chicken, cut into serving pieces
Red burgundy wine

3 cups basic stock or chicken stock from which all fat has been removed

Place all the ingredients except the chicken, wine and stock in a large bowl. Mix thoroughly. Add the chicken pieces, skin side down. Add just enough wine to cover the chicken. Place a tight cover on the bowl. Marinate for 6 hours or, preferably, overnight. Turn the chicken pieces 3 or 4 times. Do not refrigerate.

After the chicken pieces have been marinated, put them, together with the marinade, into a heavy pot and add the stock. Place a loose-fitting lid on top, and bring to a boil. Adjust heat to a simmer, and simmer for 40 to 50 minutes or until the chicken is tender.

When tender, remove the chicken pieces to a dish and keep warm. Strain the broth into a bowl through a fine sieve or 2 pieces of cheesecloth placed over a strainer. Skim off the excess fat, and prepare the following Sauce Morgan:

3 *tbs. butter*	2 *cups of the strained*
1 *small onion, peeled*	*stock*
and finely chopped	¼ *tsp. salt*
¼ *tsp. garlic, finely*	1 *tsp. guava jelly*
chopped	2 *cups finely sliced*
1 *tsp. tomato paste*	*mushrooms*
2 *tsps. potato flour*	*Lemon juice*

Heat 1 tablespoon of the butter in a heavy pan, and when hot, add the onion and cook until transparent. Remove from heat; add the garlic, tomato paste and potato flour. Stir and mix thoroughly. Add stock, salt and jelly, and stir until blended. Place over a low heat, bring to a boil, stirring continuously, and simmer 5 to 10 minutes.

Heat the remaining butter in a pan, and when foaming, add the mushrooms. Sprinkle with a few drops of lemon juice, and cook over a high heat 3 or 4 minutes, stirring and tossing. Add to the sauce. Stir.

To serve: Place the chicken pieces on a heated serving platter, and spoon over 1 cup of the sauce; serve the balance in a heated sauceboat. Serve with rice, preferably wild rice.
Serves 6.

STEAMED CHICKEN AND RUM

The combination of rum and chicken is a good one. In the tropics, rum is used generously in cooking, and it was once used more extensively in the American kitchen than it is today. I find it adds a subtle flavor to many dishes.

1 4-lb. chicken
Lemon wedge
Salt
Pepper
4 tbs. celery leaves, coarsely chopped
1 medium carrot, scrubbed and quartered

3 scallions, washed and coarsely chopped
1½ cups basic stock or chicken stock from which all fat has been removed
1 cup dark rum

Rub the inside and outside of the chicken with the lemon wedge. Sprinkle the inside with salt and pepper. Stuff it loosely with the vegetables. Truss.

Pour the stock and rum into a large pot. Place the chicken, breast side down, on a trivet or rack set over the liquid. The chicken should not touch the liquid. Place a tight-fitting lid on top, and bring to a boil. Adjust the heat to a simmer, and gently steam for 1½ to 2 hours or until tender. Remove to a heated dish and keep hot. Strain the stock into a bowl and prepare the following Rum Sauce:

2 tbs. butter
2 tbs. flour
1 tsp. shallots, finely chopped
¼ tsp. garlic, peeled and finely chopped
½ tsp. salt

1 pinch cayenne pepper
2 cups of the hot stock
½ cup heavy cream
2 tbs. rum
2 tbs. parsley, finely chopped

Melt the butter in a heavy saucepan and add flour. Cook over a low heat for 3 minutes, stirring constantly. Add shallots, garlic, salt and pepper, and cook for 2 minutes. Remove from fire and add the hot stock. Cook slowly for 10 minutes, stirring all the while. Add the cream and rum. Stir. Heat, but do not boil. This should be a thin sauce.

To serve: Carve the chicken. Arrange the pieces attractively on a warm serving platter. Spoon just enough of sauce over the chicken to coat it; then sprinkle with the parsley. Serve the remainder of the sauce in a heated sauceboat. Rice or noodles make a nice companion for this dish.

Serves 6.

STEAMED CHICKEN WITH RICE AND MUSHROOM STUFFING

1 *4- to 5-lb roasting chicken* *Lemon wedge*	1 *cup mushrooms, including stems, finely chopped*
2 *tbs. butter*	*Lemon juice*
1 *small onion, peeled and finely chopped*	½ *tsp. dried thyme*
1 *tsp. salt*	½ *cup dry white wine*
½ *tsp. pepper*	1½ *cups basic stock or chicken stock from which all fat has been removed*
½ *cup long-grain Carolina rice*	

Rub the outside and inside of the chicken well with the lemon. Remove all pieces of excess fat and set aside.

Heat the butter in a heavy saucepan, add onion and cook until transparent. Do not brown. Add salt, pepper and rice. Stir continuously over a low flame for 5 minutes. Remove from heat and add mushrooms. Sprinkle with a few drops of lemon juice, add thyme and mix thoroughly.

Stuff the chicken loosely with the rice and mushroom mixture. Space must be allowed for the rice to expand. Sew up the cavities, and truss. Place the pieces of chicken fat over the back of the chicken.

Pour the wine and stock into a steamer. Place the chicken, breast side down, on a trivet or rack set over the liquid. The chicken should not touch the liquid. Place a tight-fitting lid on top. Bring the liquid to a boil, adjust the heat to a simmer and gently steam for 1½ to 2 hours or until the chicken is tender.

Check the liquid in the steamer from time to time, and add more stock if necessary.

To serve: Untruss the chicken, place it on a bed of watercress on a large heated platter and surround it with steamed carrots and peas. Save the stock for future use.

Serves 6.

STEAMED BABY CHICKENS

Be certain that your butcher gives you the smallest birds. This is an excellent party dish.

3 1- to 1½-lb. baby chickens
Salt
Pepper
Sweet butter
3 cups dry white wine
2 cups basic stock or chicken stock from which all fat has been removed
Chicken gizzards and hearts, cut into small pieces

1 medium truffle, finely chopped
Stuffing:
12 leaves fresh tarragon, chopped, or 1 tsp. dried tarragon
1 medium clove garlic, cut into 3 pieces
3 small carrots, scrubbed and cut into 1-inch pieces
3 sprigs parsley

Sprinkle the cavities of the chickens with salt and pepper.

Mix the stuffing ingredients, and put an equal amount of it in each chicken. Generously rub the outside of each chicken with butter.

Put the wine, stock, chicken gizzards and hearts into the bottom of a steamer.

Place the chickens, breast side down, on a trivet or rack set over the liquid. The chickens should not touch the liquid. Place a tight-fitting lid on top. Bring the liquid to a boil, adjust the heat to a slow boil and steam for 1 to 1½ hours or until the chickens are tender.

When tender, remove the chickens to a heated platter and keep warm.

Strain the stock into a bowl, and prepare a tarragon sauce (see pp. 124 and 174). Save any remaining stock for future use.

To serve: Cut the chickens in half. Remove strings and discard stuffing. Arrange the chickens on a heated platter and spoon the Tarragon Sauce over them. Garnish with the chopped truffle and serve at once.

Serves 6.

BRUNSWICK STEW

An adaptation of an early American stew. The original recipe called for all of the sweet sun-ripened vegetables of the summer season. It was then, and is now, a hearty one-dish meal. With today's frozen vegetables it can be prepared in any season. Serve it with hot cornbread.

2 tbs. bacon fat
1 tbs. butter
1 3- to 4-lb. chicken, cut into serving pieces
2 tbs. brandy or dark rum
2 cups basic stock or chicken stock from which all fat has been removed
2 cups fresh tomatoes, peeled and diced, or canned tomatoes
¼ cup dry white wine
2 onions, peeled and thinly sliced

½ tsp. garlic, peeled and finely chopped
1 medium leek, including the fresh green leaves, washed and thinly sliced
1½ tsps. salt
½ tsp. pepper
½ tsp. sugar
1½ cups fresh or frozen small lima beans
1½ cups fresh or frozen corn kernels
Celery leaves, coarsely chopped

Heat the bacon fat and butter in a heavy large pot. When hot, add chicken; fry until golden brown on all sides. Remove to a plate. Discard fat. Replace chicken, and flame with the brandy or rum. Add stock, tomatoes, wine, onions, garlic, leek, salt, pepper and sugar. Stir. Cover pot with a loose-fitting lid, and simmer 40 minutes or until chicken is tender.

When tender, remove the chicken from the pot. Discard the skin and bones, and cut the chicken into large pieces. Set aside. Skim any excess fat off the stock. Add lima beans and corn. Cook 30 minutes or until vegetables are tender. Return the chicken pieces to the pot and heat.

Serve in a heated serving dish and garnish with the celery leaves.

Serves 6 to 8.

CHICKEN MARENGO

2 *2½- to 3-lb chickens,*
  cut into serving pieces
  Seasoned flour
3 *tbs. butter*
3 *tbs. olive oil*
2 *ozs. brandy*
1 *tsp. garlic, peeled and*
  finely chopped
1 *bay leaf*
6 *sprigs parsley*
½ *cup basic stock or*
  chicken stock from
  which all fat has been
  removed

½ *cup dry white wine*
1½ *cups fresh tomatoes,*
  peeled and diced, or
  canned tomatoes
1 *tsp. salt*
¼ *tsp. pepper*
½ *lb. small mushroom*
  caps, or if large,
  thickly sliced
1 *tbs. parsley, finely*
  chopped

Dredge the chicken pieces lightly in the seasoned flour.

Put the butter and olive oil into a heavy pot, heat until foaming, add the chicken pieces and brown until golden all over.

Heat the brandy, and flame the chicken. Add the garlic, tie the bay leaf and parsley together and add them to the pot with the stock, wine, tomatoes, salt and pepper. Cover the pot, and simmer gently over a low fire for 30 to 40 minutes or until the chicken is tender.

When tender, add the mushroom caps or slices; stir and cook 3 to 5 minutes.

To serve: Remove the bay leaf and parsley. Serve in the pot in which it is cooked or ladle into a heated casserole. Garnish with the chopped parsley.

Serves 6.

CHICKEN WITH WHITE ONIONS

To peel onions without tears, put them in a pan and pour boiling water over them. Leave for 10 seconds. Drain, and rinse under cold running water. Make a small cross at the root end of the onion, and the outer skin will slip off easily.

This dish can be frozen without loss of flavor, but don't put it over direct heat to reheat it. Place it in a double boiler over a medium heat. When it is piping hot, serve at once. Don't continue to cook.

¾ lb. butter	¼ cup dry white wine
4 lbs. small white onions, peeled	1½ cups rice
3 2- to 2½-lb chickens, quartered	3 tsps. salt
	½ tsp. pepper
4½ cups basic stock or chicken stock from which all fat has been removed	3 cups light cream
	4 ozs. bourbon whiskey
	1 tbs. parsley, finely chopped

Put the butter in the top of a double boiler, add onions, cover and cook over boiling water for 1 hour or until tender.

Meanwhile, put the chicken pieces in a pot, and cover

them with the stock and wine. Bring to a boil, adjust heat to a simmer, and gently simmer for 25 to 30 minutes or until tender. When tender, remove the chicken to a flameproof casserole and keep warm.

Measure the broth in which the chickens were cooked; it should be 4½ cups. If not, add additional stock. Bring to a boil, and add rice, salt and pepper. Cover and cook until the rice is tender.

When the onions are tender, pour them, together with the butter in which they were cooked, over the chicken. Add the cream and cooked rice. Carefully mix all the ingredients together, heat over a low flame and add the bourbon. Stir and heat. Do not boil.

To serve: Garnish with the parsley, and serve at once.
Serves 6.

COLD CHICKEN WITH LEMON

A superb summer dish. It should be made a day in advance so that it can set properly and so that you and your kitchen can remain cool. Serve it with crisp watercress salad and a cold dry white wine.

1 3- to 4-lb. chicken, cut into serving pieces	3 tbs. thin slivers of lemon peel
Peel of ½ lemon	¼ cup lemon juice
1½ to 2 quarts basic stock or chicken stock from which all fat has been removed	¼ cup sherry
	1 tsp. salt
	2 egg yolks
	1 cup heavy cream

Put the chicken pieces into a deep pot, and add the peel of half a lemon. Add the stock, which should barely cover the chicken. Bring to a boil. Cover pot with a loose-fitting lid. Adjust heat to a simmer, and simmer 45 minutes or until the chicken is tender.

When tender, remove the pot from the heat. Let the chicken cool in the stock.

When cooled, remove the chicken and discard the skin and bones. Cut the meat into neat, small pieces. Set aside.

Remove any excess fat from the stock, and strain stock into a bowl. Pour the stock into a pan and boil rapidly, uncovered, until it is reduced to 1½ cups. Add 2 tablespoons of the slivered lemon peel, the lemon juice, sherry and the salt. Boil gently for 5 minutes.

In a bowl combine the egg yolks with the heavy cream, and add the hot sauce bit by bit, stirring continuously. When blended, put the mixture into the pot, and stir it briskly over a low heat for 3 or 4 minutes until it is slightly thickened. Add the chicken pieces. Mix.

Pour the mixture into an attractive glass dish and chill thoroughly for at least 4 hours or, preferably, overnight. The sauce should have the texture and appearance of a custard.

To serve: Garnish with the remaining tablespoon of slivered lemon peel, and serve on chilled individual plates.

Serves 4 to 6.

CHICKEN BREASTS IN SOUR CREAM

An easy party dish, and one that can be made early and reheated; but if you reheat, do so over a very low heat or, preferably, over hot water. Serve with rice.

6 *whole chicken breasts,*   2 *tsps. salt*
    boned   ⅛ *tsp. cayenne pepper*
    Flour   2 *tsps. currant jelly*
4 *tbs. butter*   2 *tbs. grated Parmesan*
3 *tbs. hot Marsala wine*   *cheese*
2 *tbs. flour*   ¼ *lb. mushroom caps*
1 *tsp. tomato paste*   *Lemon juice*
1 *cup hot basic stock or*   1 *tbs. sherry*
    chicken stock from   1 *tbs. fresh dill, finely*
    which all fat has been   *chopped, or 1 tsp.*
    removed   *dried dill*
2 *cups sour cream*

Dust the chicken breasts lightly with flour. Put 3 tablespoons of the butter into a heavy pot, and when foaming, add the breasts, skin side down. Brown quickly all over. Add the hot Marsala wine.

Remove the chicken breasts, lower the heat and add the flour and tomato paste. Mix well. Stir in the hot stock. Cook and stir until the sauce thickens. Add the sour cream slowly, stirring briskly all the while. Add salt, pepper, jelly and cheese. Stir. Replace the chicken breasts. Cover and simmer gently for 15 to 20 minutes or until tender.

Cut mushroom caps into fine slices. Put the remaining tablespoon of butter into a pan with a few drops of lemon juice. When foaming, add the mushrooms, and cook over a high heat, stirring and shaking the pan, for 3 or 4 minutes. Add the sherry and dill. Stir. Add to the chicken breasts, and mix very gently.

To serve: Heat, and serve in the pot in which the chicken was cooked; or place the chicken breasts on a heated platter and carefully spoon the sauce over them.

Serves 6.

CHICKEN TETRAZZINI

Another Italian classic, and so easy to prepare if you have a boiled chicken in the pot. It is a delicious one-dish meal that can be frozen and reheated in the oven. If you do freeze it, don't add the cheese and glaze until ready to serve.

3 cups boiled chicken meat

7 tbs. butter

4 tbs. flour

3 cups hot basic stock or chicken stock from which all fat has been removed

2 cups heavy cream

3 tbs. sherry

3 tsps. salt

½ tsp. pepper

½ tsp. nutmeg

1 canned red pimiento, finely diced

1 cup Parmesan cheese, grated

1 lb. thin spaghetti

1 tsp. lemon juice

½ lb. mushrooms, finely sliced

1 tbs. parsley, finely chopped

Remove skin from the chicken, and discard. Dice the meat into ½-inch cubes. Discard the bones.

Melt 4 tablespoons of the butter in a heavy saucepan. Add flour and cook, stirring constantly, 2 or 3 minutes. Do not brown. Add the stock. Stir and cook until it comes to a boil. Add cream, sherry, salt, pepper, nutmeg, pimiento and ½ cup of the cheese. Continue stirring, cook over a low heat for 3 or 4 minutes. Keep warm.

Cook the spaghetti in 3 quarts of salted boiling water until tender. When tender, drain and pour into a buttered serving dish. Mix in ¼ cup of the cheese and 2 tablespoons of the butter. Keep warm.

Meanwhile, sprinkle the lemon juice over the mushroom

slices and sauté them in the remaining tablespoon of butter over a high heat for 3 or 4 minutes.

Scatter the chicken pieces and mushrooms over the top of the spaghetti, and pour the hot sauce over them. Sprinkle the remaining ¼ cup of cheese over the top, dot with butter and place under a broiler until the cheese has melted and the top is glazed.

Serve in the serving dish and garnish with parsley.

Serves 6.

CHICKEN DADO

An interesting and delicious way to use the chicken that went into the preparation of your basic or chicken stock. Serve it with rice or noodles.

2 *cups boiled chicken meat, diced*	½ *cup basic stock or chicken stock from which all fat has been removed*
3 *tbs. butter*	
3 *tbs. scallions, finely chopped*	2 *tsps. salt*
1 *cup water chestnuts, sliced*	1 *tsp. lemon juice*
2 *tsps. fresh ginger root, slivered*	½ *tsp. pepper*
	1 *tbs. scallion tops, finely chopped*
2 *cups sour cream*	

Discard the bones of chicken, and dice the meat into neat cubes.

Heat the butter in a heavy, large pot until foaming, add scallions and cook until soft. Do not brown.

Remove from the heat and add the water chestnuts,

ginger, sour cream, stock, salt, lemon juice and pepper. Return to the heat and bring to a boil. Add chicken. Heat through, but do not cook. Stir gently and as little as possible so that the chicken pieces don't break up.

Serve immediately in a heated serving dish, and garnish with scallion tops.

Serves 6.

BOILED CHICKEN WITH DILL SAUCE

Another superb use for your boiled chicken. It can be prepared days in advance and frozen. If you do freeze it, don't add the cheese and glaze until it is defrosted and reheated.

1 3½- to 4-lb. boiled chicken	1 pinch cayenne pepper
4 tbs. butter	1 tsp. dried dill or 3 tsps. fresh dill, finely chopped
4 tbs. flour	
2 cups hot basic stock or chicken stock from which all fat has been removed	1 egg yolk
	½ cup heavy cream
	2 tbs. grated Parmesan cheese
1 tsp. salt	Butter

Carve the meat into large serving pieces. Discard bones.

Butter individual casseroles or one large gratin dish, and place the chicken meat in the dishes or dish.

Melt the butter in a heavy saucepan. Add flour and cook, stirring constantly—2 or 3 minutes. Do not brown. Add stock. Stir and cook until the mixture comes to a boil. Add salt, pepper and dill. Simmer 5 minutes.

In a small bowl mix the egg yolk with the heavy cream.

Add 1 cup of hot sauce bit by bit, stirring rapidly, until blended. Pour slowly back into the sauce, and cook a minute or two, stirring constantly. Do not boil.

Spoon the sauce over the chicken pieces. Sprinkle with cheese, dot with butter and place under a broiler until the cheese has melted and the top is glazed. Serve at once.

Serves 4 to 6.

COLD HAM AND CHICKEN MOUSSE

This recipe is an elegant solution to the problem of what to do with leftover ham and chicken. Particularly good during the summer, it should be served with a chilled rosé or dry white wine.

Vegetable oil	1 tsp. tomato paste
1½ cups cooked ham, finely ground	1 pinch cayenne pepper
	¼ tsp. salt
1 cup cooked chicken meat, finely ground	2 egg yolks
	2 egg whites
1½ envelopes unflavored gelatin	1 cup heavy cream
	¼ cup sherry
¼ cup cold water	1 large cucumber, washed and cut into paper-thin slices
1 cup basic stock, chicken stock or veal stock, clarified	
	Sprigs of watercress

Lightly oil a 1-quart metal ring mold or loaf pan. Set aside.

The ham and chicken should be ground through the finest blade of the meat grinder, or cut into fine cubes and put through a blender. Set aside.

Soak the gelatin in the cold water. Bring the stock to a boil, add tomato paste, pepper and salt. Add the gelatin and stir until dissolved.

Beat the egg yolks lightly in a bowl, and add the stock bit by bit, stirring continuously. Return the mixture to the pan, and over a very low heat cook and stir until it coats the back of a wooden spoon. Remove from the heat and cool.

When cool, beat the egg whites until stiff, and fold and blend them into the stock mixture. Beat the cream until stiff, and fold and blend it into the mixture. Fold in the ham, chicken and sherry. Pour into the mold, cover and refrigerate until set.

To serve: Turn the mold out onto a chilled platter and decorate with the cucumber slices and watercress.

Serves 4 to 6.

CHICKEN LIVER PÂTÉ

We find this marvelous for a picnic. If the pâté is well chilled in a thick, covered crock, it will keep firm and cool for hours; that is, if the sun isn't too hot!

14 tbs. butter	½ tsp. dry mustard
1 small onion, peeled and coarsely chopped	¼ tsp. salt
	¼ tsp. nutmeg
¾ lb. chicken livers	¼ tsp. mace
¼ cup basic stock or chicken stock from which all fat has been removed	1 pinch cayenne pepper
	¼ tsp. anchovy paste
	1 tbs. brandy
	½ tsp. lemon juice

Melt 3 tablespoons of the butter in a medium pot, and when foaming, add onion and cook and stir until onion is transparent. Add chicken livers, stock and 4 more tablespoons of the butter. Stir and cook over a medium heat until the livers are tender—15 to 20 minutes. Add the seasonings, anchovy paste, brandy, lemon juice and the remaining 7 tablespoons of butter. Put into a blender and blend until smooth, or press through a food mill.

Pour the mixture into a crock. Cover and chill.

To serve: Serve directly from the crock with plain toast squares or a good dark pumpernickel bread.

Serves 6.

Variation:

Pâté in aspic (see recipe pp. 52–54): Cool the liver mixture, but don't let it become firm. Melt 1 cup of aspic, and pour it into the bottom of a lightly oiled metal mold. The aspic should be ¼ inch thick. Chill until set. Carefully pour and gently press the liver mixture over it. Cover and refrigerate until firm.

To serve variation: Unmold on a plate and garnish with watercress sprigs.

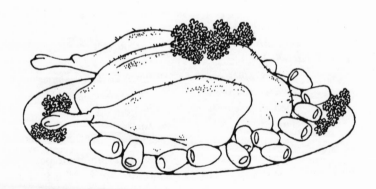

DUCK IN RED WINE

A dish that can be made early in the day and reheated or frozen for future use.

If the dish is prepared early, there is time to chill the sauce in the refrigerator; then all the fat congealed on the surface can be removed effortlessly.

2 *4-lb. ducks, cut into serving pieces*	*Red wine*
	Seasoned flour
1 *tsp. salt*	2 *tbs. butter*
½ *tsp. pepper*	*Livers of the ducks*
¼ *tsp. nutmeg*	*Gizzards and hearts of*
2 *medium onions, peeled*	*the ducks*
and finely chopped	6 *sprigs parsley*
1 *clove garlic, peeled*	1 *bay leaf*
and finely chopped	2 *stalks celery, cut into*
½ *cup brandy*	*2-inch pieces*
½ *cup basic stock or*	½ *lb. mushrooms, in-*
chicken stock from	*cluding stems, coarsely*
which all fat has been	*sliced*
removed	

Put the pieces of duck into a large bowl; add salt, pepper, nutmeg, onions, garlic, brandy and stock. Mix. Add sufficient red wine to cover the duck pieces. Place a tight-fitting lid on the bowl, and marinate 4 hours or overnight. Occasionally turn and move the pieces around so that each is well marinated.

When marinated, remove the duck pieces and dry thoroughly on paper towels. Do not discard the marinade. Dredge the duck pieces in the flour. Melt the butter in a large heavy pot, and when hot, add the duck pieces and brown on all sides. Remove and set aside.

To the same pot add the livers, gizzards and hearts, cook 10 or 15 minutes and then discard them. To this delicately seasoned fat, return the duck pieces and add the parsley, bay leaf and celery. Add the marinade. Cover and bring slowly to a boil. Adjust the heat to a simmer, and simmer for 1½ to 2 hours or until the duck is tender.

When the duck is tender, remove it from the sauce and set aside. Strain the sauce into a metal bowl; when cool, remove and discard all the fat that has congealed on the surface.

Pour the liquid into an attractive serving pot, add the duck pieces and the mushrooms. Mix. Bring to a slow boil, and simmer, uncovered, for 10 minutes.

Serve with wild rice, white rice or noodles.

Serves 6.

STEAMED DUCK

If you enjoy duck but have been avoiding it because of its excessive fat, try this recipe, which is practically fat-free. Though the preparation entails quite a few steps, it is not complicated, and the result is delicious. It can be prepared a day in advance and reheated without any loss of flavor or tenderness.

2 4- to 5-lb. ducks
   Lemon wedge
   Salt
   Pepper
½ cup crushed dried
   mushrooms, or 1 cup
   fresh mushrooms,
   finely chopped
2 carrots, scrubbed and
   quartered
2 stalks celery, cut in
   2-inch pieces
1 orange, cut in quarters

2 small onions, peeled
   and coarsely chopped
6 medium slices fresh
   ginger root, or 1 tsp.
   powdered ginger
6 sprigs parsley
1 cup basic stock or
   chicken stock from
   which all fat has been
   removed
2 cups dry white wine
   Necks, gizzards and
   hearts of the ducks
   Watercress or parsley

Rub the ducks inside and out with the lemon wedge. Sprinkle the inside of each with salt and pepper. Stuff each duck with an equal amount of the mushrooms, carrots, celery, orange, onions, ginger and parsley. Truss the ducks.

Pour the stock and wine into the bottom of a large pot or a steamer. Add the necks, gizzards, and hearts. Set the livers aside for use in the sauce. Place a rack or trivet in the pot, which should be high enough so that the ducks do not touch the liquid. Place the ducks, breast side down, on the rack. Place a tight-fitting lid on top of the pot so that the ducks cook in a heavy bath of steam. Bring the liquid to a boil, turn the heat down and steam slowly for 1½ to 2 hours or until the ducks are tender.

When tender, remove the ducks from the steamer. Cut off all the skin, but do not discard. Place the ducks in a covered container and refrigerate.

Place the skin of the ducks in a cake or bread pan, sprinkle with salt and put in a 350° F. oven. As the fat is rendered from the skin, pour it off. Continue cooking and pouring off the fat until the skin is crisp and deep golden in color. Remove from the oven, and drain on a flattened brown paper bag so that all excess fat is absorbed.

Strain into a bowl the stock over which the ducks were steamed; when cool, remove and discard all fat congealed on the surface. Heat the stock and prepare the following Orange Sauce:

2 tbs. butter	½ tsp. salt
Livers of the ducks	¼ tsp. pepper
1 tsp. shallots, finely chopped	2 tsps. ginger root, finely slivered, or ¼ tsp. powdered ginger
¼ tsp. garlic, finely chopped	
1 tsp. tomato paste	½ cup Madeira wine
3 tsps. potato flour	2 tsps. guava jelly
1½ cups of the hot stock	Watercress or parsley
Peel from ½ orange, cut into fine slivers	

Heat the butter in a heavy pan, and when foaming, add the livers and cook until brown on all sides. Remove and discard the livers. Remove the pan from the heat, and add to the butter, the shallots garlic, tomato paste and potato flour. Stir until thoroughly mixed. Add the hot stock, replace the pan over a low heat and cook, stirring continuously, until smooth. Add orange peel, salt, pepper, ginger, Madeira and jelly. Bring to a boil, and simmer slowly 5 to 10 minutes. Stir occasionally.

A half-hour before serving time, assemble the dish as follows:

Cut away and discard the congealed fat from the ducks. Discard the stuffing. Carve the ducks.

Pour the remaining stock into the steamer. If it does not measure 1½ cups, add water or wine. Place the duck pieces on the rack of the steamer. They should not touch the liquid. Bring the liquid to a slow boil, cover with a tight-fitting lid and steam 15 to 20 minutes to reheat the duck pieces.

Place the golden, crisp skin in a warm oven to reheat. Heat the sauce.

To serve: Arrange the duck pieces attractively on a heated platter, and spoon 1 cup of the sauce over them. Crush 1 cup of the crisp skin, and sprinkle it over the ducks and sauce. Crush the remainder of the skin, and serve it with the rest of the sauce in side dishes. Garnish the platter with sprigs of watercress or parsley.

Serves 6.

(5) MEAT

MEAT NOTES

Canned beef stock or a bouillon cube may be used in the following recipes, but the result will not be as good as it will if you use your own stock. Also, the can has to be recycled.

Before serving a stew or meat sauce, skim off the fat. This is easily done by firmly gripping a side of the pot with one hand and tipping it away from you. With the other hand, skim off the excess fat with a large spoon.

The leanest meats are always the best buy; use them.

Seasoned flour is 1 cup of flour combined with 2 teaspoons of salt and ½ teaspoon of pepper. Prepare 2 or more cupfuls and store in a closed container; in this way a supply is always available.

All pepper should be freshly ground.

Taste before you serve. Correct the seasoning to your taste.

BOILED BEEF

Truly one of the great dishes. I cook the potatoes sep-
arately because they tend to cloud the broth. However, if you
prefer, they can be added to the pot with the carrots and onions.
Should there be any beef left over, you'll find it is deli-
cious sliced cold, cut into thin strips and added to a mixed salad,
or cubed and added to a vegetable soup.

6 *lbs. brisket of beef*	1 *lb. peas, fresh or frozen*
3 *quarts cold basic stock*	2 *lbs. small new potatoes,*
or beef stock from	*scrubbed, or 8 regular*
which all fat has been	*medium potatoes,*
removed	*peeled and cut in half*
2 *lbs. small white*	2 *tbs. parsley, finely*
onions, peeled	*chopped*
12 *medium carrots,*	
scrubbed and cut in	
half	

Put the brisket of beef into a large pot, add the stock
and bring to a boil. Cover pot with a loose-fitting lid, adjust heat
to a simmer, and simmer for 1½ hours.

Add onions and carrots. Simmer for another hour. Add
peas. If the peas are fresh, allow 8 to 10 minutes' cooking time;
if frozen, 4 minutes' cooking time.

Steam the potatoes in a separate pot until tender, and
keep warm. If small new potatoes are used, do not peel them, for
the skin is flavorful and nutritious.

When ready to serve, remove the beef and carve it into
thin slices against the grain. Arrange the slices neatly on a large
heated platter. Surround the meat with the potatoes, carrots,

onions and peas. Spoon ¾ cup of the hot broth over the meat and vegetables. Sprinkle the whole dish with the parsley.

Taste the broth and correct the seasoning.

Serve as a first course or in cups, together with the beef and vegetables.

Serves 8.

NOTE: Many sauces—such as dill, horseradish or mustard —are excellent with Boiled Beef; but the most delicious, in my opinion, is the following Spring Sauce:

2 *hard-boiled eggs*	1 *tsp. pepper*
2 *slices white bread*	1½ *tbs. vinegar*
¼ *cup milk*	1 *tbs. lemon juice*
1 *egg yolk*	1 *medium head Boston*
3 *tbs. salad oil*	*lettuce, washed and*
1 *cup light cream*	*finely shredded*
1 *cup sour cream*	½ *cup chives, finely*
2 *tsps. salt*	*chopped*

Peel and chop the eggs. Cut off and discard the crusts of the bread. Cube the bread, put it into a small bowl, pour the milk over it and stir and soak until soft.

When the bread is soft, pour it into a large mixing bowl, add the chopped eggs and all of the other ingredients. Stir and mix thoroughly.

This is a thin sauce and should not be too piquant. If you want it to be more tart, add additional salt and lemon juice.

Serve it in a large glass bowl with a good-sized ladle or serving spoon, as each person will want an ample helping.

BOILED BEEF WITH VEGETABLE PURÉE

3 lbs. brisket of beef	4 medium potatoes, peeled and cubed
4 cups basic stock or beef stock from which all fat has been removed	2½ tsps. salt
	1 tsp. pepper
2 medium onions, peeled and sliced	3 tbs. butter
	2 tbs. parsley, finely chopped
4 medium carrots, scrubbed and sliced	

Put the meat into a large pot and add the stock. Bring to a boil, adjust heat to a simmer, cover, and simmer for 1½ hours. Add vegetables, 1 teaspoon of the salt and ½ teaspoon of the pepper, and continue simmering for 1 hour or until the meat and vegetables are tender.

When tender, remove the beef to a plate and keep warm. Strain the vegetables and reserve the broth for future use.

Put all the vegetables through a food mill or a blender with the butter, the remaining salt and pepper, and just enough broth—approximately 1 cup—to make a thick purée.

To serve: Slice the beef and arrange the slices neatly on a warm platter; surround them with the puréed vegetables and garnish with the parsley.

Serves 6.

BEEF IN RED WINE

If a burgundy wine is used in this recipe it is a Boeuf Bourguignon. *However, any good dry, full-bodied red wine can*

*be used. It is a splendid party dish and can be prepared 1 or 2
days in advance. It requires no last-minute preparations; just
reheat slowly.*

8 slices bacon, cut into 1-inch pieces	1 bay leaf
2 tbs. bacon fat	1 pinch dried thyme
2 tbs. butter	1¼ tsps. salt
4 lbs. lean beef, top round or chuck, cut into 1- to 1½-inch pieces	½ tsp. pepper
	1 tsp. tomato paste
	16 to 18 small white onions, peeled
2 tbs. brandy	1 lb. mushrooms, including stems
1½ cups dry red wine	
1½ cups basic stock or beef stock from which all fat has been removed	3 tsps. potato flour
	3 tsps. cold water
	2 tbs. parsley, finely chopped
1 carrot, peeled and finely sliced	

Cook the bacon over a low flame in a deep heavy pot
until most of the fat is rendered. Do not brown. Remove from
the pot, and drain on a flattened brown paper bag. Discard all
but 2 tablespoons of the bacon fat.

Add the butter to the bacon fat, and when hot, brown
the pieces of beef. Do not let them overlap; as they brown remove them to a plate. When all are brown, return them to the
pot and flame them with the brandy. Stir, and add the wine,
stock, carrot, bay leaf, thyme, salt, pepper, tomato paste and
bacon pieces. Bring to a boil, adjust the heat to a simmer, cover
pot with a tight-fitting lid and simmer for 45 minutes.

Add the onions to the pot. Remove the stems from the
mushrooms, and set the caps aside. Cut the stems into rings and

add to the pot. Cover and simmer for 30 minutes or until the beef is tender.

If the mushroom caps are small, add them whole; if large, cut them into thick slices and add them to the pot. Cover and cook 5 minutes.

Mix the potato flour with the cold water and add to the pot. Stir and cook until thickened. Remove the bay leaf, and garnish with parsley.

Serves 6 to 8.

B R A I S E D   B E E F

The principal elements of this dish are a spicy marinade, good stock and a lean cut of beef. It can be prepared in advance and reheated.

4½ to 5 lbs. lean chuck, round or rump of beef	2 cloves garlic, peeled and coarsely chopped
1 tbs. salt	2 tsps. dried thyme
½ tsp. pepper	1 bay leaf
2 medium carrots, washed and thinly sliced	1 whole clove
	1 tsp. dried basil
1 large onion, peeled and thinly sliced	2 tbs. parsley, finely chopped
3 stalks celery, including leaves, coarsely diced	3 cups red wine
	¼ cup brandy
	½ cup olive oil

Trim any excess fat from the meat, and rub it with salt and pepper. Mix all the ingredients in a large bowl, add the meat and turn it around so that all sides are saturated with the marinade. Cover tightly. Marinate for at least 6 hours at room temperature or, if possible, overnight. Turn the meat frequently. When marinated, proceed as follows:

4 tbs. bacon fat	10 medium carrots, peeled and quartered
1 cracked veal knuckle	25 to 30 small white onions, peeled
¼ lb. bacon rind	Parsley or watercress sprigs
1 cup canned tomatoes	
3 cups basic stock or beef or brown stock from which all fat has been removed	

Remove the meat from the marinade; dry it thoroughly. Heat the bacon fat in a deep heavy pot. When hot, add the meat and brown on all sides. Pour the marinade over the meat, and add the veal knuckle, bacon rind, tomatoes and stock. Place a tight-fitting lid on top, adjust the heat to a simmer, and simmer 3 to 4 hours or until tender. Turn the meat from time to time.

Steam the carrots and onions as directed in Chapter 7, "Vegetables" (pp. 235 and 240).

When the meat is tender, remove it to a plate, strain the liquid into a large bowl and skim off the fat. Return the liquid to a clean pot and boil it over a high heat, uncovered, until it is reduced to 4 cups. Add the meat, carrots and onions, and simmer for 5 minutes.

To serve: Carve the meat and arrange it neatly on a heated platter; surround it with the carrots and onions, and spoon 1 cup of the sauce over the meat and vegetables. Serve the balance of the sauce in a separate dish. Garnish with parsley or watercress sprigs. Serve with rice or boiled potatoes.

Serves 10 to 12.

2

POT ROAST

This is a basic pot roast. You can make it more elaborate by adding other vegetables—peas, turnips or string beans, for example—and your favorite combination of herbs. The vegetables should be added during the last hour of cooking. If you use frozen vegetables, allow for the cooking time shown on the package when you add them to the pot roast.

4 lbs. chuck, round or rump of beef	½ cup red wine
1 clove garlic, peeled and cut in half	1 cup canned tomatoes
1 tbs. bacon fat	½ tsp. pepper
1 large onion, peeled and cut in thin slices	1½ tsps. salt
1 bay leaf	½ tsp. sugar
½ cup basic stock or beef or brown stock from which all fat has been removed	6 medium potatoes, peeled and cut in half
	6 medium carrots, scrubbed and cut in half
	2 tbs. parsley, chopped

Trim any excess fat from the meat. Rub well with the cut garlic. Tie the meat with a string so that it will hold its shape during cooking and so that it can be lifted easily to and from the pot without piercing it with a fork.

Heat the bacon fat in a large heavy cast-iron pot. When hot, add the meat and brown on all sides. Remove to a plate.

Place a low rack (most cast-iron pots, which are also known as Dutch ovens, come with a rack) in the bottom of the pot, and put the onion and bay leaf on it. Place the browned meat on top, and pour in the stock, wine and tomatoes. If the tomatoes are whole, cut them in small pieces. Add pepper, salt and sugar. Place a tight-fitting lid on top, adjust heat to a simmer, and simmer for 1 to 1½ hours.

After this cooking period, the pot can be set aside. An hour before serving time, add potatoes and carrots, cover and return to a low heat for 1 hour or until vegetables are tender.

To serve: Place the meat on a heated platter and surround it with the vegetables. Discard the bay leaf. Skim off excess fat from the sauce, bring to a boil and pour the sauce over the meat and vegetables. Garnish with chopped parsley.

Serves 6.

BEEF STEW WITH GHERKINS

The addition of the gherkins and coriander give this familiar recipe an unusual and special touch.

3 tbs. vegetable oil
2½ to 3 lbs. lean chuck, cut into 2-inch pieces
2 medium onions, peeled and coarsely chopped
3 tomatoes, peeled, seeded and coarsely chopped
1 tbs. tomato paste
3 cloves garlic, peeled and finely chopped
2 tsps. salt
½ tsp. pepper
⅛ tsp. coriander powder

1 cup basic stock or beef stock from which all fat has been removed
½ tsp. dried thyme
1 bay leaf
3 sprigs parsley
3 sprigs fresh dill, or ½ tsp. dried dill
6 medium potatoes, peeled
6 large carrots, peeled and halved
4 tbs. sour gherkins, finely chopped
2 tbs. parsley, finely chopped

Heat the oil in a heavy pot, and nicely brown the pieces of meat. Do not let them overlap, and as they brown, remove them to a plate. When all the meat is browned, add the onions, stirring and cooking them until transparent. Return the meat to the pot. Add the tomatoes, tomato paste, garlic, salt, pepper, coriander powder and stock. Tie up in a cheesecloth the thyme, bay leaf, parsley, and dill, and add to the pot. Bring to a boil, stir and place a lid on top. Adjust the heat to a simmer, and simmer for 1½ hours.

Add the potatoes and carrots, and cook for 40 minutes or until tender. Add the gherkins and stir.

Serve the stew in the pot in which it is cooked or ladle it into a heated serving dish. Garnish with the chopped parsley.

Serves 6.

SWISS STEAK WITH SOUR SAUCE

The sharpness of the sauce goes well with boiled potatoes or brown rice. Add a green salad, and your dinner is ready.

2 tsps. salt	1½ cups basic stock or
½ tsp. pepper	beef stock from
3 tbs. flour	which all fat has
3 to 4 lbs. top round	been removed
steak	3 tbs. wine vinegar
¼ cup vegetable oil	2½ tsps. prepared mus-
3 medium onions, peeled	tard
and thinly sliced	1 bay leaf
	Parsley

Mix the salt and pepper with the flour, sprinkle it onto both sides of the steak and rub it in.

Heat the oil in a heavy pot, and brown the steak well on both sides. Lower the heat, add the onions and cook until transparent. Add the stock, vinegar, mustard and bay leaf. Bring to a boil, adjust the heat to a simmer, place a tight-fitting lid on top and simmer for 2 hours or until tender.

To serve: Remove the bay leaf. Place the steak on a heated platter; spoon the sauce over the meat. Garnish with sprigs of parsley.
Serves 6.

GROUND BEEF AND NOODLES

2 tbs. vegetable oil	1 6-oz can tomato paste
1 tbs. butter	2 tsps. salt
2 medium onions, peeled and thinly sliced	½ tsp. pepper
	1 bay leaf
	½ lb. medium-wide noodles
2 lbs. lean ground round or chuck beef	1 cup sour cream
3½ cups basic stock or beef stock from which all fat has been removed	1 tbs. fresh dill, finely chopped, or 1 tsp. dried dill

Melt the oil and butter in a heavy large pot, and when hot, add the onions. Cook until transparent. Add the beef, breaking it up into small pieces. Cook and stir until slightly browned. Add stock, tomato paste, salt, pepper and bay leaf. Bring to a boil, add noodles and stir. Adjust heat to a simmer, cover, and simmer for 25 to 30 minutes or until noodles are tender.

When tender, remove the bay leaf and add the sour cream and dill. Heat, but do not boil.

To serve: Serve directly from the pot in which it was cooked or pour into a covered heated serving dish.
Serves 6.

STEAMED SPICED BEEF

This is tender, spicy and delicious hot or cold. It can be prepared in the morning and reheated without any loss of flavor. The origin of this recipe is Venezuelan.

3½ to 4 lbs. bottom round of beef	8 small green olives with pimiento stuffing, halved
Vegetable oil	
Salt	½ clove garlic, peeled and cut into thin slivers
Pepper	
Prepared mustard	
1 slice bacon, cut into ½-inch pieces	Watercress or parsley

Trim excess fat from the beef. Using a sharp, pointed knife, slash many small holes in the beef, then rub it with oil, salt, pepper and mustard. Into each slash insert a piece of the bacon, together with a sliver of garlic and half an olive. Tie the meat up with a string, and put it into a bowl with the following marinade:

1 cup basic stock or beef stock from which all fat has been removed
2 cups dry red wine
½ cup olive oil
1 clove garlic, peeled and quartered
2 medium onions, peeled and sliced
2 carrots, scrubbed and sliced

2 shallots, peeled and cut in quarters
1 bay leaf, crushed
1 clove
3 sprigs parsley
7 peppercorns
2 tsps. salt
3 juniper berries
4 tsps. soy sauce
1 pinch dried basil
1 pinch dried thyme

Cover the bowl tightly, and marinate the beef for 3 hours or, if time permits, overnight. Turn the beef occasionally.

When ready to cook, remove the meat to a plate. Pour the marinade, together with spices and vegetables, into a pot. Place a rack or a trivet over the liquid. On the rack, place the following vegetables:

1 carrot, scrubbed and thinly sliced
1 medium onion, peeled and thinly sliced

8 sprigs of parsley
4 stalks of celery, coarsely cubed

Put the meat on top of the vegetables, and cover pot with a tight-fitting lid. Bring the liquid to a simmer, and steam for 1 to 2 hours. One hour's cooking time will give you rare beef; two hours cooking time will give you well done meat.

When cooked to your taste, remove the meat to a heated platter. Strain the marinade into a saucepan, and boil it rapidly, uncovered, over a high heat, until it is reduced to 2 cups.

Remove the string from the meat, and carve it in medium-thin slices. Arrange them attractively on the heated platter.

Spoon a few tablespoons of the sauce over the sliced meat and
serve the remainder in a sauceboat. Garnish with watercress or
parsley.

Serves 6 to 8.

STEAMED VEAL AND PORK PUDDING

*This pudding is delicious hot or cold; if it is to be served
cold, omit the sauce. The pudding can be made in the morning,
left in the mold and reheated over steam prior to serving. Since
the sauce, too, can be made in the morning, this is a good dish
to serve when company is coming.*

Butter	*½ tsp. pepper*
2 tbs. butter	*½ tsp. paprika*
1 medium onion, peeled and finely chopped	*2½ tbs. parsley, finely chopped*
2 lbs. ground lean veal	*¼ cup heavy cream*
¾ cup ground lean pork	*1 cup basic, chicken or veal stock from which all fat has been removed*
2 cups fine bread crumbs	
4 egg yolks	
2½ tsps. salt	*4 egg whites*
	Watercress or parsley sprigs

Generously butter the inside of a 2-quart metal mold, including the inside of the lid.

Melt the 2 tablespoons of butter in a small pan, and
when foaming, add the onion and cook until transparent. Do not
brown.

In a large bowl put the veal, pork, bread crumbs, egg yolks, salt, pepper, paprika, parsley, cream and stock. Add the onion, together with the butter in which it was cooked. With your hand, mix the ingredients thoroughly until blended.

Beat the egg whites until stiff, and with a wooden spoon, work one-third of them into the meat mixture. Fold in the remainder, and pour into the prepared mold. Cover and steam (see *Steaming Directions for Molds*, pp. 302–304) for 2½ hours.

Prepare the following Brown Sauce:

2 tbs. butter	1½ cups basic stock or
2 tbs. flour	brown stock from
½ small onion, peeled	which all fat has
and finely chopped	been removed
½ tsp. tomato paste	½ tsp. salt
	¼ tsp. pepper
	1 tsp. currant jelly

Heat the butter in a small saucepan until foaming. Add the flour and onion, and stir and cook until both are brown. Remove from the fire. Add tomato paste, stock, salt, pepper and jelly, and stir until blended. Return to the fire, and stirring continuously, cook until the sauce has thickened—about 10 minutes. When thickened, strain into a bowl and discard the onion pieces. Return the sauce to a pan and heat.

To serve: Turn the pudding out onto a heated platter, spoon the sauce over it, and garnish with watercress or parsley sprigs.

Serves 6.

Variation:

Wash and finely dice ¼ lb. mushrooms. Add them to the sauce and cook for 3 or 4 minutes.

VEAL CHOPS CREOLE

Serve these chops and the rich sauce with rice, boiled potatoes or noodles.

1 tbs. butter	4 canned whole to-
2 tbs. olive oil	matoes, diced
6 large veal chops,	1 small can tomato
lightly dusted with	paste
seasoned flour	2 tbs. parsley, finely
1 medium onion,	chopped
peeled and finely	1 bay leaf
chopped	½ tsp. sugar
2 small cloves garlic,	½ tsp. dried rosemary
peeled and finely	1½ tsps. salt
chopped	1 tsp. pepper
1 medium green pepper,	3½ cups basic stock or
its seeds and white	chicken or veal stock
membranes removed,	from which all fat
cut into 2-inch strips	has been removed
½ lb. mushrooms, in-	
cluding stems, cleaned	
and coarsely sliced	

Heat the butter and oil in a deep pot. When hot, add the chops, and cook until golden brown on each side. Do not let them overlap.

Remove the chops to a plate, and add the rest of the ingredients to the pot. Stir and bring to a boil. Place the chops in the sauce, adjust heat to a simmer, cover, and simmer for 40 minutes or until the chops are tender.

To serve: Remove the bay leaf, place the chops on a heated platter, and spoon the sauce over them.

Serves 6.

VEAL CHOPS ITALIANO

A delicious party dish that can be cooked in advance and reheated without any loss of flavor or tenderness. To complete the menu, serve with a tossed green salad, a fresh loaf of rye bread and a dessert of chocolate mousse or a Bavarian cream. A rosé wine is a lovely complement to the veal and its sauce.

6 *thick veal chops*
  Vegetable oil
2 *tbs. butter*
1 *medium onion, peeled and sliced*
1 *small clove garlic, peeled and finely chopped*
2 *carrots, scrubbed and sliced*
2 *medium potatoes, peeled and sliced*

1 *cup basic stock or chicken stock from which all fat has been removed*
2 *cups canned tomatoes*
½ *tsp. dried rosemary*
2 *tsps. salt*
½ *tsp. pepper*
  Parsley, finely chopped

Rub the veal chops with vegetable oil. Melt the butter in a heavy pot. Add the veal chops and brown them well on each side. Place over them the onion (separate the rings as you add them to the pot), garlic, carrots and potatoes. Pour in the stock and tomatoes. If the tomatoes are whole, cut them in small pieces. Add rosemary, salt and pepper. Place a tight-fitting lid on top, turn the heat to low, and simmer for 40 minutes or until tender.

Serve directly from the pot or put the veal chops in a heated gratin dish and spoon the vegetables and liquid over them. Garnish with parsley.

Serves 4 to 6.

VEAL WITH SAUSAGE

If Italian sweet sausages are not available, use plain pork sausage. This dish can be frozen.

1 tbs. vegetable oil	1½ cups rice
1 tbs. olive oil	3 tbs. parsley, finely chopped
1 medium onion, peeled and thickly sliced	4 cups basic stock, chicken stock or veal stock from which all fat has been removed
2 lbs. veal shoulder, cut into 1-inch cubes	
½ lb. sweet Italian sausages, cut into 1-inch pieces	1½ tsps. salt
	½ tsp. pepper
1 cup canned tomatoes	3 tbs. Parmesan cheese, grated

Heat the oils in a deep pot, and when hot, add onion, veal and sausages. Stir and cook 5 minutes over a medium-high heat.

Add tomatoes, rice, parsley, stock, salt and pepper. Stir and bring to a boil. Cover, adjust heat to a simmer, and simmer for 35 to 45 minutes or until the meat is tender. Add cheese. Stir and cook for 5 minutes.

To serve: Pour into a heated serving dish.
Serves 6 to 8.

VEAL PAPRIKA

Use a quality paprika in this dish. To keep paprika fresh, keep it in the refrigerator.

2½ lbs. leg of veal, cut into 2- to 3-inch pieces	2 cups basic stock or chicken stock or veal stock from which all fat has been removed
¼ cup seasoned flour	2 tbs. lemon juice
3 tbs. butter	½ tbs. salt
1½ tbs. olive oil	¼ tsp. pepper
2 medium onions, peeled and thinly sliced	1 cup sour cream
1½ tbs. paprika	2 tbs. parsley, finely chopped

Dredge the veal pieces in the seasoned flour. Heat 2 tablespoons of the butter and the olive oil in a deep heavy pot. When hot, add the veal pieces in a single layer; do not let them overlap, and brown them on all sides. As the pieces brown, remove them to a plate.

After the veal is browned, add the remaining tablespoon of butter and the onions. Separate the rings as you put them into the pot. Cook until transparent. Add paprika, stir and pour in the stock. Put the veal pieces back into the pot. Add lemon juice, salt and pepper. Adjust heat to a simmer, cover pot with a loose-fitting lid, and simmer for 1 hour or until veal is tender.

Just before serving, add the sour cream, stir thoroughly and reheat. Do not boil.

To serve: Serve directly from the pot or spoon into a heated serving dish. Garnish with the parsley.

Serves 6.

VEAL WITH MUSHROOM SAUCE

*This is a relative of the famous French Veal Blanquette.
I find it every bit as delicious and less work. One step that is
eliminated is the skimming of the veal stock. The residue from
the veal bones and meat does not discolor the sauce, and the
nutriments contained in these tiny particles enrich the sauce.*

*Use a large pot to boil the veal and bones. You will have
an ample quantity of a rich stock left over. If you use this in
an aspic or a consommé, it should be clarified.*

*The marrow should be removed from the bones; it can
be sliced and added to the sauce or, while it is hot, spread on
crackers and eaten by the cook as a special treat.*

4 to 4½ lbs. leg of veal	fat has been removed
Basic stock or chicken	(approximately 2
stock from which all	quarts)
	20 to 24 small white
	onions, peeled

Have the butcher remove the meat from the bones and
cut the bones into 4- to 6-inch pieces. The meat can be left in
large pieces.

Put the meat and bones into a large pot. Cover them by
½ inch with stock. Bring to a boil, cover pot with a loose-fitting
lid and adjust the heat to a simmer. Simmer 1½ hours or until
the meat is tender.

While the meat is cooking, steam the onions (see p. 240),
but do not discard their juices.

When the meat is tender, remove it with a fork or tongs
to a cutting board. Strain the stock into a bowl and set aside.

Cube the veal into 1- to 2-inch pieces, discarding any skin or tough gristle, and set aside.

Prepare the following Mushroom Sauce:

4 tbs. butter	1 tsp. salt
5 tbs. flour	¼ tsp. pepper
5 cups of the stock in which the veal was cooked and from which the fat has been removed	1 lb. mushrooms
	1 tbs. lemon juice

Melt the butter in a heavy saucepan, and when foaming, add the flour. Cook and stir continuously over a low flame for 3 minutes. Remove from the heat and add the stock, salt and pepper. Stir rapidly until the mixture is blended. Return to the heat, stir, and simmer over a low flame for 5 minutes.

Clean the mushrooms and remove the stems (save them for the stockpot or a stew). If the caps are larger than 1 inch in diameter, cut them into coarse slices. Add them together with the lemon juice, to the sauce and stir. Simmer uncovered for 5 minutes.

Put the cubed veal and the onions with all their juices into a flameproof serving casserole, and pour the mushroom sauce on top.

This dish may be set aside at this point, and the final step prepared as follows just before serving:

Bring the dish to a simmer over a low heat, and add the following mixture:

3 egg yolks	1 tbs. parsley, finely chopped
1 cup heavy cream	
2 tbs. brandy	¼ tsp. nutmeg

Lightly beat the egg yolks with the cream and brandy. Stirring and folding continuously, slowly pour the egg-yolk mixture into the veal. Stir gently and heat. Do not boil. Garnish with the parsley and nutmeg, and serve at once. Serve with rice, noodles or new potatoes.

Serves 6 to 8.

VEAL WITH TARRAGON AND MUSHROOM SAUCE

If you cook the veal early it can be quickly reheated in the stock, or steamed. Caution: *Reheat; do not cook. The sauce, too, can be prepared early and reheated over hot water.*

This dish is attractive served on a large platter surrounded by timbales of saffron rice. Use the extra veal stock for cooking the rice.

3½ to 4 lbs. sirloin of veal	1 clove garlic, peeled and sliced
2 cups basic stock, veal stock or chicken stock from which all fat has been removed	1 stalk celery, cut into 1-inch pieces
2 cups cold water	2 whole cloves
1 carrot, scrubbed and sliced	1 bay leaf
1 medium onion, peeled and sliced	½ tsp. dried tarragon
	7 peppercorns
	1 tsp. salt
	½ cup dry white wine

Have the butcher roll and tie the veal securely with string. Put it into a deep pot, and add the stock and cold water, which should barely cover the veal. Add additional stock or water if necessary. Bring slowly to a boil, and add all the other ingredients. Bring back to a boil, adjust the heat to a simmer, cover, and simmer for 1 hour and 45 minutes or until the veal is tender when tested with a fork. Remove from the heat, and prepare the following Tarragon and Mushroom Sauce:

2¼ tsps. dried tarragon, or ¼ cup fresh tarragon leaves, finely chopped	1 tsp. salt
	1 pinch cayenne pepper
	1 pinch nutmeg
2 tbs. brandy	2 cups of the stock in which the veal was cooked, strained
4 tbs. butter	
4 medium mushrooms, including stems, cleaned and finely chopped	1 cup heavy cream
	3 egg yolks
	2 tbs. light cream
1 tsp. lemon juice	
4 tbs. flour	

Soak the tarragon in 1 tablespoon of the brandy and set aside.

Melt the butter in a small, heavy saucepot, and when foaming, add mushrooms and lemon juice. Stir and cook for 3 minutes, remove from heat and add flour, salt, pepper, nutmeg and the veal broth. Stir until well blended. Return to heat and cook, stirring continuously until sauce comes to a boil. Stir and simmer gently 3 to 4 minutes. Add the heavy cream. Stir and heat.

Mix the egg yolks in a bowl with the remaining tablespoon of brandy and light cream. Beat 1 cup of the hot sauce into the egg mixture bit by bit. When blended, add to the sauce and cook over a low heat until the yolks thicken it slightly. Add the tarragon, together with the brandy in which it was soaked.

To serve: Remove the strings from the veal and slice it very thin. Arrange the slices neatly on a heated platter and spoon the sauce over them.

Serves 6 to 8.

VEAL SHANKS IN TOMATO SAUCE

Ask your butcher for shanks with generous pieces of meat ·on them, and have him cut the bone into 2- to 2½-inch pieces. This dish freezes perfectly.

Flour

4 veal shanks, including their meat

2 tbs. oil

2 tbs. butter

3 medium carrots, scrubbed and finely diced

1 large onion, peeled and finely chopped

1 medium clove garlic, peeled and finely chopped

1 bay leaf, crushed

1 cup tomato sauce

2 tbs. tomato paste

1½ cups basic stock, chicken stock or veal stock from which all fat has been removed

1 tsp. salt

½ tsp. pepper

1 tsp. fresh ginger root, finely diced, or ¼ tsp. powdered ginger

1 cup white wine Parsley, finely chopped

Flour the shanks lightly. Heat the oil and butter in a large pot. When hot, add the shanks and cook until golden on both sides.

Remove the shanks to a plate, and add the carrots and

onion. Stir and cook until the onion is transparent. Add the garlic, bay leaf, tomato sauce, tomato paste, stock, salt, pepper, ginger and wine. Stir and bring to a boil. Replace the shanks, adjust the heat to a simmer, cover, and simmer for 1½ hours or until tender.

To serve: Place the shanks in a large heated gratin or serving dish, remove the bay leaf, and spoon the sauce over the shanks. Garnish with parsley.

Serves 6.

OSSO BUCO

You should use a big pot or two medium pots so that all the succulent, marrow-filled bones are able to simmer freely in the sauce.

4 *veal shank bones, including their meat*
½ *cup seasoned flour*
4 *tbs. olive oil*
4 *tbs. butter*
½ *tsp. dried sage*
1 *tsp. dried rosemary*
1 *large onion, peeled and finely chopped*
1 *clove garlic, peeled and finely chopped*
2 *medium carrots, scrubbed and finely diced*
2 *stalks celery, including leaves, washed and finely diced*
1½ *tsps. salt*
½ *tsp. pepper*
1½ *cups dry white wine*
1½ *cups basic stock or chicken stock from which all fat has been removed*
3 *tbs. tomato paste*
2 *tbs. parsley, finely chopped*
1 *clove garlic, peeled and finely chopped*
1 *tbs. grated lemon peel*

Have your butcher cut and saw each shank into 3 pieces. Thoroughly coat the veal pieces with the seasoned flour.

Heat the olive oil and butter in a large pot, or heat equal parts of both in two pots. When hot, add the veal pieces and brown until golden on all sides. Do not overlap the pieces while browning. When brown, remove to a plate and discard half of the fat in the pot.

Return the veal pieces to the pot. Sprinkle with sage, rosemary, onion, garlic, carrots, celery, salt and pepper. Place a tight-fitting lid on top, and braise over a high heat for 7 minutes.

Remove the lid and add the wine, stock and tomato paste. Stir. Replace lid, turn heat down to a simmer, and simmer for 2 hours or until tender.

Combine the parsley, garlic and lemon peel.

When ready to serve, place the veal pieces in a large heated serving dish, pour the sauce over them and sprinkle the top with the mixed parsley, garlic and lemon peel.

Serve with rice or noodles.

Serves 6 to 8.

CALVES' LIVER IN WINE SAUCE

12 slices bacon	1 cup basic stock or
1½ lbs. calves' liver, cut	chicken stock from
into 6 thin slices	which all fat has been
Flour	removed
2 tbs. butter	½ cup dry red wine
2 medium onions,	½ tsp. salt
peeled and thinly	¼ tsp. pepper
sliced	1 pinch mace
	Parsley sprigs

Fry the bacon until crisp. Set aside and keep warm. Discard all but 2 tablespoons of the bacon fat.

Remove any skin or membrane from the liver, then lightly dust the liver pieces with flour.

Put the butter and the 2 tablespoons of bacon fat into a large frying pan, and when hot, add the pieces of liver and cook until brown on each side. Allow 3 to 4 minutes for each side. Remove the liver to a heated serving platter and keep warm.

Add the onions to the pan in which the liver was cooked, and stir and cook until transparent. Add the stock, wine, salt, pepper and mace. Bring to a boil over high heat, stirring continuously, and boil until the liquid is reduced to 1 cup.

To serve: Spoon a portion of the onions and sauce over each slice of liver, place the bacon slices around the edge of the platter and garnish with a few sprigs of parsley. Serve at once.

Serves 6.

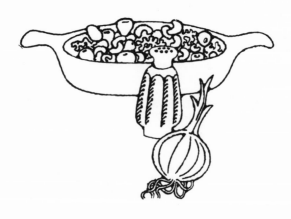

LAMB STEW

A change from the traditional spring lamb stew; in fact, I would call it an "all-seasons" stew. It can be prepared a day or two in advance, and it can be frozen.

2½ lbs. boneless lamb, neck, shoulder or shank
2 ozs. butter
1 medium onion, peeled and coarsely chopped
4 tbs. flour
4 cups basic stock or beef stock from which all fat has been removed
1 carrot, scrubbed and cut in half

1 stalk celery, washed and cut in half
4 sprigs parsley
1 clove garlic, peeled
1 bay leaf
1 tsp. dried thyme
2 tsps. salt
½ tsp. pepper
4 cups cooked and drained white kidney beans*
2 tbs. parsley, finely chopped

Trim any excess fat from the lamb and cut into 2-inch pieces.

Melt the butter in a deep pot, and when hot, add the meat and onion. Stir and cook until slightly browned. Sprinkle with the flour and continue cooking, stirring continuously, until brown. Add the stock and stir. Make a *bouquet garni* by tying a cheesecloth bag, or with a string, the carrot, celery, parsley, garlic and bay leaf, and add to the pot. Add the thyme, salt and

* Cooking instructions for the kidney beans are given in Chapter 8, "Dried Beans and Grains."

pepper. Cover pot with a loose-fitting lid, and simmer for 1½ hours. Add the beans, cover and simmer for 20 minutes.

To serve: Discard the *bouquet garni.* Ladle the stew into an attractive heated serving dish and sprinkle with parsley.
Serves 6.

LAMB SHANK STEW

This dish can be frozen, but I prefer to freeze it before adding the vegetables, because cooked potatoes, which are such a succulent part of this dish, tend to lose flavor and texture in freezing. So I suggest the meat be frozen in its sauce. When you want to serve it, defrost, add the vegetables, and continue to cook as directed.

6 to 8 lamb shanks	½ tsp. pepper
Flour	2½ cups basic stock or
2 tbs. bacon fat	beef stock from
1 tbs. vegetable oil	which all fat has
2 tbs. brandy	been removed
1 large onion, peeled	16 small white onions,
and coarsely chopped	peeled
1½ tsps. tomato paste	8 medium carrots,
1 clove garlic, peeled	peeled and halved
and finely chopped	8 medium potatoes,
2 stalks celery, diced,	peeled and halved,
including the leaves	or 16 small new po-
1 bay leaf	tatoes, washed
½ tsp. dried thyme	1 cup fresh peas, or 1
2 tsps. salt	box frozen peas
	2 tbs. parsley, finely
	chopped

Have the butcher cut the shanks into 2- to 3-inch pieces. Remove and discard any excess fat from the meat.

Lightly flour the shanks. Heat the bacon fat and oil in a large pot, and brown the shanks until golden. Remove to a plate.

Heat and flame the brandy, and pour it into the pot and deglaze. Add the onion, and stir and cook until transparent. Add the tomato paste, garlic, celery, bay leaf, thyme, salt, pepper and stock. Stir.

Return the lamb shanks to the pot. Bring to a boil, cover pot with a loose-fitting lid, adjust the heat to a simmer, and simmer for 1 hour. Add the onions, carrots and potatoes, and continue to cook for 40 minutes. If fresh peas are used, add them and continue to cook until the vegetables are tender. If frozen peas are used, follow the cooking time indicated on the package.

To serve: Remove the bay leaf and serve the stew in a large heated tureen. Garnish with the parsley.

Serves 6 to 8.

IRISH LAMB STEW

A 6- to 7-quart pot is needed for this fine stew, which can be prepared a day in advance. Serve it with a green salad, a bottle of red wine and warm French bread.

4 lbs. boneless shoulder
of lamb cut into 2- to
3-inch cubes

4 cups basic stock or
beef stock from which
all fat has been re-
moved

4 cups cold water

½ cup red wine

8 medium potatoes,
peeled

3 medium onions, peeled
and coarsely sliced

4 leeks, washed and
coarsely sliced, in-
cluding the fresh green
tops

4 stalks celery, washed
and cut into 2-inch
pieces

2 cloves garlic, peeled
and sliced

¼ tsp. cayenne pepper

5 tsps. salt

6 medium carrots,
peeled and cut into
quarters

24 small white onions,
peeled

2 tbs. parsley, finely
chopped

Wash and trim excess fat from lamb cubes. Put the lamb into a deep large pot; add stock, water and wine. Cube 4 of the potatoes, and add to the pot together with the onions, leeks, celery, garlic, pepper and 3 teaspoons of the salt. Cover pot with a loose-fitting lid, and slowly bring to a boil. Stir. Adjust heat to a simmer, and simmer for 1 hour.

With a slotted spoon, remove the pieces of lamb to a 5-quart pot. Strain the stock into a bowl and set aside.

Purée the cooked vegetables through a food mill, or

blend in a blender until smooth. Pour the purée over the lamb. Add the remaining 4 potatoes cut into quarters, the carrots, white onions and the remaining 2 teaspoons of salt.

Remove and discard the fat from the stock. Add 1 quart of the stock to the lamb and vegetable mixture. Stir. Cover and simmer over a low heat for 1 hour or until the vegetables are tender.

To serve: Serve in the cooking pot, or ladle into a heated covered serving dish. Garnish with the parsley.

Serves 8.

LAMB IN WINE SAUCE

A delicious Sunday or company dish. It can be made in advance up to the point of reducing the sauce, and this is easily done at the last moment.

3 *lbs. boneless lamb, shank, shoulder, or neck, cut into 1- to 2-inch pieces*	2 *tsps. salt*
	½ *tsp. pepper*
3 *tbs. butter*	2 *cups basic stock or chicken stock from which all fat has been removed*
1 *tbs. oil*	
2 *tbs. brandy*	
2 *medium onions, peeled and finely chopped*	½ *cup dry white wine*
	1 *bay leaf*
	1 *cup heavy cream*
2 *tbs. tomato paste*	½ *lb. mushrooms, cleaned and coarsely sliced*
½ *medium clove garlic, peeled and finely chopped*	
	Lemon juice
2½ *tbs. flour*	*Parsley*

Trim any excess fat from the meat, and dry thoroughly. Heat 2 tablespoons of the butter and the oil in a deep, heavy pot, and when foaming, add pieces of the meat; do not overlap. Brown on all sides, and remove to a plate. Flame the brandy and pour it into the pan, stir and deglaze all the bits of brown crust. Add the onions and cook until transparent. Remove the pot from the fire, and add the tomato paste, garlic, flour, salt, pepper, stock and wine. Stir until blended. Add the bay leaf, and return the meat to the sauce. Bring the sauce to a boil, adjust the heat to a simmer, cover and cook for 1 hour or until the meat is tender.

When tender, remove the meat with a slotted spoon to a heated serving platter, and keep warm. Remove and discard the bay leaf. Add the cream, stir and rapidly boil the sauce, uncovered, over a high heat until sauce is reduced to 2 cups.

Heat the remaining tablespoon of butter in a small pan, add a few drops of lemon juice, and when foaming, add the mushrooms. Cook and stir 2 or 3 minutes, and add to the sauce.

To serve: Spoon the sauce over the lamb and garnish with the parsley. Serve with noodles, rice, boiled potatoes or kasha.

Serves 6.

LAMB WITH BROCCOLI

1½ tbs. butter	1 tsp. salt
1½ tbs. vegetable oil	½ tsp. pepper
3 lbs. boneless shoulder of lamb, cut into 2-inch cubes	2 bunches fresh broccoli, washed, or 2 boxes frozen broccoli
2 large onions, peeled and coarsely chopped	4 tsps. potato starch
	Juice of 2 lemons
2 cups basic stock or chicken stock from which all fat has been removed	2 eggs

Heat the butter and oil in a heavy pot; add the lamb and brown. Add the onions, and stir and cook until transparent. Add the stock, salt and pepper. Cover, and simmer for 45 minutes. Add the broccoli, cover and cook until it and the meat are tender.

Dissolve the potato starch in the lemon juice and add to the stew. Stir and cook for 3 to 5 minutes. Remove from heat.

Beat the eggs lightly in a bowl. Add 1 cup of the sauce from the stew to the eggs bit by bit, beating continuously. Add to the stew, stir and heat until thickened. Do not boil.

To serve: Pour into a heated serving dish. Serve with kasha or couscous.

Serves 6.

BOILED LEG OF LAMB

Have your butcher do the boning and tying of the lamb. And don't forget to ask him to include the bone, which you can freeze and use in your stockpot.

½ cup butter
3½ to 4 lbs. leg of lamb, boned and rolled
2¾ cups of basic stock or beef stock from which all fat has been removed
4 carrots, scrubbed and sliced
18 small white onions, peeled
½ tsp. dried rosemary Bay leaf

3 tomatoes, peeled, seeded and quartered
1 cup dry white wine
1 small clove garlic, peeled and finely chopped
¼ cup canned tomato sauce
1 tsp. salt
½ tsp. pepper
1 tsp. sugar
1 tbs. fresh dill, finely chopped

In a heavy pot or Dutch oven melt the butter, and when foaming, add the lamb and brown on all sides. When brown, add one-quarter cup of the stock, the carrots, onions, rosemary and bay leaf. Cover tightly, and simmer over a low heat for 45 minutes. Add the tomatoes, wine, garlic, tomato sauce and the remaining stock. Bring to a boil, cover tightly, and adjust heat to a simmer. Simmer for 1 hour or until the lamb is tender.

When tender, remove the lamb to a heated platter and keep warm. Remove and discard the strings from the lamb. With a slotted spoon or tongs place the onions around the lamb. Skim the fat from the top of the sauce. Remove and discard the bay leaf. Add salt, pepper and sugar. Over a high heat reduce the sauce to approximately 2 cups. Put the sauce through a food mill or blend in a blender until smooth. Return the sauce to the pot, bring to a boil and spoon it over the lamb. Garnish with the dill and serve.

Serves 6.

NOTE: The lamb may be neatly carved in thin slices before serving, and a few tablespoons of the sauce spooned over the slices. The remainder of the sauce should be served in a side dish.

BRAISED PORK CHOPS

I suggest that the chops be accompanied by a wine applesauce. This is a delicately seasoned sweet-sour sauce that is excellent with roast pork, too.

1 tbs. vegetable oil	1 cup basic stock or
6 thick pork chops	beef stock or brown
2 large onions, peeled	stock from which all
and thinly sliced	fat has been removed
1 medium green pepper,	1½ tsps. salt
with the white mem-	½ tsp. pepper
branes and seeds re-	
moved, cut into thick	
slices	

Heat the oil in a large flat skillet, and when hot, add the pork chops and brown on both sides. Remove to a plate. Add the onions and green pepper to the pan. Stir and cook until the onions are golden. Add the stock, salt and pepper. Return the pork chops to the pan, and bring the liquid to a boil. Cover, adjust heat to a simmer, and simmer for 45 minutes or until the chops are tender.

To serve: Place the pork chops on a heated serving platter and spoon the gravy, onion and green pepper over them. Serve with the following:

WINE APPLESAUCE

4 tbs. butter

4 tsps. shallots, peeled and finely chopped

3 cups unsweetened plain applesauce

4 tbs. dry white wine

½ cup sugar

½ tsp. salt

⅛ tsp. pepper

Melt the butter in a small pot, and when foaming, add the shallots. Cook and stir over a low heat until soft. Do not brown. Add applesauce, wine, sugar, salt and pepper. Stir and bring to a boil. Simmer, uncovered, for 5 minutes.

Serve in heated individual bowls.

Serves 4 to 6.

NOTE: If a sweetened applesauce is used, omit the sugar and add 1 additional tablespoon of wine.

SAUSAGES AND ENDIVES HUGUETTE

You don't need a large pot for this recipe, which was given to me by a French friend who inherited it from her grandmother. It may be a first course, or the main course for a light supper or luncheon. It is delicious whenever it is served.

12 endives

12 small breakfast sausages

5 tbs. butter

2 tbs. olive oil

½ tsp. salt

¼ tsp. pepper

Basic stock or chicken stock from which all fat has been removed

Cut the endives in half lengthwise. Carefully hollow out the center of each half to make space for one sausage. Place the sausage in the center. Reshape the endives, and tie them up at each end with string.

Heat the butter and oil in a large heavy frying pan. Put the endives in the pan side by side. Sprinkle with salt and pepper. Cook them over a slow fire, uncovered, turning occasionally so that they can brown evenly all over.

Allow 30 to 40 minutes to braise them. The juices produced by the endives should be enough liquid, but if not, add a splash of stock so that they do not stick to the pan.

To serve: Place on a heated platter and remove strings. Serve 2 to a person.

NOTE: The breakfast sausage is a small sausage approximately 2 inches in length.

PORK AND GREEN PEPPERS

Another delicious recipe from a French friend. It is a simple dish, and if you add the potatoes, it makes a whole meal. The green peppers can be frozen in their sauce and reheated. To reheat, place the pot over hot water or in a slow oven.

6 medium green peppers, washed	1 tsp. pepper
1 cup water	1 egg
¼ cup long-grain white rice	1 tbs. flour
3 tsps. salt	1 6-oz. can tomato paste
2 tbs. vegetable oil	2 tsps. sugar
1 large onion, peeled and finely chopped	3 cups basic stock or beef stock from which all fat has been removed
1 lb. lean pork, ground	1 tbs. parsley, finely chopped

Cut the stem end off the green peppers. Remove core, seeds and membranes. Be careful not to break the forms.

Bring the water to a boil, add the rice and ½ teaspoon of the salt. Cover and cook for 10 minutes only. Rinse under cold water and drain thoroughly.

Heat in a pan 1 tablespoon of the vegetable oil, and when hot, add onions and cook until transparent.

Put into a mixing bowl the ground pork, the remaining 2½ teaspoons of salt, pepper, egg, partially cooked rice and cooked onions. Mix thoroughly with your hand. Stuff the pepper forms loosely with the mixture.

Put the remaining 1 tablespoon of vegetable oil and flour into a saucepan. Stir and cook over a medium heat until the flour is golden. Remove from the fire, add tomato paste and sugar, blend until smooth. Add stock and stir until blended.

Place the stuffed green peppers upright in a heavy pot. Pour the sauce around them; it should come up to about three-quarters of the sides of the peppers. Place a tight-fitting lid on top, and bring to a boil. Adjust the heat to a simmer, and simmer for 50 to 60 minutes.

To serve: Remove the peppers carefully with tongs or a slotted spoon, and place them on a heated serving dish. Spoon part of the sauce neatly over the top of the peppers and pour the rest around them. Sprinkle with parsley and serve.

Serves 6.

Variation:

Peel 6 medium-sized potatoes, add them to the pot and cook with the peppers in the tomato sauce.

SMOKED PORK CHOPS WITH LENTILS

The pork chops should be cut thick and be as freshly smoked as possible. Only a green salad and a fruit dessert are needed to complete the menu. The chops can be frozen.

2 lbs. lentils, washed
3 cups basic stock or ham stock from which all fat has been removed
Cold water
1 bay leaf
2 carrots, scrubbed

1 medium onion, peeled
2 tsps. salt
8 smoked pork chops
2 tbs. flour
1 tsp. vinegar
½ cup sour cream

Put the lentils into a large pot, add the stock and cold water to cover by 2 inches; add bay leaf, carrots, onion and salt. Bring to a boil, cover pot with a loose-fitting lid and turn the heat down to a simmer. Simmer for half an hour.

Add pork chops and additional cold water to cover all the ingredients by 2 inches. Bring the pot back to a boil, adjust heat to a simmer, replace lid and cook for 1 hour.

Remove bay leaf, carrots and onion.

In a small bowl mix the flour with cold water until it is smooth. Add a little of the hot liquid from the lentils, beat until blended and slowly pour the mixture into the pot, stirring continuously. Stir gently; do not mash the lentils. Add vinegar and simmer for 20 minutes.

When ready to serve, add the sour cream, stir and bring to a boil.

Serve in the pot in which it was cooked, or ladle into a heated, covered serving dish.

Serves 6 to 8.

AFRICAN RICE

*A full meal, needing only a salad and dessert as comple-
ments.*

1 lb. small pork sausages	2½ cups water
1 lb. cooked ham	2 cups basic stock or
3 large leeks	ham stock from
1 tbs. olive oil	which all fat has been
2 cups uncooked long-	removed
grain rice	2 tsps. salt
	1 tsp. pepper

Cut the sausages into ½-inch pieces. Cut the ham into
small cubes. Set aside.

Wash the leeks thoroughly, cut the white parts into thin
slices and set aside. Don't use the green tops (save them for your
stockpot).

Heat 1 teaspoon of the olive oil in a frying pan. Add the
sausages and cook until brown. Set aside.

Heat the remaining 2 teaspoons of olive oil in a deep
heavy pot, and add the rice. With a wooden spoon, stir continuously over a medium heat until the rice is coated with the oil.
Do not brown.

Add to the rice the sausages, ham, leeks, water, stock,
salt and pepper. Bring to a boil, stir, cover pot with a tight-fitting
lid and cook over a low flame 25 to 30 minutes or until the rice
is tender.

Serve directly from the pot.

Serves 6 to 8.

HAM WITH MADEIRA SAUCE

Either boiled or baked ham can be used in this recipe. It is an excellent way to use the remains of a baked ham.

2 tbs. butter
2 tbs. shallots, peeled and finely chopped
2 tsps. flour
1½ tsps. tomato paste
2 cups basic stock or ham stock from which all fat has been removed

2 tbs. Madeira
2 boxes frozen chopped spinach, or 3 cups fresh spinach, cooked, chopped and thoroughly drained
1 tsp. lemon juice
12 thin lean slices of cooked ham

Melt 1 tablespoon of the butter in a saucepan, add shallots and flour. Cook and stir until the flour is golden. Remove from the heat, and stir in the tomato paste; add the stock slowly, stirring continuously. Return the sauce to a low heat, and simmer slowly, uncovered, until the sauce is reduced to 1½ cups. Stir in the Madeira.

If frozen spinach is used, cook according to the directions on the package. Drain thoroughly. Put the cooked spinach into a saucepan over a low heat, stir in the lemon juice and keep warm.

Put the remaining butter into a pan, and heat the ham slices; do not brown.

To serve: Make a bed of the spinach on a heated serving platter or in a gratin dish, overlap the ham slices neatly on top and spoon the sauce over them. Serve at once.

Serves 6.

CREAMED HAM AND MUSHROOMS

Eighteen minutes is the complete preparation and cooking time!

4 tbs. butter	3 cups cooked ham,
2 tbs. flour	diced into ½-inch
1½ cups chicken stock,	cubes
ham stock or basic	½ lb. mushrooms,
stock from which all	coarsely chopped
fat has been removed	½ tsp. lemon juice
¼ tsp. pepper	½ cup heavy cream

Melt 2 tablespoons of the butter in a sauce pot, add flour and stir and cook until blended. Remove from heat and add stock and pepper, stir until smooth. Return to heat, and stir and simmer for 5 minutes. Set aside.

Melt the remaining butter in a skillet, and when foaming, add ham, mushrooms and lemon juice. Stir and cook until slightly golden. Add to the sauce, stir, and simmer for 5 minutes. Add heavy cream; heat, but do not boil.

To serve: Pour into a heated serving dish and serve with noodles or rice, or spoon over toast triangles on individual serving plates.

Serves 6.

HAM CASSEROLE

*This dish freezes well and is a full hearty meal in itself.
Serve it with a mixed green salad and a loaf of rye bread.*

*Taste before adding any salt to the casserole, since the
ham and stock may season it sufficiently.*

1 8-oz. package of thin noodles	½ tsp. pepper
1 tbs. vegetable oil	2 cups cooked ham, diced into ½-inch pieces
1 tbs. butter	
1 large onion, peeled and finely chopped	1½ cups mushrooms, thinly sliced
3 tbs. flour	2 tsps. scallions, finely chopped, including the fresh green leaves
1 cup milk	
2 cups ham stock, chicken stock or basic stock from which all fat has been removed	

Cook the noodles according to the directions on the
package.

Meanwhile, heat the oil and butter in a deep heavy pot.
Add the onion, and cook until transparent. Remove from heat;
stir in flour. Add milk and stock slowly, stirring constantly. Return to heat, stir and cook until the liquid comes to a boil. Add
pepper, and simmer, uncovered, for 5 minutes. Add ham and
mushrooms, stir, and simmer for 10 minutes. Add the cooked
noodles, which have been thoroughly drained. Stir and bring
to a boil.

Serve in the pot in which it is cooked or pour into a
heated serving dish and garnish with the scallions.

Serves 6.

SZÉKELY GOULASH (HUNGARIAN)

Another Székely goulash recipe! Yes, and the best you have ever eaten. It is the family recipe of a well-known Hungarian artist, Lazslo Fircha, now living in Venezuela. The paprika should be the imported variety if possible. Serve the goulash with boiled potatoes, a cucumber salad and beer.

2 tbs. vegetable oil	2 lbs. sauerkraut
1 tbs. butter	1 pinch cumin powder
2 medium onions, peeled and finely chopped	2 green peppers, with the core, seeds and white membranes removed, cut into 1-inch pieces
2 tbs. paprika	
2½ lbs. pork ribs, including the bones, cut into 2- to 3-inch pieces	1 large tomato, peeled and chopped into coarse pieces
3½ cups basic stock or beef stock from which all fat has been removed	½ cup flour
	¾ cup cold water
	1 cup sour cream

Heat the oil and butter in a large heavy pot; when hot, add the onion. Stir and cook until golden. Add paprika and stir. Add pork ribs and 1 cup of the stock. Stir and bring to a boil, cover, adjust the heat to a simmer, and simmer for 45 minutes.

Put the sauerkraut in a colander, rinse well with cold water and add to the pork mixture. Also add the cumin, peppers, tomato and the remaining 2½ cups of the stock. Stir and bring to a boil, cover, adjust the heat to a simmer and simmer for 30 minutes. Give it an occasional stir.

Mix and beat the flour with the cold water until it is a

smooth liquid. Add it slowly to the pork and sauerkraut, stirring all the while. When well blended, simmer uncovered for 10 minutes.

When ready to serve, add the sour cream, stir and blend.

Serve directly from the pot, or ladle the goulash into a heated serving dish.

Serves 6 to 8.

STUFFED ZUCCHINI ETTA

A splendid summer dish when the fresh, fat zucchini come out of your, or your neighbor's, garden. Select the larger zucchini for this recipe.

Should any of the stuffing be left over, roll it into small balls, and cook them in the sauce with the zucchini.

1 piece of white bread from which the crust has been removed	½ tsp. pepper
	1 egg
	3 to 4 lbs. zucchini
¼ cup sour cream	2 tbs. olive oil
½ lb. lean beef, ground	2 cups tomato sauce
¼ lb. lean veal, ground	1 cup basic stock or beef stock from which all fat has been removed
¼ lb. lean pork, ground	
2 tbs. onion, peeled and finely chopped	
½ tsp. garlic, peeled and finely chopped	1 bay leaf
⅛ tsp. dried thyme	2 tbs. parsley, finely chopped
2 tsps. salt	

Cut the bread into small cubes, and soak them in the sour cream.

Put into a mixing bowl the beef, veal, pork, onion, garlic, thyme, salt, pepper, egg and soaked bread. Mix thoroughly with your hand.

Wash the zucchini. Cut off each end, and with a grapefruit knife or a long spoon, remove the center seeds and core. Stuff the hollow center with the meat mixture.

Put into a heavy pot the olive oil, tomato sauce, stock and bay leaf. Place the zucchini side by side in the sauce, and bring to a boil. Adjust the heat to a simmer, place a tight-fitting lid on top and simmer for 40 to 50 minutes.

To serve: Remove the zucchini from the sauce and cut into 2-inch-wide diagonal slices. Arrange the slices attractively on a heated platter. Remove and discard the bay leaf. Spoon the sauce over the slices of stuffed zucchini and sprinkle the parsley over the top.

Serves 6.

SWEDISH MEATBALLS

If you want to add a special touch, soak the bread in heavy cream instead of light cream. This dish freezes perfectly, but add the sour cream and herbs just before serving.

4 slices white bread, trimmed and cubed	3 tsps. salt
¾ cup light cream	1 tsp. pepper
1 tbs. bacon fat	4 tbs. butter
1 small onion, peeled and finely chopped	1 tbs. tomato paste
1 lb. lean beef, ground	3 tbs. flour
½ lb. lean pork, ground	2 cups basic stock or chicken stock from which all fat has been removed
½ lb. lean veal, ground	
3 eggs	1 cup sour cream
½ tsp. garlic, finely chopped	2 tbs. fresh parsley, dill or basil, finely chopped
½ tsp. nutmeg	

Soak the bread with the light cream in a small bowl.

Heat the bacon fat in a heavy skillet, add onion and cook until transparent. Set aside.

Put into a large bowl the beef, pork and veal. Punch a hole in the center and add eggs, garlic, nutmeg, 2 teaspoons of the salt, ½ teaspoon of the pepper, the onion, and the bread and cream mixture. Thoroughly stir and mix with one hand. When completely mixed, form into 1- to 2-inch balls with wet hands.

Add 3 tablespoons of the butter to the skillet in which the onions were cooked, and when foaming, add the meatballs. Cook only one layer at a time, and cook until golden brown all over. Set aside on a plate. Remove this skillet from the heat, and add the remaining salt, pepper, butter, tomato paste, and flour. Mix and add the stock. Cook and stir until thickened.

When thickened, put the meatballs into the sauce, cover, and simmer gently for 20 minutes. Add the sour cream and parsley, dill or basil, and heat. Stir. Do not boil.

To serve: Ladle into a covered, heated serving dish and serve with noodles, rice or steamed potatoes.

Serves 6.

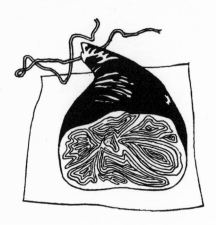

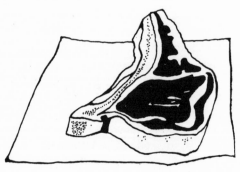

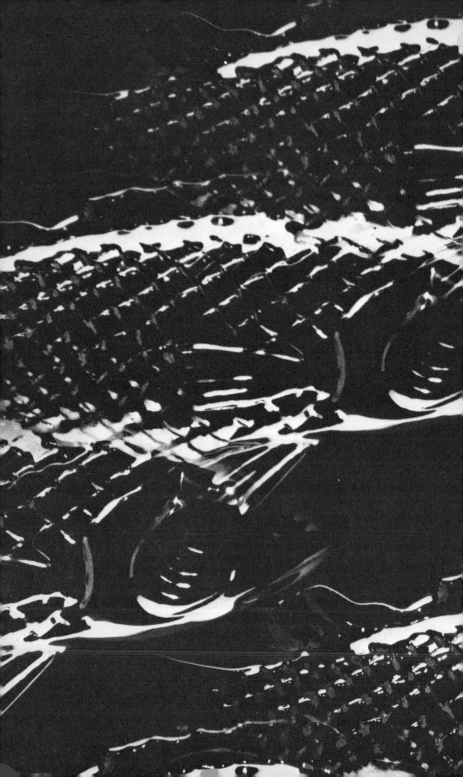

(6) FISH

FISH NOTES

Frozen fish may be substituted for fresh fish with a minimum loss of flavor. However, nothing surpasses the special taste of fish freshly caught from the sea, a mountain stream or a deep glacier lake.

The stock over which fish is steamed is enriched and can be used again. Pour it into a container and refrigerate or freeze it for future use.

Do not overcook fish.

Bottled clam juice may be substituted for your fish stock, but it's not as good.

All pepper should be freshly ground, and it is preferable to use white peppercorns in fish dishes with a white sauce.

Taste before you serve. Correct the seasoning to your taste.

FISH ASPIC

Fish aspic does not have as many uses as a meat-base aspic, but it is a real delight, particularly in the summer. If you have a supply on hand, you will not only find it simple to prepare various fish-in-aspic dishes, but will have the pleasure of chopping it into garnishes for fish salads.

5 cups fish stock	4 tbs. unflavored gelatin
1 medium carrot, scrubbed and coarsely diced	½ cup cold water
	4 tbs. lemon juice
1 medium onion, peeled and coarsely chopped	1 tsp. salt
	2 egg whites, beaten to a froth
1 bay leaf	
1 lb. fish bones and/or fish heads	1 eggshell, crushed

Put the stock, carrot, onion, bay leaf and fish bones and/or fish heads into a large pot. Bring to a rapid boil, and boil uncovered 15 to 20 minutes. Strain into a bowl.

Put the gelatin into a small bowl and add the cold water.

Pour the strained stock into a pot, add the gelatin, lemon juice, salt, egg whites and eggshell. Over heat, beat with a wire whisk until the liquid comes to a boil. Boil for 2 minutes. Remove from the heat, and leave the pot undisturbed for at least 15 minutes.

Gently strain the stock through a fine sieve, pour into a container, cover and place in the refrigerator to set.

This makes approximately 1 quart.

FISH IN ASPIC CLARA

The number of calories per serving depends entirely on the amount of sauce served, as the fish itself is without cream or fat.

Once you master the relatively easy process of coating a mold with aspic and adding a few decorations, this dish is simple to prepare. I particularly like to serve the fish, handsomely embedded in watercress and surrounded with lemon slices and capers, for a buffet, or as a first course when the menu includes an especially rich entrée.

This recipe is written in three steps. Each step may be prepared and the result put aside. The final assembly takes only a short time.

STEP 1:

1 whole 4- to 4½-lb. striped bass or trout Cold water	2 stalks celery, washed and cut into 1-inch pieces
3 tbs. salt	6 sprigs parsley
1 carrot, scrubbed and diced	1 bay leaf
1 onion, peeled and finely chopped	Juice of 1 lemon, or ½ cup dry white wine
	1 tsp. salt
	6 peppercorns

Have the fish cleaned, but do not have the head or tail removed; they add flavor to the stock. Wash thoroughly. Put the fish into a large pan and cover with cold water. Add the 3 tablespoons of salt and soak for 1 hour. Drain and rinse.

Into a large pot or fish steamer, put the carrot, onion, celery, parsley, bay leaf, lemon or wine, salt and peppercorns. Place the fish on top, and cover with cold water. Cover pot and bring to a simmer. Poach the fish at a slow simmer for 25 to 30 minutes or until it flakes easily when tested with a fork. Remove from the heat and let the fish cool in the stock.

STEP 2:

Juice of 1 lemon   ½ tsp. pepper
1 tsp. salt

When the stock is cool, remove the fish and discard the head, tail, skin and bones. Strain the stock and set it aside for the aspic or for future use if you have already made your aspic from a supply of fish stock on hand.

With your hands, finely shred the meat of the fish into a mixing bowl. Discard any small bones or pieces of skin. Add lemon juice, salt and pepper. Mix well.

STEP 3:

1 quart fish aspic
  Decorations: Select any
  combination that
  pleases your fancy:
  paper-thin carrot
  rounds, green or black
  olives cut into rounds
  or strips, thin lemon
slices, capers, thin
truffle slices, thin
slices of red pimientos,
hard-boiled white of
egg cut into rounds or
strips
Parsley or watercress

Pour ¼ inch of liquid fish aspic into a 6-cup metal mold, either a fish-form mold or a ring mold. Place the mold over a bowl of ice and tilt and turn it until the sides of the mold are evenly coated and the aspic is set. Carefully place your decorations on the set aspic and coat them with another ¼ inch of liquid aspic, then place the mold over the ice until this layer of aspic is set. Add the fish mixture by gently tapping and pressing it into the aspic lined mold. Spoon the balance of the liquid aspic over the fish mixture. Chill in the refrigerator 3 or 4 hours or until set.

Unmold onto a chilled plate and garnish with parsley or watercress or any other decorations to your liking. Serve with the following Green Sauce:

1 cup mayonnaise	*2 tbs. celery leaves,*
1 cup sour cream	*finely chopped*
½ tsp. Worcestershire	*2 tsps. lemon juice*
Sauce	*1 tsp. salt*
4 tbs. sweet gherkins,	*½ tsp. pepper*
finely diced	*½ tsp. prepared mustard*
2 tbs. fresh dill, finely	
chopped	

Combine and mix well all the ingredients in a bowl. Chill. Serves 6 to 8.

COLD SALMON MOUSSE

A really wonderful main dish for dinner in the summer or as a first course in winter. If guests are expected, it can be prepared a day in advance and unmolded and decorated an hour before they arrive. After it has been unmolded, it must be kept in the refrigerator.

Decorate with capers, lemon slices, hard-boiled eggs, watercress, parsley or chopped fish aspic.

2 lbs. fresh salmon	*½ cup sour cream*
4 cups cold fish stock	*½ tsp. Worcestershire*
2 tbs. unflavored gelatin	*Sauce*
3 tbs. lemon juice	*2 tsps. salt*
2 tbs. cold water	*¼ tsp. pepper*
⅓ cup mayonnaise	*¾ cup heavy cream*
	Vegetable oil

Put the salmon into a large pot and add the stock. Bring gently to a boil and cover. Simmer for 15 minutes or until the salmon flakes easily when tested with a fork. Remove the pan from the heat. Allow the salmon to cool in the stock.

When cool, strain the stock and set aside. Remove and discard the skin and bones of the salmon. Break the fish into small pieces and mash with a fork or put through a blender. Add ½ cup of the strained stock.

Put the gelatin into a small bowl and soften it with the lemon juice and cold water.

Put 1 cup of the strained stock into a pan and bring to a boil. Add the gelatin and stir until dissolved. Set aside until cool.

When cool, pour into a large mixing bowl and combine with the salmon mixture, mayonnaise, sour cream, Worcestershire Sauce, salt and pepper. Mix and blend thoroughly.

Beat the cream until stiff, and fold it into the salmon mixture.

Oil a fish-form mold or a ring mold of 6 cups' capacity, and gently pour the mousse into it. Cover, and put into the refrigerator to set.

Unmold the mousse onto a chilled serving platter, garnish and serve with the following Cucumber Sauce:

1	large cucumber, peeled and seeded	1	tbs. chives, finely chopped
1	cup mayonnaise	1	tbs. lemon juice
1	cup sour cream	½	tsp. salt
½	tsp. prepared mustard	¼	tsp. pepper

Grate the cucumber into a bowl, add all the ingredients and mix thoroughly. Refrigerate and serve in a chilled serving bowl.

Serves 6 to 8.

FISH PUDDING

A blender is not essential for this splendid dish, but it facilitates the preparation.

Butter
2 tbs. bread crumbs, finely ground
1¼ cups white bread pieces, or 3 hard white rolls
1 cup heavy cream
1½ lbs. fish fillets, fresh or frozen
1 small onion, peeled and sliced
1 small bay leaf
Fish stock
10 tbs. butter
2 egg yolks
1 cup Parmesan cheese, freshly grated
1½ tsps. salt
Pinch cayenne pepper
2 egg whites
3 tbs. butter, melted and browned

Generously butter the inside of a 2-quart metal pudding mold or ring mold, add bread crumbs, place the lid on top and shake vigorously. Discard excess bread crumbs. Set aside.

Soak the bread or rolls in the cream. Set aside.

Put the fish fillets into a pan with the onion and bay leaf; add just enough stock to cover. Place a cover on the pan, and gently simmer 5 to 10 minutes or until the fish flakes easily when tested with a fork. Discard the bay leaf. Strain the fish over a bowl, and press it firmly to extract as much stock as possible. Save the stock for future use.

If a food grinder is used, put the fish and onion through its finest blade. With your hands, wring the cream from the bread. Reserve the cream, and combine the bread with the fish and onion.

If a blender is used, put the fish, onions, bread and cream into it, and blend thoroughly.

Cream the butter in a mixing bowl, and add the fish mixture, egg yolks, 3 tablespoons of the Parmesan cheese, salt and cayenne pepper. (Add the reserved cream if the food grinder was used.) Mix well.

Beat the egg whites until stiff, and fold them into the fish mixture. Pour into the prepared mold, cover and steam (see *Steaming Directions for Molds*, pp. 302–304) for 1½ hours. If a ring mold is used, cover it tightly with aluminum foil, and tie it with a string.

To serve: Unmold the pudding onto a heated serving plate, dribble over it the browned butter, and sprinkle on the rest of the cheese. Serve at once.

Serves 4 to 6.

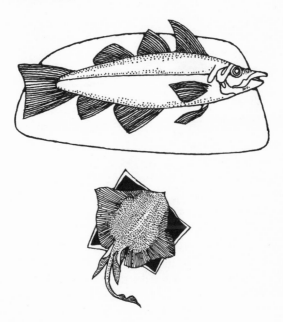

FISH STEW

This is a thick stew that originated in Peru, where it is known as Chupe de Pescado. *Because it freezes, I suggest doubling the recipe; it is a good hearty dish to have on the freezer shelf.*

I did not have the good fortune to try this dish in Peru, and I am, therefore, uninformed about the proper etiquette for eating the corn slices. My solution is to pick them up in my fingers, and I suggest my guests do likewise.

2 lbs. fresh or frozen haddock	1 tsp. dried oregano
6 cups fish stock	2 tsps. salt
1 tbs. vegetable oil	½ tsp. pepper
1 tbs. olive oil	½ cup fresh or frozen peas
1 medium onion, peeled and finely chopped	2 ears fresh or frozen corn cut into thin slices, or 1 cup of canned or frozen kernel corn
1 medium tomato, peeled, seeded and diced	
¼ cup rice	½ cup milk
2 medium potatoes peeled and diced into small cubes	1 egg
	¼ cup Parmesan cheese, grated

Poach the haddock in the fish stock until it flakes easily when tested with a fork. Strain the stock into a bowl and reserve. Shred the haddock, discarding all bones, and set aside.

In a large pot, heat the oils, add onion and cook until transparent. Add tomato and rice. Stir and cook until the rice is coated with oil. Heat and add the reserved fish stock. Bring to a boil, and add the potatoes, oregano, salt and pepper. Stir.

Cover pot with a loose-fitting lid, and cook over a low heat until the potatoes are barely tender. Add peas and corn. Cover and cook until tender. Add shredded haddock.

Lightly beat the milk and egg together, and slowly, stirring continuously, pour in a thin stream into the stew. Add the cheese, stir, and heat; do not boil.

Serve from a heated tureen or in large heated individual soup plates.

Serves 6.

Variation:

Two lbs. of cooked shrimps, deveined and cut into small pieces, can be used instead of haddock.

STEAMED COD

Hake may be used instead of cod, and it is every bit as delicious.

4- to 5-lb. piece of cod	Fish stock
Butter	½ cup dry white wine
½ clove garlic, peeled and cut into thin slivers	

Wash and dry the piece of cod. Rub with butter. Insert the slivers of garlic along the backbone of the fish. Wrap in a layer of cheesecloth.

Pour ½ inch of fish stock into a steamer, add the wine and bring to a boil. Butter the steamer rack, lay the fish on it and place the rack over the liquid. Adjust the heat to a slow boil, place a tight-fitting lid on top and steam for 45 minutes or until the fish flakes easily when tested with a fork.

In the meantime, prepare the following Tomato Sauce:

2 *tbs. butter*	1 *tsp. salt*
½ *lb. mushrooms,*	½ *tsp. pepper*
coarsely chopped	½ *cup heavy cream*
1 *tsp. lemon juice*	2 *tbs. parsley, finely*
2 *cups canned tomatoes*	*chopped*

Melt the butter in a sauce pot, and when foaming, add the mushrooms and lemon juice. Stir and cook for 2 minutes. Add tomatoes. Bring to a boil and simmer for 5 minutes. Add salt and pepper. When ready to serve, add the cream and heat. Do not boil.

To serve: Place the fish on a heated platter, carefully remove the cheesecloth and spoon the sauce over the fish. Garnish with parsley.

Serves 6.

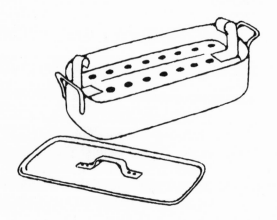

STEAMED RED SNAPPER

Cook this beautiful fish with its head and tail on if your steaming pot is long enough. If not, have the head removed, and when the fish is on the platter ready to serve, place an ample bunch of parsley or watercress sprigs in its place.

3- to 3½-lb. red snapper, cleaned	1½ cups cooked rice
1½ cups mushrooms, finely chopped	1 tsp. salt
	½ tsp. pepper
1½ cups shrimps, cooked, peeled, deveined and chopped into ¼-inch pieces	3 tbs. butter
	Fish stock
	Butter
½ tsp. dried basil	1 lemon, thinly sliced
3 scallions, including the fresh green tops, washed and finely chopped	Watercress sprigs

Wash and dry the fish.

Put the mushrooms, shrimps, basil, scallions, rice, salt, pepper and butter into a large bowl. Mix. Stuff the fish, and close by sewing with a strong thread, or use skewers. Carefully wrap the fish in 1 layer of cheesecloth.

Pour 1 inch of fish stock into a steamer. Bring to a boil.

Butter the steamer rack, lay the fish on it and place the rack over the boiling stock. The fish should not touch the stock. Adjust the heat to a slow boil, place a tight-fitting lid on top and steam for 40 to 50 minutes or until the fish flakes easily when tested with a fork.

To serve: Place the fish on a heated serving platter, carefully remove the cheesecloth, and spoon a few tablespoons of the stock over the fish. Garnish with lemon slices and watercress sprigs.

Serves 6.

FRIDAY'S FILLET OF SOLE

A light, nutritious food, perfect for the family. Buy the finest gray or lemon sole your budget permits. Serve with steamed new potatoes and creamed chopped spinach.

4 fillets of sole, approximately ½ lb. each	*Salt*
Butter	*Pepper*
¼ cup cold fish stock	*Lemon wedges*

Wash and dry the fillets. Lightly butter each side. Roll the fillets up, keeping the white side on the outside.

Bring 1 inch of water to a boil in the bottom of a double boiler. Butter the top part of the double boiler and place the rolled fillets in it side by side. Add the fish stock. Put the pot over the boiling water, cover with a tight-fitting lid, and cook 8 to 10 minutes or until the fish flakes easily when tested with a fork.

To serve: With a slotted spoon, gently remove the fillets to a heated serving platter, and spoon the juices over them. Lightly sprinkle each fillet with salt and pepper, and garnish with lemon wedges.

Serves 4.

CREAMED COD

A *quick and easy dish to be served over toast triangles or in a rice ring. The mustard adds a pleasant, piquant touch to the sauce.*

4 tbs. butter	1½ cups milk
1 large onion, peeled and finely chopped	1 tsp. salt
	⅛ tsp. cayenne pepper
4 tbs. flour	4 cups cod, cooked and flaked
1 tsp. prepared mustard	
1 cup fish stock	½ cup heavy cream
	1 tbs. parsley, finely chopped

Melt the butter in a deep heavy pot, and when foaming, add the onion and cook until transparent. Remove from heat, add flour and mustard. Stir. Add stock, milk, salt and pepper. Return to the heat, stir and bring to a boil. Simmer for 5 minutes. Add cod, stir, and simmer for another 5 minutes. Add heavy cream and heat.

To serve: Spoon over toast triangles or into a rice ring. Garnish with the parsley.

Serves 6.

NOTE: If you are going to serve the cod in a rice ring, cook the rice in fish stock.

FRESH TUNA SAINT RAPHAEL

A *classic Mediterranean dish. The ideal piece of tuna is cut from the center of the fish, near the stomach. Do not buy a piece toward the tail, where the flesh was much too nervous.*

If you cannot find small mushroom caps, use large mush-rooms and dice them into small pieces.

2- to 2½-lb. piece fresh
   tuna
2 tbs. butter
1 tbs. olive oil
2 medium onions, peeled
   and cut into thick
   slices
2 large tomatoes, cut
   into thick slices
½ cup cold fish stock
1 small clove garlic,
   peeled and finely
   chopped
6 sprigs parsley

1 bay leaf
¼ tsp. dried thyme
1 thin slice lemon
1 tsp. salt
½ tsp. pepper
2 tsps. potato flour
2 tsps. cold water
1 pinch sugar
12 pitted black olives
12 pitted green olives, unstuffed or stuffed with
   pimiento
12 small mushroom caps

With a knife, carefully remove the gray skin on the out-side of the tuna.

Heat the butter and oil in a heavy pot; add the onions and cook until transparent. Add the tuna and brown it on both sides. Don't let the onions burn; they should be golden.

Turn the heat down, and place the tomato pieces around the sides and on top of the tuna. Add the fish stock, garlic, parsley, bay leaf, thyme, lemon, salt and pepper. Place a tight-fitting lid on top, and simmer over a low heat for 40 to 50 minutes or until the fish flakes easily when tested with a fork.

Remove the tuna to a plate and keep it warm. Remove the tomato skins, bay leaf, parsley and lemon slice.

Dissolve the potato flour in the cold water and add to the sauce. Turn up the heat, cook and stir until thickened—3 or 4 minutes. Add the sugar, olives and mushrooms, and cook and stir 5 to 8 minutes. If the tuna has cooled, replace it in the sauce: this dish must be served piping hot.

To serve: Place the tuna on a heated deep platter, spoon the sauce over it and serve at once.

Serves 6.

SALMON POACHED IN RED WINE

In cooking, red wine and salmon harmonize beautifully. However, serve this salmon with a chilled dry white wine, not a red. The salmon should be a center cut and in one piece.

3 to 4 lbs. fresh salmon	¼ tsp. dried chervil
3 tbs. butter	¼ tsp. dried tarragon
6 leeks, including the fresh green tops, washed and cut into 2-inch slivers	½ tsp. salt
	¼ tsp. pepper
	6 sprigs parsley
	Lemon slices
1 cup fish stock	1 tbs. parsley, finely chopped
1½ cups dry red burgundy	

Wash and dry the salmon. Melt the butter in a shallow pot, and when foaming, add salmon. Lightly brown it on both sides, then remove it to a plate.

Add the leeks to the pot, and toss and stir until wilted.

Return the salmon to the pot, placing it on top of the leeks. Add the stock, burgundy, chervil, tarragon, salt, pepper and parsley sprigs. Bring to a boil. Adjust the heat to a simmer, cover with a tight-fitting lid, and simmer for 35 to 45 minutes or until the salmon is tender.

To serve: Place the salmon on a heated platter and keep it warm. Over a high heat reduce the sauce to approximately 1 cup, spoon it over the salmon and garnish with lemon slices and parsley. Serve at once.

Serves 6.

FILLETS OF SOLE LAROQUETTE

Ask your grocer for the fresh sweet red peppers; they do add an extra touch. However, if they are not available, the canned pimientos make a pleasant substitute. Serve with steamed new potatoes or rice.

4 tbs. butter
2 tsps. lemon juice
½ lb. mushrooms, coarsely chopped
8 scallions, including the green leaves, finely chopped

1 medium sweet red pepper, seeded and diced, or 3 canned pimientos, drained and diced
¾ cup fish stock
½ tsp. salt
¼ tsp. pepper
3 lbs. fillet of sole

Melt the butter in a deep large skillet, and when foaming, add lemon juice, mushrooms, scallions and red pepper. Stir and cook 3 or 4 minutes; add stock, salt and pepper. Adjust heat to a simmer, cover, and simmer for 5 minutes. Add fillets and cover them with a piece of buttered wax paper. Gently poach the fillets for 8 to 10 minutes or until they flake easily when tested with a fork.

To serve: Use a spatula to lift the fillets to a heated serving platter. Spoon the sauce over them.

Serves 4 to 6.

CRABMEAT AND MUSTARD RING

A marvelous luncheon dish or first course for a dinner party. Serve with crisp rounds of Melba toast and a chilled dry white wine.

Fresh, canned or frozen cooked crabmeat can be used.

Vegetable oil	2 tsps. lemon juice
4 tsps. unflavored gela-tin	1 tsp. salt
	Pinch cayenne pepper
2 tbs. cold water	½ tsp. paprika
1 cup fish stock	4 eggs
4 tbs. sugar	1 cup heavy cream
2½ tbs. dry mustard	1 lb. cooked crabmeat
1 tbs. butter	Lemon juice
1 cup dry white ver-mouth	Watercress sprigs

Lightly oil a 1-quart metal ring mold. Set aside.

Put the gelatin in a small bowl, and cover with the cold water. Bring the fish stock to a boil; add the gelatin, stir until the gelatin is dissolved. Remove from the heat and set aside.

Pour 1 inch of water into the bottom of a double boiler and heat. Do not boil. Into the top of the double boiler put the sugar, mustard, butter, vermouth, 2 teaspoons of lemon juice, salt, cayenne pepper and paprika. Stir until blended. Beat the eggs well, and stirring continuously, slowly add them to the vermouth mixture. Continue to stir and cook until the mixture is thickened.

When thick, remove from the heat, stir in the gelatin and fish stock. Chill to the point of setting, but do not set.

When chilled, beat the cream until it is stiff. Fold it into the mixture with great care; it must be completely blended. Pour into the ring mold, cover and place in the refrigerator to set.

Remove any pieces of cartilage or shell from the crab-meat, add a few drops of lemon juice, toss and chill.

To serve: Unmold the ring on a chilled serving plate. Place the crabmeat in the center and decorate with watercress sprigs.

Serves 6.

Variation:

Cooked, shelled and deveined shrimp can be used instead of crabmeat.

CRABMEAT STEW

Use fresh, frozen or canned crabmeat for this recipe. If frozen crab is used, defrost before cooking. Serve with fluffy white rice.

1½ to 2 lbs. crabmeat	2 peeled fresh to-
½ cup dry sherry	matoes, or 2 canned
¼ tsp. dried basil	whole tomatoes,
2 tbs. butter	coarsely diced
1 medium onion, peeled	1½ tsps. salt
and finely chopped	½ tsp. pepper
1 medium green pep-	1 small clove garlic,
per, seeded, with the	peeled and finely
white membrane re-	chopped
moved, finely diced	1 cup fish stock
3 tbs. flour	1 cup heavy cream

Separate the crabmeat and remove all pieces of cartilage or shell. Pour the sherry over it, add basil, mix, cover and set aside.

Melt the butter in a deep heavy pot, and when foaming, add onion and green pepper. Stir and cook until the onion is transparent. Remove from heat, add flour, tomatoes, salt, pepper and garlic. Stir and return to heat, and simmer for 5 minutes. Slowly add stock and cream. Cook and stir until the sauce comes to a boil; add the crabmeat, stir and simmer 8 to 10 minutes.

Serve directly from the pot or pour into a heated serving dish.

Serves 6.

MUSSELS IN WINE SAUCE

2 quarts fresh mussels	1 carrot, scrubbed and thinly sliced
1 cup fish stock	
1½ cups dry white wine	1½ tsps. salt
1 bay leaf	6 peppercorns
2 stalks celery, including the leaves, finely chopped	3 egg yolks
	1 tsp. potato flour
	2 tbs. brandy
1 medium onion, peeled and finely sliced	1 pinch cayenne pepper
	2 tbs. parsley, finely chopped

Scrub and remove the beards from the mussels. Discard any mussels that are open.

Pour the stock and wine into a large pot, and add the bay leaf, celery, onion, carrot, salt and peppercorns. Add the mussels, cover and bring to a boil. Steam the mussels until they are open—approximately 10 to 15 minutes. Discard any mussels that do not open.

When open, remove the mussels with a slotted spoon to a heated bowl and keep warm. Pour the liquid into a saucepot through a fine strainer lined with cheesecloth.

Beat the egg yolks lightly in a small bowl, and stir in the potato flour, brandy and pepper. Stirring continuously, pour the egg-yolk mixture into the hot, strained liquid. Place over a low heat or over hot water, and stir and cook until the sauce is thickened. Do not boil.

To serve: Remove the top shells of the mussels and arrange the mussels in a heated gratin dish or on a deep platter. Pour the sauce over them, garnish with parsley and serve at once.
Serves 6.

SHRIMP WITH WINE SAUCE

Here is a quick and delicious dish to prepare if unexpected guests show up or if just you and your family feel like celebrating with ease. Frozen shrimp are recommended. While they are being defrosted in boiling water, the rice can be cooking and you can make the sauce. Preparation should not take longer than 20 to 25 minutes.

Serve with a tomato and lettuce salad, rolls and a chilled bottle of dry white wine.

1 lb. shrimps, cooked, shelled and deveined, or frozen	½ tsp. salt
	1 pinch cayenne pepper
	4 egg yolks
3 cups rice cooked in fish stock	1½ tbs. brandy
	½ tsp. lemon juice
6 ozs. sweet butter	1 tbs. parsley, finely chopped
½ cup dry white wine	
¼ tsp. nutmeg	

Combine the cooked shrimp and rice, cover, and keep warm over hot water.

Melt the butter in a double boiler, add the wine, nutmeg, salt and cayenne pepper. Stir.

Beat the egg yolks lightly. Adjust the heat so that the water in the double boiler remains hot but does not boil. With a wire whisk, beat the butter mixture and slowly add the egg yolks, in a thread-thin stream. Continue to beat until the sauce is thickened. Add brandy and lemon juice. Stir and cook over the hot water for 1 or 2 minutes. Combine the sauce with the shrimp and rice.

Serve in a heated serving dish and garnish with chopped parsley.

Serves 6.

(7) VEGETABLES

VEGETABLE NOTES

It has been rumored that in Paradise vegetables are picked at their peak of ripeness, sped to the kitchen and immediately boiled for only a few moments in pure spring water. Our world is quite a pace away from Paradise, and for me, the finest earthly method to cook fresh vegetables is to steam them.

One of the advantages of steaming is that the vegetable will not be soggy or get cold while draining. For example, artichokes absorb a considerable amount of liquid if they are boiled, and they are tedious to drain. If they are steamed, they can be removed directly from the steamer to the serving plate when tender.

It is perfectly all right to steam your vegetables over water; if you use stock it will subtly enhance their taste, but only the most refined palate will detect this added flavor. The process of cooking by steam is what is important; however, if you use stock for steaming, it will be enriched by the vegetable. But the use of stock for steaming depends on your taste as well as on the amount you have on hand. If stock is used, return it to your supply of basic stock; if water is used, freeze it for the stockpot.

The liquids used to cook beets, cauliflower or any of the cabbage family should be kept separate. Suggestions for their use is given in the recipes, but do not add it to the stockpot.

The only vegetables not given to steaming are spinach and beet greens; these should be cooked quickly in a small amount of water or stock.

Steam your vegetables at a slow boil, not at a simmer.

All pepper should be freshly ground.

Taste before you serve. Correct the seasoning to your taste.

STEAMED ARTICHOKES

Artichokes	*Butter*
Lemon	*Salt*
Water	

Prepare 1 artichoke per person. Cut the stem even with the base. Discard any discolored lower leaves. Rinse in a pan of cold water. Drain upside down to remove excess water.

Set the artichoke on its side and cut ½ inch off the top leaves with a sharp knife. Hold the artichoke upright, and with a pair of scissors, snip off the sharp points of the other leaves.

Cut 1 thin lemon slice for each artichoke. Cut each slice into quarters and stick a piece under the leaves in 4 separate places.

Into a pot large enough to hold the artichokes side by side, pour 1 inch of water. Place a rack or trivet over the water and set the artichokes upright on it. Place a tight-fitting lid on top, and bring the water to a boil. Adjust the heat to a slow boil, and steam for 30 to 40 minutes or until a leaf can be pulled off easily.

To remove the choke, gently push open the center leaves, and with a grapefruit knife or spoon, remove the hairy choke as well as the small prickly leaves covering it. Re-form the artichoke by pressing it firmly together with your hands.

Serve with melted butter to which a few drops of lemon

juice and a good pinch of salt have been added, or with a sauce to your liking.

ARTICHOKE HEARTS AND CARROTS

This is a recipe your friends will want. Serve it with cocktails, as a first course or as a salad.

12 artichoke hearts,
   canned or frozen
½ cup olive oil
4 medium carrots,
   scrubbed and cut into
   diagonal 1- to 2-inch
   pieces
¾ cup basic stock or
   chicken stock from
   which all fat has been
   removed

2 tbs. lemon juice
1 tsp. lemon rind, grated
1 scallion, washed, with
   the root removed
1 tsp. sugar
2 tsps. salt
½ tsp. pepper
1 tbs. parsley, or chives
   finely chopped

Drain the canned artichokes or defrost and drain the frozen artichokes. Set aside.

Heat the olive oil in a pot, and when hot, add the carrots. Cover and cook until they are almost tender—about 10 minutes. Add stock, lemon juice, lemon rind, drained artichokes, scallion, sugar, salt and pepper. Cook uncovered 4 to 5 minutes.

With a slotted spoon, remove the vegetables. Cool the vegetables and sauce separately.

To serve: Remove and discard the scallion and arrange the vegetables on a serving platter. Spoon the sauce over them. Garnish with the parsley or chives and serve.

Serves 4 to 6.

STEAMED ASPARAGUS WITH
HOLLANDAISE SAUCE

Water	2½ *lbs. fresh asparagus,*
	washed and trimmed

Put 1 inch of water into a large pot or an upright steamer. Place a rack or steam basket over the water and place the asparagus in it. Cover pot with a tight-fitting lid, and bring the water to a boil. Adjust the heat to a simmer, and steam for 10 to 15 minutes or until the asparagus is tender.

Remove the asparagus with tongs to a linen towel. Wrap securely; the excess moisture will be absorbed, and the asparagus will stay warm for 10 to 15 minutes. Save the water for the stockpot.

Prepare the following Hollandaise Sauce:

½ *lb. butter*	1 *tbs. lemon juice*
4 *egg yolks*	1 *pinch salt*

Divide the butter into 3 equal parts. Heat 1 inch of water in the bottom part of a double boiler. Do not let the water boil.

Into the top of the double boiler, put 1 part of the butter, the egg yolks, lemon juice and salt. Place over the hot water and stir continuously with a whisk or wooden spoon until the butter is melted and the mixture is smoothly blended. Add the additional 2 parts of butter, one at a time, and stir each time until the sauce is thick and creamy.

If the sauce is not to be served at once, cover and place in a pan of lukewarm water.

To serve: Arrange the asparagus on a heated serving platter or on heated individual plates, and spoon over them all or part of the Hollandaise Sauce.

Serves 4 to 6.

NOTE: If salted butter is used, don't add additional salt. If a sharper Hollandaise Sauce is desired, add ½ tablespoon more lemon juice.

This recipe makes approximately 2 cups of sauce. One to 1½ cups amply serves 4 to 6 people.

STEAMED BEETS

I usually cook 2 or 3 extra beets, as they are marvelous when cold. Peel and dice them, and add them to a green salad; or slice them and serve as a salad with chopped scallions and a vinaigrette dressing (see p. 238).

6 medium beets	1 tsp. salt
Water	½ tsp. pepper
2 tbs. butter	2 tbs. parsley, finely
2 tsps. cider vinegar	chopped

Cut all but 2 to 3 inches off the tops of the beets. Wash.

Pour 1 inch of water into a deep pot. Place a rack or a steam basket over the water, and place the beets on or in it. Cover pot with a tight-fitting lid, and bring the water to a boil. Adjust the heat to a slow boil, and steam for 20 to 30 minutes or until the beets are tender when tried with a fork.

When tender, remove the beets, peel and cut into cubes.

Melt the butter in a pan, add beets, vinegar, salt, pepper and parsley. Stir and cook until thoroughly heated.

.Serve in a heated serving dish or in heated individual side dishes.

Serves 4 to 6.

NOTE: The water over which the beets were steamed is red and has a strong beet flavor. It should not be used in the stockpot, but it has other uses:

a. It can be reserved for use in a Winterborscht Soup (see p. 88).

b. An equal amount of basic stock can be added to it, heated and served with a thin slice of lemon on top as a hot beet bouillon.

BEETS WITH ORANGE PEEL

This is a variation of the preceding recipe. It is an unusual but delicious blend of flavors.

6 to 8 medium beets steamed until tender according to the preceding recipe	2 tsps. grated orange
	2 tsps. grated orange peel
	½ tsp. salt
2 tbs. butter	¼ tsp. pepper

Peel the beets and dice into ½-inch pieces. Melt the butter in a pan, and when foaming, add the beets, orange peel, salt and pepper. Toss and stir until the diced beets are thoroughly coated with butter.

Serve at once in a heated serving dish.

Serves 6.

BEET GREENS

Beet tops have such a tangy full flavor that I wish the vegetable markets would not sell beets minus their tops. As with all vegetables, the fresher the beet tops, the better the flavor.

2 slices of bacon cut into 1-inch pieces

1 small onion, peeled and finely chopped

4 to 6 beet tops, washed and cut into ½-inch diagonal strips, including the stems

2 tbs. basic stock or chicken stock from which all fat has been removed

½ tsp. salt

¼ tsp. pepper

In a large frying pan, fry the bacon until crisp; remove and drain on a brown paper bag. Discard all but 2 teaspoons of the bacon fat. Add the onion, and stir and cook until the onion is transparent. Add the sliced beet tops, stock, salt and pepper. Keep the heat high, and toss and stir vigorously until the leaves are wilted. Cover, lower the heat, and simmer 5 to 8 minutes or until the beet tops are tender. Turn into a heated serving dish. Crumble the bacon and sprinkle it over the top. Serve at once.

Serves 2 to 4.

SPICED BEETS

3½ tbs. butter

2 scallions, including the fresh green tops, finely sliced

3 tbs. wine or cider vinegar

2 tsps. sugar

1 tsp. salt

½ tsp. pepper

4 whole cloves

3 cups cooked steamed beets, sliced or diced

Melt the butter in a pot, and when foaming, add the scallions and stir and cook until wilted. Add the vinegar, sugar, salt, pepper, cloves and beets. Stir. Cover and simmer for 10 minutes.

To serve: Remove the cloves, and pour into a heated serving dish.

Serves 6.

STEAMED CARROTS

Water	*2 tsps. parsley, finely*
8 medium carrots,	*chopped*
scrubbed and halved	*1 tsp. salt*
2 tbs. butter	*½ tsp. pepper*

Pour ½ to 1 inch of water into a deep pot. Place a rack or steam basket over the water and place the carrots on or in it. Cover pot with a tight-fitting lid, and bring the water to a boil. Adjust the heat to a slow boil, and steam for 10 to 15 minutes or until the carrots are tender.

When tender, put the carrots into a heated serving dish, add the butter, parsley, salt and pepper. Toss and stir until the butter is melted.

Save the water for the stockpot.

Serves 6.

MASHED CARROTS

8 medium carrots,
   scrubbed and sliced
2 cups basic stock or
   chicken stock from
   which all fat has been
   removed

½ tsp. sugar
½ cup heavy cream
½ tsp. salt

Steam the carrots, and when tender, put them together with the stock, through a food mill, or blend in a blender until smooth. Add heavy cream, sugar and salt. Return to the pot, heat and serve.

Serves 6.

STEAMED CAULIFLOWER

Water
1 medium cauliflower,
   trimmed and washed
½ cup melted butter

1 cup bread crumbs
½ tsp. lemon juice
   Salt
   Pepper

Pour ½ to 1 inch of water into a deep pot. Place a rack or steam basket over the water, and put the cauliflower on or in it. Cover with a tight-fitting lid, and bring the water to a boil. Adjust the heat to a slow boil, and steam for 15 to 20 minutes or until the cauliflower is tender.

While the cauliflower is cooking, mix the butter, bread crumbs and lemon juice in a small pan, and cook and stir until the bread crumbs are golden.

When the cauliflower is tender, remove it to a hot serving

dish, sprinkle with salt and pepper and pour the butter and bread-crumb mixture over it.

This water should be saved for use in cauliflower or potato soup.

Serves 4 to 6.

STEAMED GREEN BEANS

2 lbs. green beans	4 tbs. melted butter
Basic stock or chicken	2 tsps. salt
stock from which all fat	½ tsp. pepper
has been removed, or	1 tbs. parsley, finely
water	chopped

Cut the ends off the beans and wash. Put 1 inch of stock or water into a large pot. Place a rack, or steam basket, over the liquid, and place the beans on or in it. Place a tight-fitting lid on top, and bring the liquid to a boil. Adjust the heat to a slow boil, and steam for 20 to 30 minutes or until the beans are tender.

When tender, put the beans into a heated serving dish and pour over them the melted butter, salt, pepper and parsley. Toss. Serve at once.

Save the liquid for the stockpot.

Serves 6.

Variation:

Wax beans may be substituted for green beans.

GREEN-BEAN SALAD

3 cups steamed green
  beans, diced into ¼-
  inch pieces
3 scallions, including the
  fresh green leaves,
  washed and finely
  chopped

2 medium tomatoes,
  peeled, seeded and cut
  into thin strips
1 tbs. fresh dill or parsley,
  finely chopped

Mix all the ingredients together in a large bowl, and chill.
Prepare the following Vinaigrette:

3 tbs. salad oil
3 tbs. olive oil
1 tbs. vinegar

1 tbs. lemon juice
1 tsp. salt
½ tsp. pepper

Thoroughly blend all the ingredients, pour the mixture
over the green-bean mixture, toss diligently and serve at once.
Serves 6.

STEAMED LEEKS

12 medium leeks
 2 cups basic stock or
   chicken stock from
   which all fat has been
   removed, or water

¾ cup melted butter
  Salt
  Pepper

Cut the tops from the leeks, leaving 2 to 3 inches of
light green leaves. Cut off the roots. Partially slice the leeks

lengthwise in order to wash thoroughly between the leaves to remove all the sand.

Pour the stock or water into a pot, and place a rack or trivet over it. Place the leeks on the rack, cover pot with a tight-fitting lid and bring the liquid to a boil. Adjust the heat to a simmer, and steam for 15 to 20 minutes or until the leeks are tender.

When tender, place the leeks on a heated platter and spoon the melted butter over them. Sprinkle with salt and pepper.

Save the liquid for the stockpot.

Serves 4 to 6.

Variation:

When the leeks are tender, chill and serve with a vinaigrette dressing.

STEAMED FRESH LIMA BEANS

Basic stock or ham stock	*2 tbs. butter*
from which all fat has	*1 tsp. salt*
been removed, or water	*½ tsp. pepper*
4 cups fresh shelled lima	
beans	

Put ½ to 1 inch of stock or water into a large pot. Place a steam basket or rack over the liquid, and put the beans in or on it. Cover pot with a tight-fitting lid, and bring the liquid to a boil. Adjust the heat to a slow boil, and steam for 15 to 18 minutes or until the beans are tender. Save the liquid for the stockpot.

When tender, pour the beans into a heated serving dish, add butter, salt and pepper. Toss and serve.

Serves 6.

STEAMED ONIONS

Perfect as a garnish for a roast.

1 cup basic stock or chicken stock from which all fat has been removed, or water	24 to 26 small white onions, peeled Salt Pepper

Pour the stock or water into a deep pot. Place a rack or steam basket over the liquid and place the onions on or in it. Cover pot with a tight-fitting lid, and bring the liquid to a boil. Adjust the heat to a slow boil, and steam for 25 to 35 minutes or until the onions are tender.

When tender, put the onions into a heated serving dish, and spoon 2 tablespoons of the liquid over them. Sprinkle with salt and pepper.

Save the liquid for the stockpot.

Serves 6 to 8.

STEAMED RADISHES

If you have not cooked radishes before, do try now. Serve them as a vegetable with any type of roast or as a first course.

30 medium radishes Water 6 tbs. shallots, or the white part of scallions, finely chopped	5 tbs. butter 1 tsp. salt ½ tsp. pepper

Wash radishes, and leave ½ to 1 inch of the green tops untrimmed.

Put ½ to 1 inch of water into a heavy pot, add a handful of radish leaves, place a steamer basket, or trivet, over the water and put the radishes in or on it. Cover with a tight-fitting lid, and bring the water to a boil. Adjust the heat to a slow boil, and steam for 10 to 15 minutes or until the radishes are tender.

Melt the butter in a small pan, and when foaming, add the shallots, or scallions, and stir and toss over a high heat for 2 to 3 minutes. Add the tender radishes, salt and pepper. Toss and stir for 2 or 3 minutes, and serve at once in a heated serving dish.

Save the water for the stockpot.

Serves 6.

MEDLEY OF STEAMED VEGETABLES

Basic stock or chicken stock from which all fat has been removed, or water

3 *medium carrots, peeled and sliced into thick rounds, or cut into 2- to 3-inch strips*

½ *lb. string beans, washed, ends removed, and cut into 2-inch pieces*

1 *small cauliflower, or ½ of a large cauli-flower, washed and broken into florets*

Salt

Pepper

½ *cup hot melted butter*

1 *tbs. parsley, dill, or chives, finely chopped*

Pour ½ to 1 inch of stock or water into the bottom of a pot. Place a rack or steam basket over it. Arrange the carrots, string beans and cauliflower florets into 3 sections on the rack or in the steam basket. Cover pot with a tight-fitting lid, and bring the liquid to a boil. Adjust the heat to a slow boil, and steam the vegetables for 15 to 20 minutes or until they are tender. Save the liquid for the stockpot.

When the vegetables are tender, arrange them in sections on a heated plate or platter, sprinkle with salt and pepper, and pour over the hot melted butter. Garnish with the parsley, dill or chives. Serve at once.

Serves 4 to 6.

STEAMED NEW POTATOES

Basic stock or chicken stock from which all fat has been removed, or water	*5 tbs. butter*
	2 tsps. salt
	1 tsp. pepper
18 to 24 small new red or white potatoes, washed	

Pour ½ to 1 inch of stock or water into a deep pot. Place a rack or steam basket over the liquid and place the potatoes on or in it. Cover pot with a tight-fitting lid, and bring the liquid to a boil. Adjust the heat to a slow boil, and steam for 20 to 25 minutes or until the potatoes are tender.

When tender, place the potatoes into a heated serving dish and toss with the butter, salt and pepper. Serve at once.

Save the liquid for the stockpot.

Serves 6.

NOTE: If you do not enjoy the fresh tender skin of the new potatoes, peel before serving.

RED CABBAGE

8 cups red cabbage,
  finely shredded
1 large apple, peeled
  and sliced
½ tsp. salt
2 cups basic stock or
  beef stock from which
  all fat has been re-
  moved

1 medium onion, peeled
  and sliced
1 bay leaf
6 whole black pepper-
  corns
4 cloves
2½ tbs. butter
6 tbs. wine vinegar
6 tbs. sugar

Put the cabbage into a heavy pot, and add apple, salt, stock, and onion. Tie the bay leaf, peppercorns and cloves in cheesecloth, and add to the pot. Bring to a boil, cover, adjust heat to a simmer, and simmer for 1 hour. Add butter, vinegar and sugar. Cover and simmer for 1 hour more. Remove and discard cheesecloth.

Serve in heated individual serving dishes.

Serves 6.

MUSHROOMS AND RICE

3 tbs. butter
1½ tbs. vegetable oil
1 medium onion, peeled
  and finely chopped
1 cup rice
2½ cups basic stock or
  chicken stock from
  which all fat has been
  removed
1½ tsps. salt

1 tsp. pepper
2 cups mushrooms, in-
  cluding the stems,
  cleaned and coarsely
  chopped
1 tbs. lemon juice
3 tbs. sherry
4 tbs. grated Parmesan
  cheese
3 tbs. parsley, chopped

Heat 1½ tablespoons of the butter and the oil in a heavy pot. When foaming, add the onion, and cook and stir until transparent. Add the rice, stock, salt and pepper. Stir and bring to a boil. Cover pot with a tight-fitting lid, turn the heat down to a simmer and cook 30 minutes or until the liquid is absorbed and the rice is tender.

In another pot, melt the remaining 1½ tablespoons of butter, and when foaming, add the mushrooms, lemon juice and sherry. Cook over a high heat for 3 to 4 minutes, tossing and stirring all the while. Pour this mushroom mixture into the cooked rice. Add the cheese and stir.

Serve in a heated serving dish and garnish with the parsley.

Serves 6.

MUSHROOMS STELLA

This recipe is the one exception: it does not use any stock. I include it in this book because it is unusual and delicious. Use the small fresh white mushrooms about the size of a quarter. If large mushrooms are used, taste will be the same, but they are not as attractive.

The prepared mushrooms can be stored 2 to 3 weeks in a closed container in the refrigerator. They are perfect as a first course or with cocktails.

1 lb. fresh mushrooms	2 scallions, including the
1 tbs. lemon juice	green tops, washed
¾ cup vegetable oil	and halved
2 tbs. soy sauce	Parsley or watercress
½ tsp. salt	

Wash the mushrooms in a large pan filled with cold water and to which the lemon juice has been added. Do not remove the stems. Drain, but do not dry. It is important that the mushrooms retain the water they absorbed during the washing process.

Heat the oil in a medium pot, and when hot, add the mushrooms. Toss and turn with a wooden spoon until all are thoroughly coated with oil. Add soy sauce, salt, scallions, and stir. Adjust the heat to a simmer, and cook uncovered 15 to 20 minutes or until the oil has separated from the water.

Remove from the heat and cool. Discard the scallions. Spoon the mushrooms, together with the sauce, into a container and cover tightly. Refrigerate until ready to serve.

To serve: With tongs or a slotted spoon, remove the mushrooms to a serving plate or individual plates, and garnish with sprigs of parsley or watercress.

Serves 6 to 8.

MUSHROOMS IN CREAM

These are so exquisitely rich and delicious that they should be shared with only your favorite guests. For my taste, because of their richness, they should accompany a roast veal or a roasted chicken. Serve 4 to 6 mushroom caps per person.

2 *lbs. large mushrooms**	2 *ozs. Madeira*
1 *tbs. lemon juice*	½ *cup basic stock or*
½ *lb butter*	*chicken stock from*
2 *tbs. shallots, finely*	*which all fat has been*
chopped	*removed*
2 *ozs. brandy*	1 *cup heavy cream*

* Two-pounds of large mushrooms should give you 32 to 36 caps.

Separate the mushroom caps and stems. Save the mushroom stems for a sauce or for the stockpot. Clean the caps and sprinkle them with the lemon juice.

In a large heavy frying pan, melt the butter, and when foaming, add the shallots and stir and cook until they are tender. Do not brown them. Add the mushroom caps and cook them, uncovered, over a low heat for 5 minutes, stirring occasionally. Add the brandy, Madeira, stock and cream. Cover, simmer for 15 minutes over a very low heat, stirring occasionally.

To serve: Spoon the mushroom caps and sauce into a heated serving dish or onto individual heated serving plates.
Serves 6 to 8.

Variation:
Place a piece of white toast, cut in half, on individual heated plates and spoon over the mushrooms and sauce.

LARDED POTATOES

If you want a change from boiled, mashed or baked potatoes, try these. They are delicious and go well with any roast. They can be prepared early and reheated prior to serving.

3 tbs. butter	2 tsps. salt
¾ cup salt pork, cubed into ¼-inch pieces	1 tsp. pepper
	1 small bay leaf
2 medium onions, peeled and coarsely chopped	½ tsp. dried thyme
	4 sprigs parsley
3 tbs. flour	6 medium potatoes, peeled and quartered
3 cups hot basic stock or beef stock from which all fat has been removed	

Melt the butter in a heavy pot, and when hot, add the salt pork and onions. Stir and cook until the pork and onions are crisp and golden brown. Remove with a slotted spoon, and set aside.

Add the flour to the fat in the pot. Stir and cook until light brown. Slowly add the hot stock, stirring continuously. Stir and cook until thickened. Add the salt and pepper. Tie up the bay leaf, thyme and parsley in a cheesecloth, and add to the pot. Stir. Add the potatoes, cover and cook 35 to 40 minutes or until the potatoes are tender. When tender, add the browned salt pork and onions. Stir. Remove and discard cheesecloth.

To serve: Spoon the potatoes and sauce into a heated serving dish.

Serves 6.

POTATOES AND CREAM

6 to 8 medium po-	½ tsp. pepper
tatoes, unpeeled	2 tbs. butter
Boiling water	½ cup heavy cream
1½ tsps. salt	1 tbs. parsley or chives,
1 cup basic stock or	finely chopped
beef stock from	
which all fat has been	
removed	

Put the potatoes into a pot, cover with boiling water and add ½ teaspoon of the salt. Place a lid on the pot, and cook until the potatoes are barely tender. Drain and peel.

Cut the potatoes into medium slices, and place them in a pot. Add the stock, the remaining salt, the pepper and butter. Bring to a boil, and cook uncovered over a medium heat for 5 minutes. Add the cream, stir, and simmer uncovered over a low heat until the potatoes are soft and the sauce is slightly thickened.

To serve: Pour into a heated serving dish, sprinkle with parsley or chives, and serve.

Serves 6.

RICE-RING MARGARET

The vegetables can be prepared early and reheated or kept hot in a double boiler. The mold of rice can be covered and set into a pan of hot water. It takes but a moment to assemble this unusually attractive and delicious dish. If the artichoke hearts are too large, cut them in half, and if small mushrooms are not available, use thinly sliced large mushrooms. The rice is especially tasty if cooked in basic stock or chicken stock.

Butter

3 cups cooked rice

12 to 14 small white onions, peeled

¾ cup basic stock or chicken stock from which all fat has been removed

8 to 10 artichoke hearts, canned or frozen

2 tbs. butter

¼ lb. small whole mushrooms, including stems

1 tsp. lemon juice

2 tbs. parsley, finely chopped

Butter an 8-inch-diameter ring mold, and gently pack the rice in it. Cover and set in a pan of hot water.

Put the onions into a small pot with ½ cup of the stock, cover and cook until tender. Drain and set aside.

If canned artichoke hearts are used, drain thoroughly; if frozen artichokes are used, defrost and drain.

Melt the butter in a medium pot, and when foaming, add mushrooms and lemon juice. Toss and cook over a high heat 2 or 3 minutes. Add onions and artichoke hearts. Lower the heat, and add the remaining ¼ cup of stock. Stir and simmer uncovered 5 to 10 minutes.

To serve: Unmold the rice ring on a hot platter, spoon the onions, mushrooms and artichokes into the center of the ring and garnish with the parsley.

Serves 6.

STEWED TOMATOES

2½ cups canned tomatoes
  1 cup basic stock or chicken stock from which all fat has been removed
  1 green pepper, finely diced, with the seeds and membranes removed

5 scallions, including the fresh green tops, finely sliced
4 stalks celery, washed and finely diced
1 tsp. salt
½ tsp. pepper
2 tbs. butter

If the canned tomatoes are whole, cut them into 1-inch pieces.

Put the tomatoes, stock, green pepper, scallions, celery, salt and pepper into a pot, and bring to a boil. Adjust the heat to a simmer, and simmer uncovered 8 to 10 minutes. Add butter. Stir.

Serve in individual heated bowls.

Serves 6.

HOT TOMATO SALAD

3 *large tomatoes*

6 *scallions, including the fresh green tops, finely chopped*

½ *cup parsley, finely chopped*

3 *medium stalks celery, finely diced*

½ *medium green pepper, finely diced, with the seeds and white membranes removed*

2½ *tbs. fresh dill, finely chopped, or 1½ tsps. dried dill*

½ *tsp. salt*

¼ *tsp. pepper*

4 *tbs. butter*

½ *cup basic stock or chicken stock from which all fat has been removed*

Cut a thin slice off the top and bottom of each tomato. Cut each tomato crosswise, making 2 thick slices. Set aside.

In a bowl mix the scallions, parsley, celery, green pepper, dill, salt and pepper.

Heat the butter in a large, flat, heavy skillet, and when foaming, add the tomato slices. Do not overlap. Cover them with the mixed vegetables and add the stock. Cover and cook over a medium-high heat 10 minutes.

To serve: With a spatula, remove the tomato slices to a heated serving platter or heated individual salad plates, and spoon the vegetables over them. Serve piping hot.

Serves 6.

(8) DRIED BEANS AND GRAINS

DRIED BEAN NOTES

If you want a help in keeping your food budget balanced and yet want to continue to eat deliciously, serve cooked dried beans more often. These wonderful small dried kernels, of which there are approximately 10,000 varieties, have been a basic food throughout history. They contain an extraordinary amount of the nutriments our bodies require; they can be stored for years, and they can be prepared easily in countless succulent ways. The recipes that follow are merely an introduction to the culinary possibilities of beans. I hope they will tempt you sufficiently so that you will seek out and use a few of the treasury of bean recipes in existence.

It is possible to buy many types of canned and prepared beans. However, you pay a great deal more for them than if you buy and prepare the dried beans. Aside from the money saved, I believe that the home-cooked beans are far more tasty.

You will note that in my recipes the first step is to "cull"; dried beans are culled by slowly pouring them into a strainer or bowl and picking out and discarding any stones or shriveled beans. The beans are then washed. Further, you will note that I do not recommend a long soak for the beans—that is, washing and soaking them the night before cooking. I find that the method of dropping the beans into boiling water or stock and steeping them for 2 hours has two advantages: First, you don't have to remember to put them to soak the night before; and, second, it aids in reducing the intestinal discomfort that beans supposedly cause.

The cooking time of dried beans depends on their age. It is impossible to know if you are purchasing this season's dried beans or beans harvested many seasons ago. Therefore, to test a bean's doneness, take two or three from the pot and bite into them; if they are soft, they are done.

I have yet to find any cooked dried beans that do not freeze beautifully. Therefore, when I cook beans I cook a pound or two and freeze what is not needed in the recipe. They can be defrosted at room temperature or by putting them into a pot with a bit of water or stock, and placed directly over a low heat.

GRAIN NOTES

Just as "diamonds are a girl's best friend," so grains have been, and are, man's best friend in the realm of sustenance. To set down the past and present benefits that mankind has derived, and still derives, from these tiny seeds would be a vast undertaking encompassing the long history of man and beast.

I hope that the following collection of recipes will introduce you to unfamiliar grains, and give you new ideas in the preparation and serving of one of civilization's oldest and most nutritious foods.

BABY LIMA BEAN NOTES

These delightful beans are the refined offspring of the fava, or broad, bean. They are prepared in the following manner.

Cull 1 cup of baby lima beans and wash thoroughly in cold water. Into a large pot, put 3 cups of water, basic stock or chicken stock from which all fat has been removed and bring to a boil. Add the baby lima beans slowly to keep the liquid at a continuous boil. Place a cover on the pot, adjust the heat to a simmer, and simmer for 40 to 50 minutes or until tender. Do not overcook. Stir occasionally; if necessary, add more water or stock.

If drained cooked baby lima beans are used in a recipe, do not discard the liquid in which they were cooked; add it to your stockpot.

One cup of dried baby lima beans makes 2¼ cups of cooked beans.

BABY LIMA BEANS WITH SHORT RIBS OF BEEF

Ribs of beef and all beans marry well. The brown sugar and lemon gives this dish an old-fashioned flavor. It is a full meal and needs to be accompanied by only a crisp green salad.

2 tbs. bacon fat	1 cup basic stock or beef
4 lbs. short ribs of beef	stock from which all fat
cut into serving pieces	has been removed, or
1 medium onion, peeled	water
and thinly sliced	2 tsps. salt
½ cup brown sugar	1 tsp. pepper
1 tbs. flour	1 bay leaf
½ cup lemon juice	3 cups cooked and
	drained baby lima
	beans

Put the bacon fat into a heavy pot (a Dutch oven is perfect), and when hot, brown the ribs on all sides and remove them to a plate. Add the onion to the pot and cook until transparent. Pour off all but about 1 tablespoon of the fat. To the onion add the brown sugar and flour, and stir until smooth. Add the lemon juice, stock or water, salt, pepper and bay leaf. Continue to stir until the mixture boils, and then return the browned ribs to the pot. Cover and cook over a low heat for 2 hours or until the meat is tender. Add the cooked baby lima beans, stir well and continue to cook uncovered for half an hour. There should be about 2 inches of liquid in the pot when the dish is completed; if not, add a bit more stock or water.

To serve: Ladle into a large heated serving dish.
Serves 6 to 8.

BABY LIMA BEANS WITH HERBS

This is a good dish to serve with a roast. Or serve for a summer luncheon with a soup, dark brown bread and a dessert.

2¼ cups cooked and drained baby lima beans
½ cup of the liquid in which the beans were cooked
¼ lb. butter
½ cup parsley, finely chopped

½ cup green onions, finely chopped
1 tsp. dried basil, or 3 tsps. fresh basil, finely chopped
2 tsps. salt
½ tsp. pepper
1 large tomato, peeled and finely chopped

Put the baby lima beans into a bowl and add the liquid; stir gently to moisten the beans.

Put the butter into a large pot to heat, and when foaming, add the parsley, onions, basil, salt, pepper and baby lima beans. Keep the heat high and toss and stir until the beans are hot and coated thoroughly with the butter and herbs.

A moment before serving, reheat the beans if necessary, and toss in the chopped tomato. The tomato should be nicely mixed with the beans, but should not be cooked.

Serve at once in a heated serving dish.

Serves 4 to 6.

BABY LIMA BEANS WITH BACON

6 *slices bacon, cut into 1-inch pieces*	4 *cups cooked dried baby lima beans*
2 *shallots, peeled and finely chopped*	1 *tsp. salt*
	¼ *tsp. pepper*
½ *medium green pepper, seeded, with white membranes removed, and finely diced*	1 *cup basic stock or ham stock from which all fat has been removed*

Fry the bacon pieces in a skillet until crisp. When crisp, remove with a slotted spoon and reserve.

Discard all but 2 tablespoons of the bacon fat from the skillet. Add the shallots and green pepper. Stir and cook for 3 minutes. Add the lima beans, salt, pepper and stock. Simmer uncovered for 10 minutes or until most of the stock has been absorbed.

To serve: Pour into a heated serving dish and crumble the bacon over the top. Serve at once.

Serves 6.

BLACK BEAN NOTES

These beans are also known and marketed as black turtle-soup beans.

Black beans are one of the staple foods of Cuba, Venezuela and Brazil, and they are usually served with rice. In Venezuela one way of eating black beans is to mash them thoroughly with your fork after they are served on your plate, and sprinkle a little sugar on top. I have tried this and find it very good.

These beans require a good washing and long, slow cooking of at least 3 to 3½ hours. They do not have to be soaked.

One cup of dried black beans makes approximately 3 cups of cooked beans.

BLACK BEANS CUBANO

Black beans and rice, the staple food for so many of our neighbors to the south. This dish has traveled well; you will enjoy it. It can be frozen without any loss of flavor.

2½ cups dried black beans

10 cups boiling water, basic stock or chicken stock from which all fat has been removed

2 medium green peppers, seeded, cored and finely diced

2 medium onions, peeled and coarsely chopped

4 cloves garlic, peeled and finely chopped

4 tsps. salt

½ tsp. pepper

½ tsp. dried oregano

1 bay leaf

2 tsps. sugar

¼ tsp. Tabasco Sauce

2 tbs. vinegar

2 tbs. dry red wine

2 tbs. olive oil

White rice, for 6 to 8 servings

Cull the beans and put them into a large bowl. Cover generously with cold water and discard any beans which float to the surface. Pour the beans into a strainer and wash thoroughly under cold running water.

In a large pot, bring the water or stock to a hard boil, and slowly add the beans so that the water boils continuously. Continue boiling, uncovered, for 2 minutes. Remove from the heat and let stand, uncovered, for 2 hours.

Return the beans to the heat, and add one of the green peppers and one of the onions. Bring the pot to a boil, cover, adjust the heat to a simmer, and simmer for 1 hour. At this time add the other green pepper and onion, together with the garlic, salt, pepper, oregano, bay leaf, sugar and Tabasco Sauce. Cover and simmer for 1 hour.

Add the vinegar and wine and continue to cook for 45 minutes or until the beans are tender. If there is a lot of liquid on the beans at this stage, remove the cover and continue to cook. When the beans are ready to serve, they should be in a thick sauce. Stir occasionally.

When the beans are tender and their sauce is thick, add the olive oil.

Meanwhile, cook white rice for 6 to 8 servings.

To serve: Place an ample serving of beans on a large heated serving plate and top with a serving of rice. Or the beans and the cooked rice may be served in separate large heated serving dishes and passed to each person.

Serves 6 to 8.

BLACK BEAN SOUP

This soup is a true delicacy. It is not much work, but it does require slow and long cooking. As it freezes perfectly, it

*should be a staple on the freezer shelf for a party luncheon or
a Sunday supper.*

2 cups dried black
beans

3½ quarts of water, basic
stock or chicken stock
from which all fat
has been removed

1 ham bone with ap-
proximately ½ lb.
meat on it

2½ tbs. olive oil

4 cloves garlic, peeled
and coarsely chopped

4 medium onions, peeled
and coarsely chopped

2 medium carrots,
scrubbed and
coarsely chopped

1 medium green pepper,
cored, seeded and
coarsely chopped

½ cup celery leaves,
chopped

3 large fresh tomatoes,
quartered, or 4 canned
tomatoes, quartered

1 bay leaf

2 tbs. salt

¼ tsp. dried ground chili
peppers

2 tsps. paprika

2 tbs. butter

4 tbs. sherry
Thin lemon slices, or
slices of hard-boiled
eggs

Cull the beans. Put them into a large bowl with cold
water, and discard any of the beans which float. Pour the beans
into a strainer, and wash thoroughly under cold running water.
Put the water or stock into a large pot, bring to a boil, and
slowly add the beans so that the liquid continues to boil. Boil
uncovered for 2 minutes. Remove from the fire, cover, and let
stand for 2 hours.

Put the pot back on the stove and add the ham bone.
Bring to a boil, cover, adjust the heat to a simmer, and simmer
for 3 hours.

Put the olive oil into a pan, and when hot, add the garlic,
onions, carrots, green pepper and celery leaves. Stir and cook

for 15 minutes. Add this mixture to the beans, together with the tomatoes, bay leaf, salt, chili peppers and paprika. Stir, cover and simmer for 1 hour.

NOTE: To save time, the olive oil, vegetables and condiments may be added to the beans together with the ham bone, and the soup slowly simmered for 4 hours. However, I find the soup more flavorful if the vegetables are sautéed and then added to the beans. Experiment for yourself.

After the beans have cooked for 4 hours, remove the ham bone and bay leaf. Leave in any small lean pieces of ham, as they will be blended into the soup.

Pour the soup into a blender and blend until smooth, or put it through a food mill. Return the soup to the pot, add the butter and heat thoroughly. Just before serving add the sherry.

To serve: Pour into heated large soup bowls and garnish with a slice of lemon or a slice of hard-boiled egg.

This recipe makes approximately 3½ quarts of soup.

FAVA BEAN NOTES

Fava beans are also known as haba beans or *havas grandes* in Spanish-speaking countries, and as the broad bean, which is also known as the large lima bean. Fava beans are one of the oldest known beans; they have been eaten for sustenance by both man and beast for centuries.

Do not overcook this bean; cook until soft but not mushy. I find it extremely succulent when combined with herbs or sauces. Do try it. To cook fava beans, use the following method:

Cull 1 cup of fava beans and wash thoroughly in cold water. Bring to a boil 4½ cups of water, basic stock or chicken stock from which all fat has been removed, and slowly drop the beans into it. Cover, and reduce the heat to a simmer. Cook for 30 to 40 minutes or until tender.

If drained fava beans are used in a recipe, do not discard the liquid in which they were cooked; add it to your stockpot.

One cup of dried fava beans makes 2½ cups of cooked beans.

FAVA BEANS WITH BACON

This dish is an easy and delicious main course for either lunch or dinner. Serve it with hot cornbread and a salad.

½ lb. sliced bacon
1 large onion, peeled and finely chopped
4 medium tomatoes, peeled and coarsely chopped, or whole canned tomatoes
1 cup of basic stock or chicken stock from which all fat has been removed
1 medium clove garlic, peeled and finely chopped

1 pinch sugar
1 tsp. dried basil, or 1 tbs. fresh basil, finely chopped
2 tsps. salt
½ tsp. pepper
4 cups drained and cooked fava beans
2 tbs. parsley, finely chopped

Fry the bacon until crisp. Drain and set aside.

Put 2 tablespoons of the bacon fat into a pan, and when hot, add the onion and cook until transparent. Add the tomatoes, stock, garlic, sugar, basil, salt and pepper. Stir and bring to a boil. Reduce the heat to a simmer, and gently simmer, uncovered, for 10 minutes. Add the cooked beans. Crumble the bacon and add it together with the parsley. Stir and cook for 3 to 5 minutes until thoroughly heated.

Serve in a large heated serving dish.

Serves 6.

KIDNEY BEAN NOTES

There are red kidney beans and there are white kidney beans and, except where noted, they are interchangeable in any recipe. White kidney beans are also known as "Great Northern" beans.

There are various brands of kidney beans on the market which are boldly labeled "No Soaking Necessary." If you use this brand of beans, proceed directly with the recipe. Of course, all beans should be culled and washed before being cooked.

If the above-mentioned label does not appear on the package of beans, prepare them as follows:

Cull 1 cup of beans and wash thoroughly in cold water. In a large kettle bring to a boil 4 cups of water, basic stock or chicken stock from which all fat has been removed, and slowly drop the beans into the liquid. Boil, uncovered, for 2 minutes. Remove the kettle from the heat, cover and let stand for 2 hours. Return the ketttle to the heat, bring to a boil, cover, adjust the heat to a simmer, and simmer for 1 to 1½ hours or until the beans are tender.

If drained kidney beans are used in a recipe, do not discard the liquid in which they were cooked; add it to your stockpot.

One cup of dried kidney beans makes 2½ cups of cooked beans.

RED KIDNEY BEANS IN RED WINE

Red wine, herbs and beans are a lovely combination. This is a fine bean dish to serve as a main course or as an accompaniment to any roasted meats. I do not recommend using white kidney beans in this recipe.

3 tbs. butter	1 medium clove garlic,
1 large onion, peeled and	peeled
finely chopped	3 cups drained and
2 cups red wine	cooked red kidney
1 bay leaf	beans
Celery leaves	2 tsps. salt
Parsley sprigs	½ tsp. pepper

In a large pot, melt the butter until foaming, add the onion, stir and cook until transparent. Add the red wine. Tie the bay leaf, celery and parsley together. Add them and the garlic, cover, and simmer for 15 minutes.

Add the cooked beans, salt and pepper. Stir. Cook uncovered for 8 to 10 minutes.

Remove the bay leaf, celery, parsley and garlic.

To serve: Pour into a heated serving dish.
Serves 4 to 6.

Variation:
Add 1 cup of finely cubed sharp cheddar cheese to the beans when they are in the serving dish; toss and serve at once.

SMOKED PORK AND BEANS

*To cook 2 meals in one, double the amount of beans.
Serve half of the beans with the pork, and refrigerate the remainder for a cold bean salad, or reheat and serve later in the
week with a tomato sauce. An economical—and nutritious—dish.*

2 cups dried white kidney beans	3 tbs. fresh celery leaves, finely chopped
3 cups basic stock or ham stock from which all fat has been removed	Cold water
	2 lbs. smoked boneless pork butt (Porkette)
1 medium onion, coarsely chopped	1 tbs. scallions or parsley, finely chopped
2 tsps. salt	
1 tsp. pepper	

Cull the beans and wash thoroughly in cold water. In a
large kettle, bring the stock to a boil and slowly drop the beans
into the liquid. Boil uncovered for 2 minutes. Remove the kettle
from the heat, cover, and let stand for 2 hours. Return the kettle
to the heat, and add the onion, salt, pepper and celery leaves. If
necessary add additional hot water or stock to cover the beans
by 2 inches. Bring to a boil, cover, adjust the heat to a simmer,
and simmer for 45 minutes. Add the pork butt, replace cover and
simmer for 1½ hours. Add additional stock if needed.

To serve: Ladle the beans into a heated deep platter or
gratin dish. Carve the pork butt into ¼-inch slices and overlap
them down the center on top of the beans. Garnish with the
scallions or parsley.
Serves 6 to 8.

WHITE KIDNEY BEAN SALAD

Red kidney beans can be used in this recipe, but I prefer the white. If the recipe is made a day in advance and refrigerated, the beans marinate in the dressing, which enhances the flavor immensely.

4 cups cooked white kidney beans, thoroughly drained	1 small clove garlic, peeled and finely chopped
3 tbs. olive oil	¼ cup scallions, finely chopped
3 tbs. lemon juice	¼ cup parsley, finely chopped
1 tsp. salt	
¼ tsp. pepper	
Pinch dried basil	
¼ tsp. dried thyme	

Chill the beans. Thoroughly mix the oil, lemon juice, salt, pepper, basil, thyme, garlic, scallions and parsley. Put the beans into an attractive serving dish, and toss and mix thoroughly with the dressing. Refrigerate until ready to serve.

To serve: Toss the beans and dressing once again just before serving.
Serves 6 to 8.

RED KIDNEY BEANS WITH CHEESE

This recipe lends itself perfectly to either the red or the white kidney bean.

6 slices of bacon cut into
  1-inch pieces
1 large onion, peeled and
  finely chopped
1 cup canned tomatoes,
  drained, and if whole,
  cut into small pieces
1 cup basic stock or
  chicken stock from
  which all fat has been
  removed

2 tsps. salt
½ tsp. pepper
1 tsp. prepared mustard
2 cups cooked and
  drained red kidney
  beans
½ tsp. sugar
1 cup sharp cheddar
  cheese, diced into
  small cubes

Fry the bacon in a pan until crisp. Drain, crumble and set aside.

Heat 1 tablespoon of the bacon fat in a large pot; add the onion, stir and cook until transparent. Add the tomato, stock, salt, pepper, mustard, kidney beans and sugar. Cover, adjust the heat to a simmer, and simmer for 30 minutes.

Remove from the heat, stir in the cheese, pour into a heated serving dish and sprinkle the crumbled bacon on top. Serve at once.

Serves 4 to 6.

PEA BEAN NOTES

The pea bean is also known as the navy bean, and it is prepared as follows:

Cull 1 cup of beans and wash thoroughly in cold water. In a large kettle bring to a boil 5 cups of water, basic stock or chicken stock from which all fat has been removed, and slowly drop the beans into the liquid. Boil uncovered for 2 minutes. Remove the kettle from the heat, cover and let stand for 2 hours. Return the kettle to the heat, bring to a boil, cover, adjust the heat to a simmer, and simmer for 1½ to 2 hours or until the beans are tender.

If drained cooked pea beans are used in a recipe, don't discard the liquid in which they were cooked; add it to your stockpot.

One cup of pea beans, or navy beans, makes 3 cups of cooked beans.

PEA BEAN SOUP

Not for the calorie-counter but for anyone who enjoys a hearty, rich soup. This soup can be made with white kidney beans too. It freezes perfectly.

4 cups pea beans, cooked and drained

1 cup of the liquid in which the beans were cooked

1 cup basic stock or chicken stock from which all fat has been removed

1 tsp. lemon juice

1 tsp. salt

½ tsp. pepper

1 cup tomato sauce (canned)

1 cup cooked rice

1 cup watercress leaves, stemmed and washed

Butter

Heavy cream

Put the beans, stock and bean liquid together through a food mill or into a blender and blend until smooth. Pour the mixture into a large heavy pot, and add the lemon juice, salt, pepper, tomato sauce and rice. Stir and bring to a boil. Add the watercress leaves, stir and cook until they are wilted approximately 2 to 3 minutes.

Serve piping hot in heated individual soup bowls, and

top each serving with a small nugget of butter and a teaspoon of heavy cream.

Serves 6.

Variation:

Sorrel can be added instead of watercress and is prepared as follows:

Wash and finely shred enough fresh sorrel leaves to make ½ cup. Add them to the hot soup and simmer for 10 to 15 minutes.

PEA BEANS ITALIAN STYLE

This may be served as a first course; it is aromatic and delicious. If macaroni is added, it becomes a zestful main course.

¼ cup olive oil

1 cup parsley, finely chopped

3 medium cloves garlic, peeled and finely chopped

3 large onions, peeled and finely chopped

2 medium carrots, scrubbed and finely diced

4 slices bacon, cut into small pieces

2 tbs. dried basil, or 6 tbs. fresh basil leaves, finely chopped

1 tsp. oregano

3 large tomatoes, peeled and coarsely chopped

1 cup basic stock or chicken stock from which all fat has been removed

1 tsp. pepper

2½ tsps. salt

3 cups cooked dried pea beans

In a large pot heat the olive oil, and when hot, add the parsley, garlic, onions, carrots, bacon, basil and oregano. Stir and cook until the vegetables are soft. Add the tomatoes, stock, pepper and salt. Cover, and simmer over a low heat for 10 minutes or until the vegetables are tender. Add the cooked beans, toss and stir until the beans are hot and thoroughly mixed with the vegetables.

Serve in a heated serving dish.

Serves 6.

Variation:

Add 1 cup cooked small elbow macaroni which has been mixed with a generous amount of butter and ½ cup grated Parmesan cheese. The macaroni should be added at the same time the beans are added to the vegetables.

PINTO BEAN AND PINK BEAN NOTES

Pinto beans and pink beans are products of Mexico and the Southwest. The pinto bean is speckled and slightly larger than the pink bean. The pink bean is lighter in color than the red kidney bean and smaller in size.

From where I sit, pinto beans and pink beans can be used interchangeably in any recipe.

The dried pinto and pink beans were the main fare for the pioneers of the Southwest. The beans did not spoil, they were easy to transport and they provided abundant nourishment. On long cattle or sheep drives, and at roundup time, the beans were cooked in the cast-iron Dutch ovens. At dawn the beans, which had been put to soak the night before, were put into the Dutch oven, together with water and whatever dried or fresh meat was available, and brought to a good boil on the breakfast campfire. Then a hole was dug in the ground, and the glowing wood coals were shoveled into it. The cover was placed on the pot of beans, and the pot was lowered into the hole to nestle directly into the bed of coals. Earth was shoveled over the pot, and the beans cooked slowly throughout the day. At grub time the beans were tender and ready to eat.

An interesting aside about the old black cast-iron pots: these pots were standard equipment in most country kitchens 50 years ago. Besides their practical use they supplied, unbeknownst to their owners, additional nutriment in their diets. It has been ascertained that the bits and specks of rust, which all these pots develop, were incorporated into the cooked foods and gave the family an extra dose of iron. Maybe that is why they had so much energy! At any rate, if your modern cast-iron pot shows a few specks of rust, let them be absorbed into the food and your family will be getting a supplement of iron. Of course, to care for these cast-iron pots properly, they should be treated with a vegetable oil, washed, rinsed and dried immediately after every use.

Pinto beans and pink beans are cooked as follows: Cull 1 cup of beans and wash thoroughly in cold water. In a large kettle bring to a boil 4 cups of water, basic stock or chicken stock from which all fat has been removed, and slowly drop the beans into the liquid. Boil, uncovered, for 2 minutes. Remove the kettle from the heat, cover and let stand for 2 hours. Return the kettle to the heat, bring to a boil, cover, adjust the heat to a simmer, and simmer for 1 to 1½ hours, or until the beans are tender.

If drained pinto beans or pink beans are used in a recipe, don't discard the liquid in which they were cooked; add it to your stockpot.

One cup of dried pinto beans makes 3 cups of cooked beans.

One cup of dried pink beans makes 3 cups of cooked beans.

PINTO BEAN SOUP

Here is an authentic Mexican soup, and a good one it is! It is a splendid first course for any meal, and if you have a supply of pinto beans in the freezer, it can be prepared on a moment's notice. I prefer it with the croutons instead of the cream.

3 tbs. butter
1 medium onion, peeled and finely chopped
1 small clove garlic, peeled and finely chopped
2 cups pinto beans, cooked and drained

2 cups basic stock or chicken stock from which all fat has been removed
2 tsps. salt
½ tsp. pepper
½ cup tomato juice
Croutons, or heavy cream

Put the butter into a saucepan and heat, and when foaming add the onion and garlic. Cook and stir until the onion is transparent. Add the cooked pinto beans, stock, salt and pepper. Bring to a boil, cover, adjust the heat to a simmer, and simmer for 15 minutes.* Put the mixture through a food mill, or put it in a blender and blend until smooth. Return the soup to the pan and add the tomato juice. Heat thoroughly.

To serve: Pour into heated individual soup bowls and serve with croutons, or top each bowl with a generous teaspoon of heavy cream.

Serves 6.

* If frozen cooked beans are used, simmer 20 to 25 minutes.

CHILI BEANS

This is a good hot chili, so if you prefer a blander chili, use less chili powder. If you have a supply of frozen pinto beans on hand, this is an easy dish to prepare for a hearty Sunday night supper. Serve it with hot cornbread and a mixed green salad.

¼ lb. salt pork, cut into small cubes
2 large onions, peeled and finely chopped
3 medium cloves garlic, peeled and finely chopped
1 tsp. salt
½ tsp. pepper
2 tbs. chili powder
1 6 oz.-can tomato paste
1 8 oz.-can tomato sauce
1 tsp. dried oregano
¼ tsp. cumin
3 cups cooked pinto beans
1 cup of the stock in which the beans were cooked, or basic stock or chicken stock from which all fat has been removed
1 tsp. sugar

Put the pork cubes in a large heavy pot and cook them until they are nicely browned. Add the onions and stir and cook until they are transparent. Add the garlic, salt, pepper, chili powder, tomato paste, tomato sauce, oregano, cumin, beans, stock and sugar. Stir well. Bring to a boil, cover, adjust the heat to a simmer, and simmer for 2 hours. Stir occasionally.

Serve in a large heated serving dish or in heated individual bowls.

Serves 6 to 8.

FRIED PINK BEANS

Quick and easy. And a nice way to use up any leftover baked ham. Additional chili powder may be added if you like a stronger flavor.

4 tbs. vegetable oil	1½ cups finely cubed
4 tbs. butter	cooked ham
1 large onion, peeled	½ tsp. salt
and finely chopped	½ tsp. pepper
3 cups cooked and	¼ tsp. chili powder
drained pink beans	

In a large frying pan melt the oil and butter, and when hot, add the onion and stir and cook until transparent. Add the cooked beans, ham, salt, pepper and chili powder. Stir and fry 8 to 10 minutes over a medium heat. Do not let the beans brown.

Serve at once in a heated serving dish.

Serves 6.

SOYBEAN NOTES

These are truly "miracle beans." Besides many other nutrients, they contain 97% protein and are known as "the meat of the soil." These beans have been cultivated and consumed by civilizations of the Far East for the past 5,000 years, and were brought to this country in the middle of the nineteenth century. I wish a few of the Eastern recipes had been imported with them.

The Western world has only recently begun to appreciate the versatility of these beans. A few of the food products made from them are flour, cheese, paste, milk and sauce. In addition to being a part of man's diet, they have innumerable important uses in agriculture, industry and medicine.

These beans can be boiled or baked; served hot or cold. Their nutritional value is high and their cost is low. The flavor of the soybeans is determined by the condiments and sauces in which they are cooked. Without any added flavorings they are, like pastas, bland and tasteless. They are a food that you and your family should be enjoying regularly.

And enjoying them regularly may soon become a national habit because of the development within the last ten years of "analogs" (so named because the textured vegetable protein is supposedly analogous to meat protein). Analogs are foods made from soybeans that look and taste like roast beef, ham, turkey, fish (which flakes when served), bacon and even fresh strawberries. These foods are made by processing the minute fibers of the beans and then spinning them to simulate the textures of meats and other foods. As these fibers are tasteless and colorless, synthetic colorings and flavorings are added. These foods are, of course, high in protein, economical, and have only to be heated before serving. I am told they are delicious. I feel they have an important place in institutional kitchens and certain diets. However, if analogs were served as a steady diet, I would become quite concerned about the synthetic flavorings and colorings added to them; how healthful are they?

For the present I prefer starting from scratch in my home with my own pot of soybeans and adding my own natural condiments and flavorings.

To prepare soybeans, cull 1 cup of them and wash thoroughly in cold water. In a large kettle, bring to a boil 5 cups of water, basic stock or chicken stock from which all fat has been removed, and slowly drop in the soybeans. Boil for 2 minutes. Remove from the fire, cover and let stand for 2 hours. Return to the fire, bring to a boil and cover. Adjust the heat to a simmer, and simmer for 2½ to 3 hours or until the soybeans are tender. Remove and discard any loose bean skins.

If drained cooked soybeans are used in a recipe, don't discard the liquid in which they were cooked; add it to your stockpot.

One cup of dried soybeans makes approximately 3½ cups of cooked soybeans.

STEAMED SOYBEANS AND CRACKED WHEAT

Do you enjoy a meatless dinner? If so, this is a splendid entrée. Serve it with a green salad and crusty French bread.

½ cup uncooked dried soybeans

2 cups of basic stock or beef stock from which all fat has been removed, or water

3 tbs. butter

1 medium onion, peeled and finely chopped

1 medium green pepper, with the white membranes and seeds removed, finely diced

1 cup of cracked wheat
2-quart metal mold
Butter

2 tsps. salt

1 tsp. pepper

3 tbs. parsley, finely chopped

½ tsp. Tabasco Sauce

6 fresh tomatoes peeled and coarsely chopped, or whole canned tomatoes coarsely chopped

1 tsp. ground cumin

1 cup feta cheese, crumbled

Cull and wash the soybeans. Bring 1 cup of the stock or water to a boil and slowly add the beans; boil for 2 minutes, cover, remove from the heat and set aside for 2 hours.

Drain the soybeans over a container. Pour ½ cup of the

liquid into a blender, add the beans and blend. Blend into coarse small pieces, not to a mush. Save the rest of the bean liquid for the stockpot.

Put the butter into a pan and heat, and when foaming, add the onion and green pepper; stir and cook until tender. Add the cracked wheat. Stir and cook over a low heat for 2 minutes. Bring the other cup of stock or water to a boil and add to the cracked-wheat mixture. Stir, cover and set aside until all the liquid is absorbed by the cracked wheat. This will take about 5 minutes.

Thoroughly butter the 2-quart metal mold and set aside.

Put the blended soybeans into a bowl, add the cracked wheat mixture, salt, pepper, parsley and Tabasco Sauce. Stir thoroughly.

In a small bowl, mix the chopped tomatoes and cumin.

Spoon half of the soybean mixture into the buttered mold. Sprinkle half of the feta cheese over it and add half of the tomatoes. Spoon the balance of the mixture into the mold, and cover it with the rest of the cheese and tomatoes. Cover tightly. Steam (see *Steaming Directions for Molds*, pp. 302–304) for 1½ to 2 hours or until done.

When done, remove the cover and run a knife around the edge of the mixture. Gently ease it into a heated serving dish (this recipe does not make a firm mold).

Serves 6.

SOYBEAN AND HAM SOUP

This soup is a rich full meal. A bowl of it served to hungry children after school is nourishing and satisfying. I like to serve it with Steamed Molasses Cornmeal Bread; the flavors of each are nicely complemented.

3½ cups cooked soy- beans, and the water in which they were cooked

1½ to 2 lbs. ham bone

4 cups basic stock or chicken stock from which all fat has been removed

2 tsps. salt

½ tsp. paprika

¼ tsp. cayenne pepper

4 large stalks of celery, washed and finely chopped

2 large onions, peeled and finely chopped

1½ cups of canned tomatoes

¼ cup parsley, finely chopped

In a large pot put the soybeans and the water in which they were cooked (which should be approximately 3 to 4 cups), the ham bone, stock, salt, paprika, and cayenne pepper. Bring to a boil, cover, adjust the heat to a simmer, and simmer for ½ hour. Add the celery, onions, tomatoes and parsley, and stir. Cover and simmer for 1 hour.

To serve: Remove the ham bone to a plate. Remove the ham from the bone and cut it into small cubes. Return the ham pieces to the soup, and serve in large heated soup bowls.

Serves 6 to 8.

SOYBEANS WITH MUSHROOMS

This dish pleasantly complements roast beef or a roasted chicken. It can be frozen without loss of flavor or texture.

3 *tbs. vegetable oil*	½ *lb. mushrooms, washed and coarsely chopped*
2 *tbs. butter*	
3 *medium onions, peeled and finely chopped*	4 *cups soybeans, cooked and drained*
2 *medium green peppers, seeded, cored and cut into strips*	2 *tsps. salt*
	1 *tsp. pepper*
1 *large clove garlic, peeled and finely chopped*	4 *tbs. parsley, finely chopped*

In a large pan, put the oil and butter, and when hot, add the onions, peppers and garlic. Cook and stir until the onions are transparent. Add the mushrooms and toss and stir 3 minutes. Add the cooked soybeans, salt and pepper, and toss and stir until the soybeans are thoroughly heated.

To serve: Spoon into a heated serving dish and sprinkle the parsley over the top.

Serves 6.

SOYBEAN PURÉE

This is a delicate and refined purée. It is a suitable accompaniment to any roast meat or fowl.

2 cups cooked soybeans,
 drained
¾ cup of the liquid in
 which the beans were
 cooked
3 tbs. butter

1½ tsps. salt
1 pinch cayenne pepper
¼ tsp. grated nutmeg
1 tbs. chives, or
 parsley, finely
 chopped

Blend the soybeans and liquid in a blender until they are smooth or put them through a food mill, adding the liquid bit by bit. Pour this mixture into a saucepan and add the butter, salt, cayenne pepper and nutmeg. Stir continuously until the purée comes to a boil.

To serve: Spoon the purée into a heated serving dish and garnish with the chives or parsley.
Serves 4 to 6.

BLACK-EYED PEA NOTES

There is a legend in the South that if you eat black-eyed peas on New Year's Day, good luck will be yours throughout the coming year. Whether you eat them on this holiday to assuage the gods or not, it is a lovely dish that goes particularly well with ham or pork.

To prepare black-eyed peas: Cull 1 cup of dried black-eyed peas and wash thoroughly in cold water. Bring to a boil 4 cups of water, basic stock or chicken stock from which all fat has been removed, and slowly drop the peas into it. Boil for 2 minutes. Remove from the heat, cover, and let stand for 2 hours. Return to the heat, bring to a boil, cover and adjust the heat to a simmer, and simmer for 30 minutes or until the peas are tender.

One cup of dried black-eyed peas makes 2½ cups of cooked peas.

BLACK-EYED PEAS WITH HAM

This dish is far above the category of a "leftover," but good menu-planning makes it an ideal dish to serve if you are wondering how to use up the rest of that baked ham.

4 tbs. butter	6 cups cooked black-eyed peas
1 large onion, peeled and thinly sliced	½ cup of the liquid in which the peas were cooked
2 cups canned tomatoes (1 16-oz. can); if the tomatoes are whole cut them into small pieces	6 medium slices baked ham
1 tsp. dried basil	2 tbs. parsley, finely chopped
½ tsp. dried thyme	
2 tsps. salt	
½ tsp. pepper	

Put the butter into a pan and heat, and when foaming, add the onion and cook and stir until transparent. Add the tomatoes, basil, thyme, salt and pepper. Cook over a low heat, stirring occasionally, until it is a thick sauce. Add the cooked black-eyed peas and the half cup of liquid in which they were cooked; toss and stir until the sauce is well mixed with the peas. Place the ham slices on top, cover, and simmer over a low heat until the ham slices are heated through.

To serve: Remove the ham slices to a plate and pour the peas into a heated serving dish; place the ham slices on top and sprinkle with the parsley.
Serves 6.

CHICK-PEA NOTES

These peas, which to me look more like a nut than a pea, are widely used in South American cooking where they are called *las garbanzas.*

Cooked chick-peas are a pleasant addition to soups, stews and casseroles, and when marinated in a French dressing, make a good salad. I find that chick-peas are quite bland, so be certain to add plenty of seasoning.

To prepare chick-peas: Cull 1 cup of chick-peas and wash thoroughly in cold water. Bring to a hard boil 4 cups of water, basic stock or chicken stock from which all fat has been removed, and slowly drop in the chick-peas. Boil for 2 or 3 minutes. Remove from the heat, cover, and let stand for 2 hours. Return to the stove, bring to a boil, adjust the heat to a simmer, and simmer for 1½ hours or until tender.

If drained chick-peas are used in a recipe, don't discard the liquid in which they were cooked; add it to your stockpot.

One cup of dried chick-peas makes 2 cups of cooked chick-peas.

PURÉE OF CHICK-PEAS

The French consider the chick-pea the perfect ingredient for a purée, and I must say that I agree with them. It is delicious. Serve it with any meat or poultry. If your chick-peas are cooked, the purée can be prepared in 5 minutes.

4 cups cooked chick-peas	3 tbs. butter
1¼ cups of the water in which the chick-peas were cooked	4 tbs. heavy cream
	1 tsp. dried basil
	2 tsps. salt
	¼ tsp. cayenne pepper

In a blender, blend the chick-peas with the water until it is a smooth mixture.

In a saucepan melt the butter, add the blended chick-peas, cream, basil, salt and pepper. Stir and cook over a low heat until it comes to a boil; continue to stir and cook for 3 or 4 minutes.

To serve: Pour into a heated serving dish.
Serves 6.

Variation:
Add ¼ tsp. of curry powder.

LENTIL AND SPLIT PEA NOTES

I have been unable to locate in my neighborhood markets any package of dried lentils or green or yellow split peas that is not marked "Fast Cooking" or "No Soaking Necessary."

To cook the "fast cooking" lentils or split peas, wash 1 cup of lentils or peas thoroughly in cold water, put them into a pot and add 3 cups of cold water, basic stock or chicken stock from which all fat has been removed. Bring to a boil, cover, adjust the heat to a simmer, and simmer for 45 minutes or until the lentils or peas are tender.

If "fast cooking" lentils or split peas are not available in your market, cook them as follows: Wash them in cold water. Put them in a pot and cover them by 1 inch with cold water or chicken stock from which all fat has been removed, and soak for 2 hours. Place the pot on the stove, cover, bring to a boil, adjust the heat to a simmer, and simmer for 1 to 1½ hours or until tender.

If you have a good supply of stock on hand, I urge you to use it to cook lentils or split peas; at least use half stock and half water, as they really are so much tastier if all, or part, of the liquid in which they are cooked is stock.

If drained cooked lentils or split peas are used in a recipe, don't discard the liquid in which they were cooked; add it to your stockpot.

One cup of dried lentils or split peas make 2¼ cups of cooked lentils or split peas.

CURRIED LENTILS

A fine combination; serve it cold as an appetizer, or serve it hot with a succulent roasted leg of lamb.

4 tbs. butter
4 medium onions, peeled and finely chopped
2 tbs. curry powder
2 cups basic stock or chicken stock from which all fat has been removed
2 tsps. salt
½ tsp. pepper
2 cups cooked lentils
1 tbs. lemon juice
½ cup sour cream
1 small head iceberg lettuce, shredded
Parsley or chives, finely chopped

Heat the butter in a medium-sized pot, and when foaming, add the onions; stir and cook until transparent. Add the curry powder and cook over a low heat for 5 minutes, stirring often. Add the stock, salt, pepper, and cooked lentils. Stir and cook uncovered over a low heat until the lentils have the consistency of a purée, but they should not be mashed. Remove from the fire and stir in the lemon juice.

To serve cold: Spoon the lentils into a bowl and chill thoroughly. Arrange the shredded lettuce on 6 individual plates and place a serving of lentils on each. Top with a generous spoonful of sour cream, and garnish with the parsley or chives.

To serve hot: Spoon the lentils into a heated serving dish, garnish with the parsley or chives, and omit the lettuce and sour cream.

Serves 6.

LENTILS WITH SHORT RIBS OF BEEF

Do cook the short ribs early in the morning or on the day before so that they may become thoroughly cooled. This makes it easy to remove the fat from the meat and broth and to cut the meat into neat cubes. This is a highly nutritious and toothsome dish.

4 *lbs. short ribs of beef*	2½ *tsps. salt*
6 *cups basic stock, or beef stock from which all fat has been removed*	¼ *tsp. dried thyme*
	2 *cups cooked tomatoes (one 16-oz. can)*
2 *stalks celery, washed, and cut into 1-inch pieces*	1½ *cups lentils, culled and washed in cold water*
3 *medium cloves of garlic, peeled and finely chopped*	6 *medium potatoes, peeled*
½ *cup dry red wine*	2 *tbs. parsley, finely chopped*
1 *bay leaf*	
½ *tsp. pepper*	

Put the short ribs, stock, celery, garlic, wine, bay leaf, pepper, salt and thyme into a large pot. Bring to a boil, adjust the heat to a simmer, and simmer 1 hour and 45 minutes.

Remove the pot from the stove and, with tongs or a fork, remove the meat to a plate. Cool the broth and meat. When cool, remove the fat from the broth and cut all the excess fat from the meat. Cut the meat into 3-inch cubes. If any of the bones are still attached to the meat, leave them on; discard any bones which have fallen away from the meat.

Return the meat to the broth. If the tomatoes are whole, slice them into strips and add them, together with their juice, to the meat. Bring to a boil, add the lentils, and adjust the heat to a simmer; cover pot with a loose-fitting lid and cook for 45 minutes or until the lentils are tender.

While the lentils are cooking, boil the potatoes until tender.

To serve: Spoon the meat and lentils into a large heated serving dish and surround them with the potatoes. Sprinkle the parsley over the entire dish.

Serves 6.

LENTIL SOUP

A fine soup for any time of the year. It freezes well, and there are so many variations possible in serving it that, with a quart or two on hand, a nutritious and tasteful dinner can be rapidly prepared.

1 lb. dried lentils
7 cups cold water
1 ham bone
2 stalks celery, washed and coarsely chopped
2 carrots, washed and quartered
2 medium onions, peeled and coarsely chopped

1 small clove garlic, peeled and chopped
4 tsps. salt
1 tsp. pepper
3 sprigs parsley
1 small bay leaf
2 tbs. lemon juice
2 cups basic stock or ham stock from which all fat has been removed

Wash lentils and put them into a large heavy pot. Add all the other ingredients except the stock. Stir. Put a loose-fitting lid on top of the pot, bring to a boil, adjust heat to a simmer, and simmer for 45 minutes to 1 hour. Remove the ham bone.

Put the soup through a food mill and don't be lazy in extracting all the goodness from the lentils; you should have to discard no more than the tough husks.

Return the purée to the pot and add the stock. Stir and bring to a boil.

This recipe makes 2 quarts.

To serve: Select one of the following variations:

a) Add neatly diced cubes of cooked ham.

b) Add frankfurters cut in ½-inch pieces and simmered 10 minutes in the soup.

c) Serve with croutons (see p. 103).

d) Float a thin lemon slice on each bowl.

e) To each quart of soup, add 1 cup of light cream, stir, heat and serve.

GREEN OR YELLOW SPLIT PEA SOUP

These tasty peas can be substituted for one another in any recipe, and what good soup they make!

2 cups of green or yellow split peas	1 large onion, peeled and quartered
10 cups basic stock or chicken stock from which all fat has been removed	1 ham bone
	2 tsps. salt
	1 tsp. pepper
	Diced ham

Wash the peas thoroughly in cold water. Put them into a large pot with the stock, onion and ham bone. Bring to a boil, stir, cover pot with a loose-fitting lid, and adjust the heat to a simmer. Simmer for 1½ to 2 hours or until the peas are tender.

When the peas are tender, remove the ham bone as well as any loose pieces of ham. Cut the ham from the bone and set aside.

Put the peas and stock through a food mill. Do not blend in a blender. Pour the soup back into the pot, and add the salt and pepper. Neatly dice the ham into small cubes and add to the soup. Stir and bring to a boil.

To serve: Pour into a heated tureen or into heated individual soup bowls.

Serves 6 to 8.

BARLEY NOTES

This is one of the most hardy of all cereals, and it has been cultivated since ancient times. It can be served as a soup or added to any meat or vegetable soup, as well as to chowders, stews and casseroles. It is so nutritious that the water in which it is cooked is often fed to infants.

Barley has many uses, but it does require an hour or more cooking time. Therefore, I always cook up the amount given in the following recipe. After it is cooked and cooled, I spoon it into 1-cup containers and freeze it. In this way I have "instant barley" on hand. When frozen, it can be added directly to any soup or stew, or it can be defrosted at room temperature.

To prepare barley, put 7 cups of water, basic stock or chicken stock from which all fat has been removed into a large kettle, and bring to a boil. When boiling, add 1 cup of barley, stir, and cover. Adjust the heat to a simmer, and simmer for 1 hour or until the barley is tender. Drain into a container, and freeze the barley water for the stockpot.

One cup of uncooked barley makes approximately 4 cups of cooked barley.

BARLEY SOUP

This is an adaptation of an old Viennese recipe, and it is just marvelous. If you have a supply of cooked frozen barley and stock on hand, this soup can be prepared in 8 minutes.

8 cups of basic stock or chicken stock from which all fat has been removed	3 tbs. flour
	1 tbs. lemon juice
	1½ tsps. salt
	½ cup milk
3 cups cooked barley	2 egg yolks
3 tbs. butter	Thin lemon slices

Pour the stock into a pot, add the cooked barley, and bring to a boil. Put this mixture through a food mill or preferably, blend it in a blender until smooth.

Meanwhile, melt the butter in a large kettle, add the flour, stir and cook over a low heat until well mixed. Don't let the flour brown. Pour the blended barley and stock slowly into the butter and flour, stirring continuously, and cook until thickened. Add the lemon juice and salt.

In a small bowl, beat the milk and egg yolks lightly and slowly pour them into the hot soup, stirring continuously. Stir and cook for 2 or 3 minutes, remove from heat and serve.

To serve: Pour into a heated tureen, or into heated individual soup bowls. Garnish each serving with a lemon slice.
Serves 6 to 7.

YOGURT AND BARLEY SOUP

So nutritious. The yogurt gives this soup a zest which is a nice contrast to the bland smooth taste of barley. The mint adds sparkle.

1 tbs. butter

1 small onion, peeled and finely chopped

4 cups basic stock or chicken stock from which all fat has been removed

2 cups cooked barley

1 egg

2 cups plain yogurt

2 tbs. parsley, finely chopped

1 tsp. salt

½ tsp. pepper

3 or 4 fresh mint leaves, finely chopped, or ½ tsp. dried mint leaves

Heat the butter in a pan; when foaming, add the onion, and cook and stir until transparent. Do not brown the onion. Add the stock and cooked barley; bring to a boil, cover, adjust the heat to a simmer, and simmer for 10 minutes.

Meanwhile beat the egg and yogurt together, and slowly pour it into the stock, stirring all the while. Continue stirring until the soup is thoroughly heated; do not boil. Add the parsley, salt, pepper and mint.

Serve in a heated tureen or in heated individual soup bowls.

To reheat the soup, pour into a double boiler.

Serves 6.

COUSCOUS

Sometimes spelled "kouskous"—but whichever spelling is used, it is semolina, which has been a North African specialty for a long time. Semolina is made with cereals, mostly wheat, milled to various grades of coarseness. In parts of North Africa it is cooked in a couscous receptacle, which is an earthenware or metal steamer. However, the couscous I'm able to find on the American market is so finely ground that to hold it in any of our traditional steamers would be an impossibility.

Couscous has a variety of culinary uses: as a cereal with cream and sugar; as an accompaniment to lamb, chicken or beef; and as a main dish mixed with ground or cubed meats. Also, it can be cooked in fruit juices with sugar and mixed with nuts and raisins to be served as a dessert.

I find it especially nice to serve with lamb. If you plan to serve it with a meat, I recommend that it be cooked in a stock.

To cook couscous, bring to a boil 2 cups of basic stock, lamb stock from which all fat has been removed, or water, and slowly pour in 1 cup of couscous. Add 2 tablespoons of butter and 1 teaspoon of salt, stir and boil for 2 or 3 minutes until nearly all the liquid is absorbed. Remove from the fire, cover securely and let sit for 10 to 15 minutes. Stir it up with a fork before serving.

Serves 6.

One cup of uncooked couscous makes 3 cups of cooked couscous.

CORNMEAL NOTES

Cornmeal is a real American grain so "ingrained" in our diet that it needs no introduction. I found the following century-old steamed cornmeal bread recipe and it is so delicious I hope you will try it. If you like a strong molasses flavor, use a blackstrap molasses to make this bread. If not, use any unsulphured molasses.

CORNMEAL BREAD

This bread is marvelous hot or cold, and it can be frozen without any loss of flavor or texture.

Butter	2 *cups yellow cornmeal*
1 *2-quart metal mold*	1½ *cups milk*
1 *cup all-purpose flour*	1 *cup molasses*
1 *tsp. baking soda*	1 *egg*
½ *tsp. salt*	¼ *cup melted butter*

Generously butter the mold and set aside.

Sift the flour together with the baking soda and salt into a mixing bowl. Add the cornmeal, milk and molasses. Mix well. Beat the egg and add it to the mixture. Add the melted butter and mix it in well. Pour this batter into the prepared mold, cover and steam (see *Steaming Directions for Molds*, pp. 302–304) for 3 hours.

To serve: Remove the cover of the mold and run a knife around the edges; place a plate on top and turn the mold upside down. Remove the mold and serve.

Serves 6 to 8.

CRACKED WHEAT NOTES

This grain has a lovely flavor. Its name is *bulghur* or *ala* in the Middle East, where it is one of the staple foods. It can be served at any meal in place of rice; it can be mixed with mushrooms, onions, green peppers and any ground or diced meats. It can be added to soups, stews, stuffings—and a half cup of cooked cracked wheat tossed into a green salad adds a very special taste.

To prepare cracked wheat, melt 2 tablespoons of butter in a pan and add 1 cup of cracked wheat. Stir until the grains are covered with butter. Add 2 cups of boiling water, basic stock or chicken stock from which all fat has been removed, and ½ teaspoon of salt. Cover, adjust the heat to a simmer, and simmer for 15 to 20 minutes or until all the liquid is absorbed and the cracked wheat is tender. Stir up with a fork.

Serves 6.

One cup of uncooked cracked wheat makes 3½ cups of cooked cracked wheat.

CRACKED-WHEAT PILAF

This rich and full-flavored dish is an excellent accompaniment to meats or poultry. I think you will find it a welcome change from the usual rice or potato dishes.

3 *cups basic stock or chicken stock from which all fat has been removed*	1 *small green pepper, cored, seeded and finely chopped*
1 *cup cracked wheat*	¼ *cup raisins*
3 *tbs. butter*	1 *tsp. salt*
1 *medium onion, peeled and finely chopped*	¼ *tsp. pepper*

Bring the stock to a boil, add the cracked wheat, cover, and cook over a low heat 20 to 25 minutes or until the cracked wheat is tender and all the stock is absorbed.

Meanwhile, melt the butter in a pan, add the onion and green pepper, stir and cook until the onion and pepper are soft; add the raisins and stir and cook for 2 or 3 minutes. Add this mixture to the cooked, cracked wheat; add the salt and pepper. Stir up with a fork.

To serve: Turn into a heated serving dish.

Serves 6.

CRACKED WHEAT AND BROCCOLI

This is a pleasant switch from potatoes or rice. It goes well with either a chicken or meat entrée.

3 cups basic stock or
chicken stock from
which all fat has been
removed
2 tbs. vegetable oil or
butter
1 tsp. garlic, finely
chopped
1 cup cracked wheat

1 cup fresh or frozen
broccoli, finely
chopped
3 fresh tomatoes
peeled and coarsely
chopped, or whole
canned tomatoes
1½ tsps. salt
½ tsp. pepper

Bring the stock to a boil.

Heat the oil or butter in a pan, and when hot add the cracked wheat and stir and cook until all the grains are thoroughly coated. Add the garlic and boiling stock. Cover, and cook over a low heat for 10 minutes. Add the broccoli, tomatoes, salt and pepper. Stir, cover and cook for 15 minutes or until all the liquid has been absorbed by the cracked wheat.

To serve: Spoon into a heated dish and serve.
Serves 6.

Variation:
Add 10 to 12 stemmed whole cherry tomatoes instead of the large tomatoes; do not peel or chop them.

KASHA NOTES

Kasha, which has a sweet nutty flavor, is the Russian name for buckwheat groats. It is a staple food in middle Europe and the

Middle East. It is sold in three grades: small, medium and coarse. I find each equally tasty.

On almost every package and in practically every recent cookbook, the recipe for cooking kasha requires an egg. It is an excellent recipe, but if you wish to omit the egg, try the following recipe, which I find very good too.

Vegetable oil	2 *tbs. butter*
1 *cup of kasha*	2 *tsps. salt*
3 *cups of boiling basic*	½ *tsp. pepper*
stock or beef stock from	
which all fat has been	
removed, or water	

Oil a heavy pan, preferably a black cast-iron Dutch oven which has a snug-fitting lid, and heat it until it is smoking. Add the kasha, and with a large metal spoon, stir vigorously and cook until the grains are toasted; be very careful not to burn them. When toasted, add the boiling stock or water, butter, salt and pepper. Cover, reduce the heat to a simmer, and simmer 10 to 12 minutes or until all the liquid is absorbed and the kasha is tender.

Serves 6.

One cup of uncooked kasha makes approximately 3½ cups cooked kasha.

KASHA WITH MUSHROOMS

I find this a good dish to serve with a baked ham or a roasted leg of lamb.

3 tbs. butter
1 tbs. vegetable oil
1 medium onion, peeled
    and finely chopped

½ lb. mushrooms,
    washed and finely
    sliced
3½ cups cooked kasha
1 tsp. salt

Put the butter and oil into a pot, and when hot, add the onion, stir and cook until it is transparent. Add the mushrooms, stir and cook 2 to 3 minutes. With a fork, stir the kasha into the onions and mushrooms and heat through.

To serve: Spoon into a heated serving dish.
Serves 6.

RICE NOTES

I have not included any white-rice recipes in this chapter, since the method of preparing this lovely common grain is universally known.

Brown rice, which is unpolished white rice, is considered more healthful and can be substituted in practically all white-rice recipes. However, more cooking time is required for brown rice.

Wild rice is the caviar of all grains. It is harvested mainly from the lakes in northern Minnesota. When it is properly prepared, it flowers, and by just a little stretch of the imagination, each grain resembles a fleur-de-lis.

When wild rice is done it should be moist, with all the grains separate, not mushy. It is particularly good with poultry and game. When cooked, it can be used in stuffings or added to a soup. Also, it freezes perfectly, but it should be reheated in a steamer or in the top of a double boiler.

I recommend that wild rice be given two hot washes instead of one. This method cleans it more thoroughly and increases the flowering.

Prepare wild rice as follows: Wash 1 cup of wild rice thoroughly in cold water. Put it in a pan and add 3 cups of hot water. Bring it to a boil and boil for 2 minutes. Remove it from the fire and pour it through a strainer. Return it to the pan, add 3 cups of hot water and bring to a boil. Boil for 2 minutes, strain, and rinse quickly under the hot-water faucet. Return the rice to the pan and add either 3 cups of hot basic stock, chicken stock from which all fat has been removed or water. Bring to a boil, cover, adjust the heat to a simmer, and simmer for 25 to 30 minutes or until the rice is tender. Drain into a container and save the water for the stockpot.

One cup of uncooked wild rice makes 3 cups of cooked rice.

SIMPLE BROWN RICE

A sturdy dish which can accompany meat or fowl.

2 tbs. oil	2 cups basic stock or
1 tbs. butter	beef stock from
2 medium onions,	which all fat has been
peeled and finely	removed
chopped	2½ tsps. salt
1½ cups brown rice	½ tsp. pepper
1½ cups tomato juice	

Put the oil and butter into a pot, and when it is hot add the onions; stir and cook until they are transparent. Add the rice, and stir until each grain is covered with the oil and butter.

Meanwhile, pour the tomato juice and stock into a pan and bring to a boil. When boiling, add it to the onions and rice; add the salt and pepper and stir. Adjust the heat to a simmer, cover, and cook for 45 minutes, or until all the liquid is absorbed by the rice. Do not remove the cover or stir while the rice is cooking.

> *To serve:* Spoon the rice into a heated serving dish.
> Serves 6.

WILD RICE AND MUSHROOMS

How well mushrooms complement wild rice! This is a very special dish and should be served only on a festive occasion.

3 cups cooked wild rice	1 tsp. lemon juice
4 tbs. butter	2 tsps. salt
1½ tbs. shallots, peeled and finely chopped	½ tsp. pepper
¼ lb. mushrooms, washed and coarsely chopped	

Put the wild rice into the top of a double boiler and heat.

Melt the butter in a pan and add the shallots; cook and stir over a low heat until they are transparent. Add the mushrooms and lemon juice. Cook and stir for 5 minutes. With a fork, stir this mixture into the heated wild rice, add the salt and pepper, and stir until thoroughly mixed.

Serve in a heated serving dish.

Serves 6.

(9) DESSERTS

DESSERT NOTES

A cookbook without a chapter of desserts is like a romantic novel without a happy ending.

In compiling this book of stock recipes, I felt it appropriate to add a few desserts that could be cooked in the stockpot. These are the steamed puddings. Cooking a dessert by steam is much easier than cooking it in the oven. All that is demanded is that sufficient water be in the pot to make the steam. Puddings may be held for an hour or two after the cooking time has elapsed; turn off the heat, leave the mold in the covered steamer, and the pudding will be warm and light when it is unmolded.

Other desserts are included, and except for the Savoy Trifle, they all are prepared on top of the stove.

To whip cream without failure, put a few cubes of ice into a large metal bowl, pour the cream to be whipped into a smaller-size metal bowl, place over the ice, and beat.

STEAMING DIRECTIONS FOR MOLDS

Equipment: Metal molds are used for steaming; they are called pudding molds, and are available in various forms. A coffee or lard can, a ring mold or any metal pan can be converted into a mold. If the mold has no cover, substitute a layer of aluminum foil. The foil should overlap the top by 1 inch and be tied tightly with string. The steam should not seep into the mold.

Molds are available in sizes from ½-cup capacity to 4 quarts. For most recipes in this book, only 1- or 2-quart molds are required.

The rack, or trivet, is the rest on which the mold sits. It may be a trivet, a cake rack, a roasting rack, an opened steam basket or any perforated metal stand. Its legs should be at least ¼ inch in height.

The container for steaming the mold should be a large pot with a secure lid. The lid should not fit tightly, because a small amount of steam should escape. If the pot lid has an indentation in the center which touches the top of the mold, invert the lid, place it on top of the pot, and place a light weight on it to keep it in place.

Preparation of Mold: The mold should be buttered, sugared or floured according to the directions given in the recipe. It should not be filled more than two-thirds full. A mold of a larger capacity may be substituted for a smaller mold—but remember, never fill a mold to the brim, or part of the ingredients will ooze out into the water.

Steaming: Put 4 to 6 inches of water into the pot. Bring the water to a boil. Adjust the heat to a slow boil. Place the rack or trivet into the pot. The water should cover the rack and come quarter or halfway up the sides of the mold. Place the mold on the rack; it should sit comfortably inside the pot, leaving space for the steam to flow freely around it. Cover the pot and steam according to directions.

NOTE: Four inches of water at a slow boil, in a covered pot, will need 4 to 4½ hours to evaporate. However, it is wise to check the

water level once or twice during the steaming time and, if necessary, add additional boiling hot water, since cold water would
lower the cooking temperature.

STEAMED CHERRY PUDDING

*An unusual delicacy that can be served hot or cold. The
dark, burgundy-colored juice of the cherries is absorbed into the
bread, and when it is unmolded it has an impressive red and
white design.*

Butter	3 eggs
Sugar	1 cup sugar if fresh
2½ cups firmly packed	cherries are used; 6 tbs.
white bread cubes	sugar if Bing cherries
2 cups fresh cherries,	are used
halved and pitted, or	1 cup scalded milk
canned Bing cherries	1 tbs. brandy or dark rum

Generously butter and sugar a 2-quart metal pudding
mold, including the inside of the lid.

Cut off the crusts of the bread, and cube it into ¼-inch
pieces. If canned cherries are used, drain off the juice.

Put a layer of bread cubes into the bottom of the mold,
and cover with a layer of cherries. Continue the layers until all
the bread and cherries are used. The first and last layers should
be of bread.

Lightly beat the eggs and sugar, and slowly add the
scalded milk, stirring all the while. Add the brandy or rum.
Gently pour this mixture over the layers of bread and cherries.
Place the cover on the mold and steam (see *Steaming Directions
for Molds*, pp. 302–304) for 1 hour.

To serve: Unmold onto a platter and decorate with sweetened whipped cream sauce (see p. 307), or dribble over it the following Raspberry Sauce:

1 cup fresh or frozen	*1 tbs. cold water*
raspberries	*½ tsp. lemon juice*
3 tsps. red currant jelly	*1 tbs. kirsch*
1 tsp. cornstarch	

Mash the raspberries through a sieve so that all the seeds are extracted. Put the purée into a small pot, add the jelly and bring to a boil. Dissolve the cornstarch in the cold water and lemon juice, and add it slowly to the raspberry purée. Stir and cook until thickened. Add the kirsch. This sauce may be served hot or cold.

Serves 6 to 8.

Variation:
For the pudding, use fresh blueberries instead of the cherries.

STEAMED CHOCOLATE PUDDING 1

This is delicious hot or cold. Besides being easy to pre-pare, it is a marvelous way to use up extra egg whites. One of the delights in serving it hot for a party is that it can be made well in advance and left to sit in the steamer for an hour or more after the cooking time has elapsed; it stays warm, and its delicate soufflé quality is not spoiled.

Butter	8 *egg whites*
8 *tbs. sugar*	1 *tbs. bread crumbs,*
8 *ozs. semisweet choco-*	*finely ground*
late	1 *pinch salt*
2 *tbs. apricot jam*	

Generously butter a 1-quart metal pudding mold, including the inside of the lid; add about 3 tablespoons of the sugar, replace lid and shake vigorously so that the entire surface is coated. Shake out any excess sugar. Set aside.

Melt the chocolate over hot water. Stir. When melted, remove from heat to cool slightly.

Put the jam and 2 of the egg whites into a large bowl, and beat until blended. Add 4 tablespoons of the sugar, and continue to beat until well mixed. Add the bread crumbs and melted chocolate. Mix thoroughly.

Beat the remaining 6 egg whites with the salt. When soft peaks have formed, add the remaining tablespoon of sugar and continue beating until stiff.

Beat 4 tablespoons of the egg whites into the chocolate mixture, and fold the remainder in gently. Pour into the prepared mold, cover and steam (see *Steaming Directions for Molds*, pp. 302–304) for 1 hour.

If the pudding is to be served hot, leave the mold in the steamer, with the heat turned off, until serving time. If it is to be served cold, remove from the steamer, cool and refrigerate. Do not remove the pudding from the mold until ready to serve.

When ready to serve, run a knife around the edges of the pudding, and unmold onto a serving plate.

Serves 6.

Serve with the following Sweetened Whipped-Cream Sauce:

1 cup heavy cream	*1 tbs. brandy or dark rum*
1 tbs. powdered sugar	

Whip the cream, and when it begins to thicken, add the sugar. Continue to beat until stiff, and fold in the brandy or rum.

STEAMED CHOCOLATE PUDDING 2

The men in our house say this is the best of all the steamed chocolate puddings. It has a light cake texture and is a real delight.

Butter	*3 tbs. butter*
Sugar	*2 tbs. flour*
1½ cups light cream	*5 egg yolks*
1-inch vanilla bean, or	*10 tbs. sugar*
1 tsp. vanilla extract	*2 tbs. dark rum or*
5 ozs. semisweet choco-	*brandy*
late, cut into small	*5 egg whites*
pieces	

Generously butter a 1-quart metal pudding mold, including the inside of the lid. Add sugar, place the lid on tightly and shake vigorously. Remove the lid, and discard any excess sugar.

Put the cream into a small pot, add vanilla bean, or extract, and chocolate. Place over a low heat, and stir from time to time. Cook until the chocolate is melted. Set aside.

Melt the butter in a small pot, and add the flour. Stir and cook until blended. Slowly, stirring continuously, add the milk and chocolate mixture. Cook and stir until thickened. Remove vanilla bean.

Put the egg yolks and sugar into a mixing bowl. Beat until thick and lemon-colored. Slowly beat in the chocolate mixture. Add the rum or brandy.

Beat the egg whites until stiff. Beat 4 tablespoons of the egg whites into the chocolate mixture. Gently, but thoroughly, fold in the rest of the egg whites. Carefully pour the pudding into the prepared mold, and place the lid on top. Steam (see *Steaming Directions for Molds*, pp. 302–304) for 1 hour.

Prepare the following Sabayon Sauce:

3 egg yolks	*2 tbs. brandy or dark rum*
3 tbs. sugar	*Pinch salt*

Put 1 inch of water into the bottom of a double boiler, and bring it to a gentle simmer over a slow fire. Put all the ingredients into the top of the double boiler, and place it over the hot water. With an electric hand beater, or a whisk, beat the mixture until it is thick and holds its shape. To hold the sauce, cover and place it in a shallow pan of lukewarm water.

To serve: Turn the pudding out onto a warmed serving platter and pass the sauce in a sauce dish.

Serves 6 to 8.

Variation:

The pudding may be served with sweetened whipped-cream sauce or scoops of vanilla ice cream.

STEAMED CHOCOLATE
BREAD-CRUMB PUDDING

Do you save stale bread or crusts to make crumbs? If you haven't done so, you will want to, once you have tried this delectable and easy-to-prepare pudding. It is a fine treat for teen-agers. It can be served hot or cold, and it can be reheated.

	Butter	2 *eggs*
	Sugar	½ *tsp. salt*
3	*cups milk*	1 *tbs. butter*
3	*ozs. unsweetened chocolate*	1 *tsp. vanilla extract, or* 1 *tbs. dark rum*
1	*cup sugar*	
2	*cups white bread crumbs*	

Generously butter a 2-quart metal pudding mold, including the inside of the lid. Add sugar, place the lid on tightly and shake vigorously; remove the lid and discard any excess sugar. Set aside.

Put 2 cups of the milk and the chocolate into a small pot, and bring to a boil. Add the sugar and bread crumbs, and place the pot over hot water. Stir and cook for 10 to 15 minutes until the mixture forms a thick paste.

Beat the eggs slightly in a small bowl, and add the remaining cup of milk and salt. Stir into the chocolate mixture. Add the butter; stir and cook 3 to 4 minutes. Add the vanilla or rum. Pour into the prepared mold and place the lid on top. Steam (see *Steaming Directions for Molds*, pp. 302–304) for 1 hour.

To serve: Unmold and serve with vanilla ice cream or sweetened whipped-cream sauce (see p. 307).

Serves 6 to 8.

STEAMED CHOCOLATE NUT PUDDING

Delicious hot or cold. The nuts should be finely chopped, not powdered. The old-fashioned nut grinder is perfect for this, but a quicker and easier method is the electric blender. If you use a blender, grind only 3 to 4 tablespoons of the nuts at a time at a high speed for 20 to 30 seconds. Don't grind them to a thick, oily paste.

Butter	5 egg yolks
2 tbs. bread crumbs finely ground	4 ozs. almonds, un-blanched, finely chopped
4 ozs. semisweet chocolate	
4 ozs. butter	½ tsp. baking powder
½ cup sugar	4 egg whites
	Pinch salt

Generously butter a 1-quart metal pudding mold, including the inside of the lid. Add bread crumbs, replace lid and shake vigorously. Remove the lid, and discard any excess bread crumbs.

Melt the chocolate over hot water. In a mixing bowl cream the butter and sugar until fluffy. Add the egg yolks, and continue to beat until well blended. Add the chocolate, almonds, and baking powder, and mix thoroughly.

Beat the egg whites with the salt until stiff. Beat one-third of them into the chocolate mixture, and gently fold in the remainder. Pour the pudding into the prepared mold, cover tightly and steam (see *Steaming Directions for Molds*, pp. 302–304) for 1 hour.

To serve: Turn out onto an attractive serving plate and serve with sweetened whipped-cream sauce (see p. 307).
Serves 6.

STEAMED FRUIT PUDDING

*This is extremely easy to prepare. It is a rich and dra-
matic dessert for holiday occasions if served with flaming brandy
or rum. It can be made a week in advance and reheated over
steam prior to serving. The hard sauce can be made 2 or 3 days
in advance and stored in the refrigerator.*

Butter	⅔ cup brandy or dark
Flour	rum
¾ cup raisins	½ cup butter
¾ cup apples, peeled and finely diced	¾ cup sugar
⅓ cup dried apricots, finely diced	3 eggs
⅓ cup dates, seeded and finely diced	¾ cup flour
¼ cup fresh or preserved orange rind, finely diced	½ cup fine bread crumbs
1 tsp. lemon peel, finely diced	½ tsp. mace
	½ tsp. nutmeg
	¼ cup kidney or beef suet, finely diced

Generously butter a 1-quart metal pudding mold, including the inside of the lid. Add flour, place the lid on top, and shake
the mold vigorously. Remove the lid, and discard excess flour.

Put into a bowl the raisins, apples, apricots, dates,
orange rind, lemon peel and brandy or rum. Stir and cover. Marinate 6 hours or overnight.

Cream the butter and sugar in a large bowl, and beat
in the eggs one at a time. When well mixed, add the flour, bread
crumbs, mace, nutmeg and suet. Stir well, and add the marinated

fruits, together with the brandy or rum. Stir and pour into the prepared mold. Steam (see *Steaming Directions for Molds,* pp. 302–304) for 3 hours.

Meanwhile, prepare the following Hard Sauce:

½ cup softened sweet butter	1 pinch salt
2 cups confectioners' sugar	2½ tbs. brandy or dark rum
1 tsp. vanilla	½ cup heavy cream

Put the butter into a large bowl and cream until fluffy. Gradually work in the sugar. Continue to beat, and when creamy add the vanilla, salt and brandy or rum. Beat and mix well.

Whip the cream until stiff, and fold it into the butter and sugar mixture. Pour into a serving bowl, cover and refrigerate until set.

To serve: Turn the pudding out onto a heated serving plate and pass the sauce separately.

Serves 6 to 8.

Variations:

a. A moment before serving heat ¼ cup of brandy or rum, flame and pour over the pudding. Serve at once.

b. Serve with sweetened whipped-cream sauce (see p. 307) instead of the hard sauce.

STEAMED SCOTCH-CHOCOLATE PUDDING

This pudding should be served hot, and as it is not light in texture, serve small portions and let your guests return for seconds. It has a splendid flavor, and the orange whipped-cream sauce complements it perfectly.

Butter	1 cup sugar
Flour	10 egg yolks
5 ozs. semisweet choco-	2 tbs. brandy
late	5 tbs. sifted flour
10 tbs. butter	1 pinch salt

Generously butter a 1-quart metal pudding mold, add flour and place the lid on tightly. Shake vigorously until coated with flour. Discard excess flour.

Melt the chocolate over hot water, and set aside to cool.

Put the butter and sugar into a mixing bowl, and beat until smooth and creamy. Add and beat in 1 egg yolk at a time. Continue to beat until the mixture is fluffy. Add the cooled, melted chocolate slowly, beating continuously. Add the brandy, and fold in the flour and salt. Pour into the prepared mold, and steam (see *Steaming Directions for Molds*, pp. 302–304) for 45 minutes.

To serve: Turn out onto a serving plate, and serve with the following sauce:

ORANGE WHIPPED-CREAM SAUCE

1 orange	4 tsps. confectioners'
1 cup heavy cream	sugar

Grate the rind of the orange. Whip the cream, and when it starts to thicken, add the sugar. Continue to beat until it is stiff. Fold in the grated orange rind. Serve in a chilled bowl.

Serves 6 to 8.

STEAMED RICE PUDDING

A family dessert. The rice can be cooked and the mold prepared before shepherding the children to school, and it can be mixed with the eggs and steamed while dinner is being prepared. Should company show up, dress it up with sweetened whipped-cream sauce (see p. 307) and dribble over it a bit of raspberry sauce (see p. 305). We prefer it warm, but it is good cold too.

When you eat this rice pudding, you taste the rice kernels. Nothing is mashed, blended or disguised.

6 **Graham crackers**	½ **tsp. salt**
1 **tbs. sugar**	4 **egg yolks**
Butter	6 **tbs. sugar**
2 **cups cold milk**	1 **tsp. lemon juice,**
½ **cup Carolina long-**	**strained**
grain rice	4 **egg whites**
1 **tsp. vanilla, or ½-inch**	
vanilla bean	

Finely crush the Graham crackers, and mix them with the sugar. Generously butter a 1-quart metal pudding mold and the inside of the top. Add the cracker and sugar mixture, put on the lid and shake and coat all sides as well as the top. Discard any excess.

Put the milk into a pot, and add the rice, vanilla or vanilla bean, and salt. Bring to a boil. Stir. Place a tight-fitting lid on top, adjust the heat to a simmer, and simmer for 30 minutes, or until the milk has been absorbed into the rice.

Beat the egg yolks lightly, and add the 6 tablespoons of sugar and lemon juice. Stir into the cooked rice. Beat the egg whites stiff, and fold into the rice mixture.

Pour the pudding into the prepared mold, and steam (see *Steaming Directions for Molds*, pp. 302–304) for 30 to 40 minutes. With the heat turned off, the pudding will stay warm if left in the hot water for 1 to 2 hours.

To serve: Turn out onto a plate.
Serves 6.

STEAMED VANILLA BREAD PUDDING

Butter	*2 cups light cream*
Sugar	*2-inch piece vanilla bean,*
4 cups white bread, from	*scraped, or 1½ tsps.*
which the crusts have	*vanilla extract*
been removed, cut into	*4 eggs*
¼-inch cubes	*1 cup sugar*

Generously butter a 1½- to 2-quart metal pudding mold, including the inside of the lid. Add sugar, place the lid on tightly and shake vigorously. Remove the lid and discard any excess sugar.

Put the bread cubes into the prepared mold.

Scald the cream with the vanilla bean or the extract.

Lightly beat the eggs and sugar. Slowly add the cream to the eggs, beating continuously. Remove the vanilla bean, and pour the mixture over the bread cubes. Place the lid on top and steam (see *Steaming Directions for Molds*, pp. 302–304) for 1 hour.

To serve: Unmold onto a serving plate and spoon over the pudding a few tablespoons of raspberry sauce (see p. 305). Pass the rest of the sauce in a separate dish.

Serves 6 to 8.

Variation:

Instead of the raspberry sauce, serve the pudding with the following Hot Chocolate Sauce:

2 ozs. unsweetened chocolate	1 pinch salt
6 tbs. water	3 tbs. butter
½ cup sugar	1 tbs. brandy or dark rum

Put the chocolate and water into a small heavy pot and stir and cook over a low heat until the chocolate is melted. Add sugar and salt. Stir and cook until the sugar is dissolved and the sauce is slightly thickened. Add butter and brandy or rum. Stir, heat and serve.

APPLESAUCE PUDDING

If you eliminate the whipped cream, this is a good dessert to serve to weight watchers, since it is relatively low in calories and high in nutriments.

2 lbs. apples	2 tbs. brandy or dark rum
1 thin slice lemon	
Cold water	2 egg whites
½ cup brown sugar	1 cup heavy cream
½ cup white sugar	2 tbs. powdered sugar
3 tbs. butter	¼ tsp. nutmeg
2 egg yolks	¼ tsp. cinnamon

Wash and quarter the apples, and put them into a heavy pot. Add lemon and sufficient water, about ½ inch, to prevent the apples from burning. Bring to a boil, stir, cover with a lid and cook over a medium heat until the apples are soft.

When soft, work the apples through a strainer or food mill. Return the sauce to the pot, and add the sugar and butter. Stir and cook until the sugar is dissolved. Taste for sweetness. If the apples are tart, additional sugar should be added.

Lightly beat the egg yolks with the brandy or rum. Remove the applesauce from the heat, and slowly add 1 cup of it to the egg yolks, beating them all the while. Return this mixture slowly to the hot applesauce, and stir rapidly until well blended. Pour into a mixing bowl and cool.

Beat the egg whites until stiff, and fold them thoroughly into the applesauce. Pour into an attractive glass or crystal serving dish. Chill.

When ready to serve, whip the cream until stiff and add the powdered sugar, nutmeg and cinnamon. Cover the applesauce entirely with the whipped cream, and decorate with a sprinkle of nutmeg.

Serves 6 to 8.

Variation:

Add 1 teaspoon of nutmeg and 1 teaspoon of cinnamon to the hot applesauce.

APRICOT MOUSSE

12 ozs. dried apricots	*1½ tbs. dark rum*
6 tbs. sugar	*3 tbs. almonds,*
1 cup heavy cream	*blanched and slivered*
2 tbs. confectioners'	
sugar	

Cover the apricots with cold water, and bring to a boil. Adjust the heat to a simmer, and simmer uncovered until the apricots are tender. Add the sugar, stir and cook until the sugar is dissolved. Put the apricots through a food mill, or blend in a blender until smooth. Chill.

Whip ½ cup of the cream until stiff, adding slowly 1 tablespoon of the confectioners' sugar, and the rum. Fold the cream into the apricot purée. Pour into an attractive serving dish, or spoon into individual serving glasses.

Shortly before serving, whip the rest of the cream with the remaining tablespoon of confectioners' sugar until stiff. Spread the cream evenly over the apricot mousse. Sprinkle the almonds over the top.

Serves 6.

CHOCOLATE MOUSSE CURTIS

I like the light texture and the strong chocolate flavor of this mousse. Because the whipped cream is folded into the mousse, no last-minute sauce has to be prepared. It is an elegant and easily prepared dessert.

1 tbs. plus 1 tsp. un-flavored gelatin	10 tbs. sugar
¾ cup cold water	5 egg whites
6 ozs. semisweet chocolate	1 pinch cream of tartar
1 oz. bitter chocolate	2 tbs. dark rum or brandy
	1 cup heavy cream

Soak the gelatin in ½ cup of the cold water.

Melt the chocolate in a heavy pot over a low heat. When melted, add sugar, gelatin and the remaining ¼ cup of water.

Stir and cook until the sugar is dissolved. Remove from the heat, and cool slightly.

Put the egg whites into a large mixing bowl, add cream of tartar and beat until stiff. Beat 3 tablespoons of the egg whites into the chocolate mixture, and gently fold in the remainder, together with the rum or brandy.

Whip the cream until stiff and fold into the mousse.

Pour the mousse into an attractive crystal serving dish, cover and chill until set.

Serves 6 to 8.

CREAM VICTORIA

Measure the gelatin carefully so that the cream has the texture of cream cheese and does not become stiff and rubbery.

Vegetable oil	*½ cup sugar*
2 tsps. unflavored	*1-inch piece vanilla bean,*
gelatin	*or 1 tsp. vanilla extract*
2 tbs. cold water	*1 tbs. dark rum or brandy*
1 cup heavy cream	*1 cup sour cream*

Lightly oil a 1½-pint dessert mold and set aside.

Put the gelatin into a small bowl and soften with the cold water.

Put into a saucepan the heavy cream, sugar, gelatin and vanilla bean or extract. Place over the heat, and bring to a boil. Stir and cook until the sugar and gelatin are dissolved. Add the rum or brandy. Remove from the heat, and stir in the sour cream. Mix until thoroughly blended, remove the vanilla bean and pour the mixture into the prepared mold. Cover, and refrigerate until set.

Prepare the following Apricot Sauce:

1 10-oz. jar apricot jam   *2 tbs. dark rum or brandy*
2 tbs. water

Put the jam into a small pot, add water and rum or brandy. Place over the heat, and stirring continuously, bring to a boil. Cook and stir for 2 or 3 minutes. Remove from the heat and rub the mixture through a fine sieve. Cover and refrigerate.

To serve: Turn the mold out onto an attractive chilled serving plate, spoon half the apricot sauce over it and serve the rest in a side dish.
Serves 4.

Variation:
Pile a mound of fresh-washed and hulled strawberries or raspberries in the center or around the mold and serve with Raspberry Sauce Thérèse (see p. 327).

FRUIT COMPOTE

For a really exquisite compote, use only the ripest, sweetest fruit in season. The combination of fruit can vary with the seasons and your tastes. The fruit can be prepared early, covered and set to chill in the refrigerator.

The sauce, which I call "fruit stock," can be made and stored in a covered container in the refrigerator for a week or two. It also adds a special touch to a canned fruit compote. However, drain and chill the canned fruit thoroughly before adding the "stock."

4 large oranges   *2 medium pears*
2 medium grapefruit   *1 medium apple*
2 medium bananas   *1 cup strawberries*

Peel the oranges and grapefruit. Remove the skin and seeds from the sections. Peel and score the bananas, and slice into ¼-inch slices. Peel the pears and apple, remove cores and dice into ¼-inch cubes. Wash the strawberries and remove the stems; if the berries are large, cut them in half.

Place all the fruit into an attractive glass serving dish, cover and chill.

Prepare the following "fruit stock":

2 oranges	*1 cup sugar*
1 lemon	*1½ cups cold water*

Thinly peel the rind from the oranges and lemon. Remove any of the white membrane from the rind. With a small, sharp knife finely shred the rind into 2- to 3-inch pieces.

Put the sugar and cold water into a small pot, and add the shredded rind. Stir and cook until the liquid boils, adjust the heat to a simmer, and simmer until the rind is translucent.

Remove from the fire, pour into a container, cover and chill.

Just before serving, pour the sauce over the fruit and stir gently.

Serves 6 to 8.

Variations:

a. Add and cook in the sauce 1 inch of fresh ginger, peeled and finely shredded.

b. Garnish with a few finely shredded mint leaves.

c. Add 1 cup of defrosted and thoroughly drained raspberries.

PEARS IN RED WINE

This recipe may be prepared a week or two in advance. Store the pears in their sauce in the refrigerator.

6 medium cooking pears	½ cup sugar
1½ cups dry red wine	1 slice lemon
1 cup water	1 medium stick cinnamon

Thinly peel the pears; do not remove the stems. Core the pears from the underside so that the stems remain intact.

Put the wine, water, sugar, lemon and cinnamon stick into a pot, and bring to a boil. Place the pears into the sauce, adjust the heat to a simmer, cover and poach the pears for 10 minutes, or until just tender, not mushy. If the pears are not completely immersed in the sauce, gently turn them from time to time with a wooden spoon.

When tender, remove the pot from the heat; discard the cinnamon stick and cool the pears in the sauce. When cool, put the pears into a container, pour the sauce over them and chill.

To serve: Put each pear into an individual bowl and spoon enough sauce over it to cover one-third to one-half the pear.

Serves 6.

Variation:

Apples may be cooked in the same wine sauce. Wash, peel, quarter and remove the core from the apples; cook according to the directions given for the pears.

FLOATING ISLAND

The custard can be prepared in advance and chilled. The meringue can be made in the morning and kept in the refrigerator.

3 cups milk	1½ cups sugar
1-inch vanilla bean, or 1	Pinch salt
tsp. vanilla extract	6 egg whites
6 egg yolks	

Pour the milk into a pan, add the vanilla bean or extract, and scald.

Beat the egg yolks with ½ cup of the sugar until lemon color. Pour the milk bit by bit into the egg yolks, stirring continuously. Pour this mixture into a pan or a double boiler, and place over hot water. Cook and stir continuously over a low heat until the custard coats the back of a wooden spoon. This takes about 30 minutes. Remove from the heat, and still stirring, pour the custard into a container. Cover and refrigerate.

To prepare the mold, melt 10 tablespoons of the sugar in a heavy small cast-iron pan. Stir, and when the sugar is a deep amber color, pour it into a metal ring mold 8 inches in diameter. Turn the mold and coat the bottom, center and sides with the carmelized sugar.

Add the salt to the egg whites, and beat until stiff. When stiff, add the remaining 6 tablespoons of sugar very slowly, beating all the while.

Spoon the egg whites into the prepared mold. Press and tap them down gently so that there are no large air pockets. Place the mold, uncovered, in a pan of simmering water. The water should come halfway up the mold. Simmer for 25 to 30 minutes or until a knife blade inserted into the whites comes out clean. Remove from the water and cool.

When ready to serve, remove the vanilla bean, and pour the custard into an attractive glass bowl. Be sure the bowl is large enough to hold the meringue. Run a knife around the inner and outer edges of the egg whites and turn the mold upside down on top of the custard. Allow the liquid carmelized sugar to dribble over the meringue. Discard that which remains in the mold.

Serves 6.

COLD BURNT-SUGAR SOUFFLÉ

I advise using a metal spoon with a wooden handle to stir the hot melted sugar.

1	*tbs. unflavored gelatin*		*Pinch salt*
¼	*cup cold water*	4	*egg whites*
¾	*cup sugar*	1½	*cups heavy cream*
⅓	*cup boiling water*	3	*tbs. red currant jelly*
4	*egg yolks*	2	*tsps. hot water*
¼	*cup sugar*		

Soak the gelatin in the cold water.

Melt the sugar in a heavy cast-iron pot and cook until golden amber. Stir occasionally. When it is the right color, remove from heat and add the boiling water; stand aside, as the hot sugar will spit and bubble. When the sugar and water are mixed, add the gelatin and return to the heat. Stir for a moment until the gelatin is dissolved.

Beat the egg yolks and the remaining ¼ cup of sugar until light and fluffy. Pour the burnt sugar into a heatproof measuring cup, and slowly, in a fine thin thread, pour it into the egg yolk mixture, beating continuously. (Don't try to pour the sugar into the egg yolks directly from the hot pan, because you would need a heavy hotpot holder to hold the pan and this is too clumsy to control the pouring.)

Add salt to the egg whites and beat until soft peaks are formed. Beat 2 tablespoons of the egg whites into the yolk and sugar mixture. Gently fold in the rest. Whip until stiff 1 cup of the cream, and fold it in.

Pour the soufflé into a 1½-quart soufflé dish or an attractive serving dish. Cover. Place in the refrigerator until set.

When set, and shortly before serving, put the jelly and hot water into a small pan. Heat and stir until blended. Remove from heat and cool.

Whip the remaining ½ cup of cream and spread it evenly over the top of the soufflé.

Pour the jelly into a pastry tube or a waxpaper cone. Draw thin lines of jelly, about ½ inch apart, over the layer of cream. With the back of a dinner knife draw lightly across the jelly lines to form a lattice pattern. Serve at once.

Serves 6 to 8.

MIRABELLE FROZEN SOUFFLÉ

A real party dessert. Because it is frozen, it can be made long in advance. It is beautiful to the eye and most pleasing to the taste. It dresses up a simple dinner, or is the grand finale to a sophisticated menu.

The ideal mold for the soufflé is a metal melon mold, but any attractive metal mold may be used.

The liqueur, Mirabelle, is made from a tiny golden yellow plum grown in Europe. If this liqueur is not available, substitute brandy or a dark rum.

9 egg yolks	½ cup Mirabelle, brandy
1¼ cups sugar	or dark rum
	2 cups heavy cream

Beat the egg yolks until lemon color. Add the sugar bit by bit, and continue beating until the mixture forms ribbons.

Place the egg yolk mixture over hot water; do not let the water boil. Continue to beat until the mixture begins to stick to the side of the bowl and is warm to the touch. I use an electric hand beater for this step. Do not overcook. Remove from the hot water, and continue to beat, slowly adding the Mirabelle, brandy or rum.

Beat the cream until stiff. Beat 2 tablespoons of it into the custard and gently fold in the rest. Pour the soufflé into a 1-quart metal mold, cover and freeze.

To serve: Turn the soufflé out on a chilled platter. The individual dessert plates should be thoroughly chilled too.

Serves 6.

Variation:

Surround the unmolded soufflé with fresh hulled and washed strawberries or raspberries.

FROZEN HONEY MOUSSE

As with so many fine recipes, this mousse is simple to prepare. The only step that may demand your full attention is the cooking of the egg yolks and honey. Make it a day or a week in advance, and freeze.

I recommend an orange blossom or clover honey for this recipe.

6 *egg yolks*	3 *egg whites*
1½ *cups honey*	1 *pint heavy cream*
3 *tbs. lemon juice,*	
strained	

Put the egg yolks into a mixing bowl and slowly beat in the honey. Continue beating until the mixture is lemon-colored and fluffy.

Place the egg and honey mixture over hot water; do not let the water boil. Continue to beat with a beater until the mixture is slightly thickened, warm to the touch and begins to show a trace of hardening at the edges. Remove from the hot water, and place over a bowl of cold water or ice. Add the lemon juice, and beat for 2 or 3 minutes. Set aside to cool.

When cool, beat the egg whites until peaks are formed. Fold the whites into the mixture.

Whip the cream until stiff and fold it into the mixture. Pour into a 2-quart metal mold and freeze.

To serve: Turn the mousse onto a chilled plate.
Serves 6 to 8.

Variations:

a. Serve the mousse surrounded by fresh washed and hulled strawberries or raspberries.

b. Serve the mousse surrounded by peeled and thinly sliced fresh peaches.

c. Serve the mousse with the following Raspberry Sauce Thérèse:

2 *cups fresh or frozen*	½ *cup sugar*
raspberries	2 *tbs. kirsch*

If frozen raspberries are used, defrost and strain off the juice.

Mash the fresh or defrosted raspberries through a fine sieve to extract all seeds. Pour the raspberry purée into a small pot, add sugar and bring to a boil. Stir and cook until the sugar is dissolved. Add the kirsch and chill.

Dribble about ¼ cup of the sauce over the mousse and serve the rest in a sauce dish.

NOTE: If the frozen raspberries are sweetened, add only 3 tablespoons of sugar.

SAVOY TRIFLE

This recipe is the only dessert I've included that requires the use of the oven. It is given because it is my husband's favorite. It is a beautiful combination of cake and custard cream, a perfect party dish that can be made a day, or even two, in advance.

A tip on preparing the 2 pieces of wax paper on which the cake is turned out: Lap one piece halfway over the other, and secure them together with Scotch tape.

CAKE:

Melted butter	*⅔ cup flour*
3 *eggs at room temperature*	1 *tsp. baking powder*
	4 *tbs. superfine sugar*
½ *cup sugar*	10-oz. *jar currant jelly*
1 *pinch salt*	

Preheat the oven at 350° F.

Brush a 11-by-15-inch jelly-roll pan with melted butter. Cover with a strip of wax paper, leaving a 2-inch overlap at each end, and brush with butter.

Into the mixing bowl of an electric mixer, put the eggs, sugar and salt. Beat at a high speed until the mixture holds its shape.

Meanwhile measure the flour, add the baking powder and sift twice. When the egg mixture is stiff, sift the flour and baking powder over it, and fold in gently with a rubber spatula.

Spread the mixture evenly on the prepared jelly-roll pan. Place it on the middle shelf of the oven, and bake for 12 minutes.

Remove. Take each end of the overlapping wax paper, and carefully loosen the cake. Dust the top with 2 tablespoons of the superfine sugar. Turn the cake out onto 2 pieces of overlapping wax paper. Carefully peel off the paper that is now on top of the cake. Sprinkle with the remaining 2 tablespoons of superfine sugar. Roll up tightly in the wax paper, and chill in the refrigerator.

Stir the jelly through a sieve or strainer. When the cake is chilled, carefully unroll and spread the jelly evenly on the top. Roll up again in the wax paper and chill. Prepare the following Cream Custard:

1½ cups light cream	2 tbs. cold water
1-inch scraped vanilla bean, or 1 tsp. vanilla extract	6 egg whites
	2 cups heavy cream
6 egg yolks	2½ tbs. brandy or dark rum
6 tbs. sugar	
1¼ tbs. unflavored gelatin	1 tbs. powdered sugar

Scald the light cream with the vanilla bean or extract.

Put the egg yolks and sugar into a mixing bowl, and beat until light and fluffy. Soak the gelatin in the cold water.

Stirring all the while, slowly mix the egg yolks into the

scalded cream. Add the gelatin, and over a low heat or over hot water, cook and stir until the mixture coats the back of a wooden spoon. Turn into a dish and cool; do not set.

When cool, beat the egg whites until they form soft peaks. Whip 1 cup of the heavy cream until it is stiff. Carefully blend the egg whites into the custard, and gently fold in the cream and 1 tablespoon of the liquor.

Cut enough of the jelly roll into thin slices to line the bottom and sides of a deep glass serving dish. Sprinkle the slices with ½ tablespoon of the liquor. Slowly pour the custard into the dish. Cover and place in the refrigerator until set. When set, cover the top of the custard with thin slices of the jelly roll. Cover and refrigerate until serving time.

To serve: Whip the remaining cup of heavy cream with the powdered sugar until stiff. Fold in the remaining tablespoon of liquor and spread evenly over the top of the cake slices.

Serves 6 to 8.

Variation:
Instead of covering the top with the whipped cream, put the whipped cream into a pastry bag with a star tube and decorate the top of the trifle with rosettes and fresh strawberries.

INDEX

[331]

egg ribbon, 50–51
jellied, 49–50
pancake, 51–52
vegetable garnishes for, 47–48
Cornmeal, 292–293
bread, 293
Couscous, 291–292
Crab
chowder, 95–96
and mustard ring, 221–222
stew, 222–223
Cracked wheat, 293–295
and broccoli, 295
pilaf, 294
Cream custard, 329–330
Cream Victoria, 319–320
Croutons, 103
Cucumber
and cold beet soup, 59
sauce, 209
and yogurt soup, 58–59
Culling beans, 254–255
Curry
chicken with, sauce, 121–122
chicken soup, 74–75
lentils, 285–286
spinach soup, 67
Custard, cream, 329–330

Desserts, 302–330
cream Victoria, 319–320
floating island, 323–324
fruit compote, 320–321
mousse
apricot, 317–318
chocolate, Curtis, 318–319
frozen honey, 326–327
pears in red wine, 322
pudding
applesauce, 316–317
cherry, 304–305

chocolate I, 306–307
chocolate II, 307–308
chocolate bread crumb, 309
chocolate nut, 310
fruit, 311–312
rice, 314–315
Scotch chocolate, 313
vanilla bread, 315–316
Savoy trifle, 328–330
soufflé
cold burnt sugar, 324–325
Mirabelle frozen, 325–326
Dill
sauce, chicken with, 141–142
and tomato soup, 76–77
Dishwashing, 8–11
Dried beans, 254–268
See also Bean(s)
Duck, 145–149
in red wine, 145–146
steamed, 147–149

Egg soup
celery and, 71–72
meat and, 82–83
ribbon consommé, 50–51
Endives and sausages Huguette,
188–189
Escarole soup, 60

Fava beans, 262–264
with bacon, 263–264
Fillet of sole
Friday's, 216
Laroquette, 220
Fish, 204–225
aspic, 204–205, 207
in aspic Clara, 205–208
Higgins' chowder, 97–98
pudding, 210–211

641.7   Loebel, Alice Devine
LOE
        The simmering pot
        cookbook

c.1